A Guide to Faculty Development

A Guide to Faculty Development

Practical Advice, Examples, and Resources

Kay Herr Gillespie, Editor

Linda R. Hilsen, Associate Editor

Emily C. Wadsworth, Associate Editor

ANKER PUBLISHING COMPANY, INC.
Bolton, Massachusetts

A Guide to Faculty Development

Practical Advice, Examples, and Resources

Some material in this book is based on *A Handbook for New Practitioners* published by New Forums Press in 1988.

ISBN 1-882982-45-2

Composition by Vicki Czech
Cover design by Vicki Czech

Anker Publishing Company, Inc.
176 Ballville Road
P.O. Box 249
Bolton, MA 01740-0249

www.ankerpub.com

The POD Mission Statement

History

The Professional and Organizational Development Network in Higher Education (POD) was founded in 1976 in response to the need expressed by faculty members, administrators, and others working in faculty, instructional, and organizational development in higher education for a source of professional information and support.

Purposes

As envisioned by POD, **faculty development** encompasses activities that focus on individual faculty members first as teachers engaged in fostering student development. A second theme in faculty development focuses on faculty members as scholars and professionals and involves such tasks as career planning and development of various scholarly skills. A third area of faculty development addresses faculty members as persons, and involves activities that enhance a person's well-being such as wellness management, interpersonal skills, stress and time management, and assertiveness training.

Instructional development strives to enhance individual faculty members'—and their institutions'—effectiveness by focusing on courses, the curriculum, and student learning. Instructors serve as members of a design or redesign team, working with instructional design and evaluation specialists, to identify course or curriculum strategies or processes appropriate to achieving stated outcome goals.

Organizational development focuses on the organizational structure and processes of an institution and its subunits. Organizational development seeks to help the organization function in an effective and efficient way to support the work of teachers and students. Leadership training for department chairpersons; effective use of group processes; review, revision, and active use of the mission statement; implementing organizational change processes; and institutional governance are representative topics that fall within the purview of organizational development.

Drawing on these three kinds of development, the main purposes of POD are:

- to provide support and services for members through publications, conferences, consulting, and networking;

- to offer services and resources to others interested in faculty development;

- to fulfill an advocacy role, nationally, seeking to inform and persuade educational leaders of the value of faculty, instructional, and organizational development in institutions of higher education.

(Adopted, 1991)

Table of Contents

Preface

Recognizing the growing awareness within the academy of the importance of faculty development, inclusive of both instructional and organizational development, this publication is intended for those who are new to faculty development as well as those who are already working in the field. Administrators interested in promoting and better understanding faculty development will also find it useful. As our academic world and the challenges with which we are presented become ever more complex, it becomes increasingly critical that we undertake expanded efforts to assist faculty members in fulfilling their responsibilities. This is the task of faculty development and of faculty developers as well as the administrators who support them.

Faculty development has long been a part of higher education, but efforts were generally limited in scope until the 1960s. It was at that time that we began to give increased attention to more purposeful and intentional faculty development, and our knowledge and understanding of this emerged field has steadily increased over the years. The contributing authors of this volume have been pioneers and innovators in forming the field of faculty development through their practices, research, and articulation of theory. They willingly and gladly share their knowledge and experience.

The six parts of *A Guide to Faculty Development* provide practical guidance and useful information and resources relating to important aspects of faculty development. The four chapters of Part I, "Setting Up a Faculty Development Program," present an introduction to the field—its meaning, scope, and forms. People and institutions who are just getting started will find this section of particular interest. Part II, "Assessing Teaching Practices," and its five chapters address issues of critical importance in both assessing and enhancing teaching effectiveness. It is only relatively recently that we have come to recognize the importance of assessment of teaching performance, which is essential if our ultimate intent is to promote enhancement and improvement. The practical strategies presented in the five chapters of Part III, "Practical Strategies," cover common program features of faculty development efforts such as the promotion of programs, the presentation of workshops, and the preparation of newsletters. In Part IV, "Reaching Specific Audiences," three chapters present ideas for reaching specific audiences such as chairpersons or those seeking a particular kind of course/curricular development—in this instance, problem-based learning. The promotion of diversity goals is yet another kind of specific effort, and it is becoming increasingly important in faculty development programs in support of institutional goals. The three chapters of Part V, "Addressing Diversity," offer a framework of thought and explanation of practical approaches for addressing this area of endeavor. Finally, in the four chapters of Part VI, "A Guide to Faculty Development Committees," we present a significant structure for the implementation of a faculty development program; i.e., the faculty development committee.

This publication has been prepared under the auspices of the Professional and Organizational Development Network in Higher Education (the POD Network), a professional association devoted to promoting faculty, instructional, and organizational development. Some of the material found here is new, and some of it is revised from earlier POD publications no longer available. Our thanks are extended to Emily C. Wadsworth and Linda Hilsen, who initially guided the revision and expansion of an earlier handbook, the predecessor of this publication.

On behalf of the POD Network, we express the hope that readers benefit from the ideas and experiences presented here. Indeed we hope that readers are both excited and inspired about doing more to assist and encourage our faculty members and administrators across North America and beyond in doing their jobs as well as possible.

Kay Herr Gillespie, Editor

Kay Herr Gillespie is Professor Emerita at Colorado State University, where she served as a tenured faculty member in the Department of Foreign Languages and Literatures and began working in faculty development in 1976. She served on the POD Core Committee and was president of the organization in 1998-1999. Currently she is working independently as a higher education consultant and editor.

Questions or comments can be directed to the editor, Kay Herr Gillespie, CKF Associates, Higher Education Development, 2900 Tulane Drive, Ft. Collins, CO, U.S.A. email: <kaygi2@aol.com>, or to The POD Network, c/o David Graf, Manager of Administrative Services, Nova Southeastern University, 1750 NE 167th Street, North Miami Beach, FL 33162, U.S.A., email: [podnet@nova.edu]. Readers are also invited to consult the POD web site: <http://www.podweb.org>

Part I

Setting Up a Faculty
Development Program

I

Faculty, Instructional, and Organizational Development: Options and Choices

Robert M. Diamond

THE ISSUE

Over the past years, important reports by the National Institute of Education (1984), the National Endowment for the Humanities (Bennett, 1984), the Association of American Colleges and Universities (1985), Ernest Boyer of the Carnegie Foundation (1986), and the National Education Association (1996) have focused national attention on a number of problems facing higher education in the United States. These and other reports and commentaries cited a narrowness in the content and scope of courses and curricula, an overspecialization in faculty preparation and focus, and a lack of attention to teaching and learning effectiveness at many colleges and universities. As a direct result of such reports and of increased pressures from students, their parents, and state and national leaders, a growing number of institutions have begun to explore ways in which they can improve both the quality and the effectiveness of their academic programs. Thus, the issue is a pressing need to address matters of faculty, instructional, and organizational development in order to enhance institutional effectiveness.

A more recent study (Gray, Diamond, & Adam, 1996) found that research universities are indeed paying greater attention to teaching and teaching-related activities. However significant change does not happen by chance. It requires the commitment of dedicated and talented faculty working within a supportive environment. Such an environment cannot exist without systematic administrative leadership.

OPTIONS

The options open to an administration and a faculty committed to improving the quality of instruction are several and can range from a number of independent activities to the establishment of an office formally charged with coordinating or directing all major activities that focus on the improvement of instruction. Therefore, it is essential that those responsible for overall academic quality explore the range of options open to them and the strengths and limitations associated with each approach. If a decision is made to establish a formal office or center charged with supporting and facilitating instructional improvement and student learning, the approach taken will determine the following:

- The amount of fiscal support that will be required

- The type of impact that can be reasonably expected and, therefore, the criteria upon which the new program or center will be evaluated

- The expectation of benefits or outcomes and the broadness of the effect of these benefits upon the overall instructional program

- The anticipated duration of the specific desired outcomes

THREE ALTERNATIVES

Generally, the efforts to improve instructional quality focus on three approaches to instructional improvement. The focus of each of these distinguishes it from the others:

- Faculty development—focus on the faculty

- Instructional development—focus on the student (courses and curriculum)

- Organizational development—focus on structure and process

While some overlap can be anticipated, each approach has its own characteristics and potential outcomes. In addition, the talents and experiences of the staff required to implement each approach differ significantly. The most salient points can be summarized as follows.

Faculty Development

Faculty development emphasizes improving the teaching skills of individual faculty members. Common activities include classroom visits by professional staff, personal consultation, workshops and seminars, and the use of video to analyze teaching styles and techniques. The concept of peer review, which is having an impact both nationally and internationally, might also be considered a part of this approach. There are several major outcomes:

- Demonstration of the institution's concern for the individual

- Improvement in the productivity of individual faculty members through improvement of their teaching effectiveness

- Facilitation of focused change with more emphasis on what students learn and less on what the faculty member covers

- Improvement of faculty attitudes toward teaching

Instructional Development

Instructional development focuses primarily on the student by improving the course or the curriculum. Common activities include course and curriculum design, implementation, and evaluation. Incorporation of information and educational technologies into courses and curricula is also a part of this approach. The major outcomes of this approach are as follows:

- Improvement of academic effectiveness and efficiency

- Maximized resource utilization

- Focus on students' learning

- Potential for increasing enrollment and decreasing attrition

- An increase in faculty and student satisfaction with courses and programs

Organizational Development

Organizational development focuses upon the institution's structure and the relationship among its units. Common activities include workshops, seminars, and individual consultation with administrators and faculty members. Development activities for chairpersons and deans fall into this category as well. Its major outcomes are the following:

- Clarification of relationships among units

- Diagnosis of institutional problems

- Enhancement of communication and feedback among units

- Clarification of institutional or unit goals

- Facilitation of program implementation

- Improvement of institutional climate

Professional Development

Professional development is a term that is loosely used and generally refers to faculty and instructional development together. However, it might also be understood to encompass organizational development as well.

OTHER CONSIDERATIONS

There are several factors that should be considered in the choice of an approach to enhance an institution's developmental efforts. For example, faculty development is perhaps the easiest of the three approaches to implement. It can have a direct impact in a shorter time than either instructional or organizational development. It is also less political and the administration can benefit from being perceived as having taken quick, direct, and positive action to address problems.

Instructional development—which supports faculty in the systematic design, implementation, and evaluation of courses, curricula, and programs—takes longer to get underway. It can, however, have greater impact on the total instructional program than can faculty development alone. This approach questions what is taught and whether or not the overall goals of an academic program are being met. In instructional development, the final determination as to whether or not an effort has been successful rests with student performance. Thus, it is connected to institutional and unit assessment efforts as well.

Organizational development, unlike either faculty or instructional development, may involve the use of external consultants. With the goal of improvement in structure and process, it might well involve efforts that go beyond the direct academic enterprise. For example, attention is often given to administrative operations and student affairs. There are instances in which faculty and instructional development programs cannot be successfully implemented until other fundamental organizational problems are dealt with. Institutional strategic planning might well be part of an overall organizational development effort. A basic principle of the recently established National Academy for Academic Leadership is that if major and fundamental change is to occur all leaders at an institution must be working together toward that change, and the process must be carefully planned. Leaders should be understood to include board members, presidents, provosts, deans, chairpersons, and faculty leaders.

These three approaches are not mutually exclusive. Each effort to support student learning can, under certain circumstances, focus on activities more typical of one approach or the other. A faculty development program, for example, might identify significant course changes that should be undertaken or highlight communication problems within a department or institution that must be dealt with. An instructional development project may reveal the need to establish a new instructional support agency or improve the teaching skills of a particular faculty member, and an organizational development expert or institutional strategic planning committee may recommend the establishment of a faculty or instructional development unit or initiatives.

Quite often the specific focus of the unit can be seen in the title given it. For example, within the POD Network, the North American professional association for faculty, instructional, and organizational development, one finds members from offices with titles such as Centers or Offices for Teaching Effectiveness, for Teaching and Learning, for Instructional Development, for Teaching Excellence, for Educational Development, and for Faculty Development, among others. However, most important is the specific charge given to the unit and its placement within the institutional structure. The higher the unit is in the hierarchy of the institution and the more central it is to the structure of the university or college, the greater is its potential impact.

The administration of each institution must select which approach or combination of approaches should be supported. This decision should consider the needs and priorities of the institution within the context of its mission, the benefits or outcomes that can be reasonably

Figure 1.1 *The Growing Overlap Among Approaches*

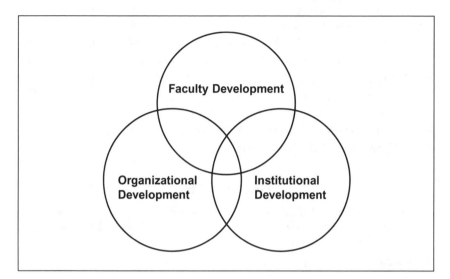

expected from a particular approach, and the balance between costs and benefits. The best approach for one institution may not be the best for another.

ADDITIONAL OBSERVATIONS

While the titles of units supporting institutional effectiveness and developmental efforts have been relatively constant over the last decades, several basic changes are taking place in the units themselves. These changes relate directly to the increased importance of teaching and learning effectiveness in many institutions, and examples of such changes are as follows:

- Units are increasingly located within the office of the provost or academic vice president, which increases the potential for impact and success.

- Resources are increasing, and the head of the unit is being placed higher in the administrative structure of the institution.

- The three functions of faculty, institutional, and organization development often blur (as illustrated in Figure 1.1).

In the long run, it is the integrated approach that may prove to be the most effective and cost efficient. It is also the one that we see being established more and more frequently.

Once a unit is established, it is the responsibility of its director to determine how to use existing resources most effectively so as to meet the priorities established for the unit. One must understand the need for exploration of alternatives and, at times, the need for trade-offs. This is never an easy task, but it is an essential one. The ensuing chapters of this volume elaborate upon aspects of faculty, instructional, and organizational development.

REFERENCES

Association of American Colleges and Universities. (1985). *Integrity in the college curriculum: A report to the academic community.* Washington, DC: Association of American Colleges and Universities.

Bennett, W. J. (1984). *To reclaim a legacy.* Washington, DC: National Endowment for the Humanities.

Boyer, E. (1986). *College: The undergraduate experience in America.* Princeton, NJ: Carnegie Foundation for the Advancement of Teaching.

Gray, P. J., Diamond, R. M., & Adam, B. E. (1996). *A national study on the relative importance of research and undergraduate teaching at colleges and universities.* Syracuse, NY: Syracuse University, Center for Instructional Development.

National Education Association. (1996). *The politics of remedy: State legislative views on higher education.* Washington, DC: National Education Association.

National Institute of Education. (1984). *Involvement in learning: Realizing the potential of American higher education.* Washington, DC: National Institute of Education.

Robert M. Diamond is President of the National Academy for Academic Leadership and Professor Emeritus, Syracuse University, Syracuse, New York. He is the author of numerous publications and has served as a member of the Core Committee of the POD Network.

Email: rdiamond@thenationalacademy.org

2

Ten Principles of Good Practice in Creating and Sustaining Teaching and Learning Centers

Mary Deane Sorcinelli

BACKGROUND

The 1990s may be remembered as the decade of teaching and learning. The research in both areas has exploded, resulting in findings that promise to improve practice inside and outside the college classroom. As more colleges and universities have accorded higher priority to student learning, they have also begun to offer enhanced teaching support through consultation services, funding incentives, workshops, and institutes—faculty, instructional, and organizational development undertakings. Increasingly, institutions have looked to teaching centers to take on the responsibility of administering these initiatives because centers are in a unique position to help teachers put new knowledge about pedagogy to work. Such centers already exist at many colleges and universities, with more established each year.

As a faculty developer, I have had the experience of starting two teaching centers at major research universities over the past two decades (Sorcinelli, 1988; Sorcinelli & Aitken, 1995). I have also visited a number of campuses to explore with faculty and academic leaders the feasibility of creating a teaching center or enhancing current faculty development offerings. Several questions have guided my own practice and my consultations with others.

- What should be the key goals of a center?
- What staff, faculty, and administrative issues need to be addressed in developing a center?
- What teaching, learning, and faculty development issues would individuals most like to explore with colleagues?
- What are the institution's biggest assets in developing a center?
- What are the biggest challenges to making things work?

These questions form a foundation for the guiding principles that have directed my work in teaching centers; in fact, their answers are implicit in the principles discussed below.

PRINCIPLES OF GOOD PRACTICE

The experience of any one individual or campus cannot be generalized to all institutions. Individuals need to shape a faculty development center to fit their institutional culture. Still, it is important to share our best ideas so that thinking about what works at one institution might provoke creative ideas and spinoffs on other campuses. The goal is to help us all do our work better. To that end, I offer ten principles of good practice in faculty development, directed toward creating new programs and strengthening established ones.

A few caveats should be mentioned. These principles are not ten commandments; they are guidelines for getting started. They also are not perfectly linear; rather they follow a loose progression, starting from before a center exists and moving to when a center is in place. The grouping of principles is loose as well. Many deal with leadership issues (e.g., getting faculty and administrators involved, suggesting what the center should offer) while a few deal with the nuts and bolts of managing a center (e.g., getting space, funds). Under each principle, I outline best practices in the field of faculty development, based on research, and describe different approaches to good practice that have been used by our own Center for Teaching and other centers as well (Ambrose, 1995; Eble & McKeachie, 1985; Eison & Sorcinelli, 1999; Lindquist, 1978; Nelson & Siegel, 1980; Nemko & Simpson, 1991; Sorcinelli, 1988; Sorcinelli & Aitken, 1995; Wheeler & Schuster 1990; Zahorski, 1993).

Principle 1: Build Stakeholders by Listening to All Perspectives

Teaching centers often occupy a unique place in the structure of an institution because their mission is to address the interests and needs of the entire academic community in support of the education that students receive. The best programs maintain a neutral posture. They are primarily faculty-based—a role which is different from most administrative offices. While they are first and foremost advocates for faculty in their role as teachers, they are also part of the administration. Ideally, the center should provide support and service to academic leaders—without being perceived as an arm of the administration—as well as to faculty in order to further the agenda for teaching excellence. In determining issues to address and priorities to set, a center stands a better chance if it is designed in direct response to the concerns of all constituencies—faculty, teaching assistants, administrators, and students. The faculty developer must be prepared to sometimes walk the tightrope in a delicate balancing act but must also recognize that the center needs the assistance of all of these constituencies to build consensus on the best use of its resources.

How might a center figure out the concerns of various constituencies, especially the faculty? Some institutions test the interest in a center through a needs assessment that can be conducted internally or by an external consultant. Such an assessment can be helpful in identifying important assets and challenges that face the proposed center. As soon as the center opens, it should develop ongoing structures for soliciting ideas. In our center, we first interviewed faculty who had been involved in informal teaching development activities. Over time, we interviewed and surveyed new, midcareer, senior, and retired faculty to help fit our programs to differing faculty needs (Sorcinelli, 1988, 1992). We also established focus groups to assess the needs of department chairs and attended Deans' Council meetings to gain understanding of the needs of schools and colleges (Sorcinelli, 1999a). At a personal level, my interviews, focus groups, and surveys of faculty, teaching assistants, students, and academic leaders have been invaluable. They have allowed me to immerse myself in the culture of the institution, offering me a more expansive view of both faculty and student cultures. These connections also helped develop friends of the center.

Principle 2: Ensure Effective Program Leadership and Management

Building stakeholders is difficult without someone designated to lead the way. Studies of teaching development programs indicate that having someone in the position to both manage and lead a program is critical for success (Eble & McKeachie, 1985; Sorcinelli, 1988; Zahorski, 1993). It is essential to have an individual who has the vision, commitment, time, and energy to take the lead in creating, developing, maintaining, and evaluating services. In larger centers, the appointment of a full-time director is the ideal. A full-time director position allows that individual to be present in the center and to find time to assess needs, develop meaningful contacts and activities, manage day-to-day office tasks, and conduct program evaluation. Most centers are small; even long-established, large research university centers typically have only two to four full-time faculty/staff professionals, a clerical staff person, and sometimes a teaching assistant or more. At smaller institutions, the model of a faculty member on release time has proved workable. In either case, because faculty usually call a person not an office, it is important for the director and staff to be highly visible and accessible so that faculty get to know the center.

I started both of my teaching centers from the beginning and directed them solo for a number of years. It can get lonely, so I encourage new directors to seek help with leading and managing programs early on. For example, before acquiring full-time staff, I brought distinguished teachers in as faculty associates to help out. Such individuals enriched the activities of the center by offering expertise on topics such as writing across the curriculum, teaching technologies, and multicultural issues. They also provided a sounding board for my ideas and concerns. Finally, they were exceedingly cost effective, requiring only one course released per year. In addition to professional support, clerical support, even half-time, is absolutely essential for routine activities such as answering the telephone and duplicating and for such time-consuming activities as workshop and conference management.

Once the institution appoints a director, and, hopefully, support staff, it is time to focus on the two key conditions necessary for moving a new center forward—faculty ownership and administrative support.

Principle 3: Emphasize Faculty Ownership

Studies indicate that faculty development programs are most effective when they have strong faculty ownership and involvement (Eble & McKeachie, 1985; Lindquist, 1978). Optimally, key leadership is provided by effective, respected teachers and scholars. Faculty ownership can ensure that the center remains responsive to faculty needs. It also provides a channel for the emergence of faculty who can take a leadership role in teaching development and renewal and student learning. While the director of a center must oversee and guide initiatives, the final product needs to be faculty inspired.

How might one engage faculty with an interest in teaching? Even before a formal center is proposed, most institutions have a core of committed and outstanding teachers who have been working at a grassroots level to address issues of effective teaching and learning. As suggested earlier, a first step for the new director of a teaching center is to seek out such well-respected faculty. These faculty can serve as allies to the center, raise its visibility, and assist in shaping and implementing programs. In several of our center's ongoing programs (e.g., teaching development workshops, new faculty orientation, tenure and promotion seminars), we invite seasoned faculty to share their insights with pretenure faculty. Faculty also take a primary role in evaluating candidates for annual fellowships, grants, and awards. Modest incentives are not essential, but they do encourage involvement. These might include a title such as faculty associate or teaching mentor, a modest stipend, small funds for professional development, or release time from a course.

Establishing a dedicated advisory committee also can be helpful in ongoing governance. Such committees always have representation from faculty, and some include administrators as well. Some committees are elected and others appointed; either way, the inclusion of faculty and administrative opinion leaders is important. Committees should strive for diversity by balancing such factors as discipline, rank, gender, and race. At the same time, successful committees are often fairly small, usually consisting of eight to 12 members. My own experience suggests that a streamlined committee can more easily schedule meetings, develop into a collaborative working group, and deal with substantive issues than can a larger committee. The more substantive the role of the advisory committee, the more likely it is that faculty as a whole will support and use the program.

Principle 4: Cultivate Administrative Commitment

An administration that is committed to the concept of faculty development and takes an active role in creating a positive environment for teaching is as crucial as faculty involvement (Eble & McKeachie, 1985; Green, 1990; Sorcinelli & Aitken, 1995). Optimally, the administration provides the budgetary support for the center's staffing and programs. Additionally, senior academic officers give tremendous credibility and visibility to the program by participating in its activities (e.g., programs, award ceremonies) and by naming these activities as important values of the institution. Stated simply, everyone on campus might agree that teaching is important, but campus constituencies must also believe that teaching is valued. Key academic officers play a crucial role in indicating the value of teaching.

The development and growth of the center may also hinge on evidence of a strong, credible ally or allies among the senior academic officers. Centers are well served by the support of an institutional administrator who is genuinely interested in faculty development and understands the needs and accomplishments of the center. This individual can serve as a liaison between the chief academic officer, other campus administrators, and the center. On our campus, for example, our deputy provost was an early mentor to the Center for Teaching, seeking opportunities for demonstrating support for initiatives, providing ongoing feedback to the provost and the center, and providing guidance on future program development. In turn, our center gives credit back to advocates in the administration, inviting them to speak, helping them to solve teaching and learning problems in the larger organization, and seeking to acknowledge their influence and express thanks (e.g., a tribute at a dinner, a plaque, flowers).

Centers also can involve chairs and deans in developing and encouraging participation in important programs. For example, some center directors meet with each department chair on an annual basis to assess needs and gather ideas for programs. At our center's orientation for new faculty, we invite chairs and deans to accompany their new faculty member to a luncheon or reception. In turn, department chairs call on our center to offer customized workshops for departments on topics such as student diversity, teaching technologies, and assessment/learning outcomes (Cook & Sorcinelli, 1999; Sorcinelli, 1999b).

Principle 5: Develop Guiding Principles, Clear Goals, and Assessment Procedures

Many directors, after receiving input from the appropriate constituencies, draft a statement expressing their guiding principles or basis for faculty development activities, a definition of faculty or teaching development, and a list of essential goals. Such a statement need not be elaborate, but it is important that the rationale and goals of the center be laid out clearly and communicated regularly to the institution (e.g., through an annual report, a program brochure, a unit plan).

In our center we outlined the following guiding principles:

- Focusing on better learning as well as more effective teaching

- Making sure that the program is voluntary, confidential, and developmental rather than evaluative

- Building a firewall between teaching development work and personnel decision-making processes

- Developing a variety of ways to share the talent, energy, and expertise of our instructors

- Blending campus-wide services with discipline-specific programs for improving teaching

- Increasing communication about teaching and student learning within and between departments and colleges

- Acting as agents for change within the organization in the arenas of teaching and learning, and assuring that the center is not identified as a clinic for sick teachers

The center is similar to a research institute where the best faculty come together for professional opportunities to learn (University of Massachusetts, 1998). This conceptual framework can also help in outlining goals and core activities, guiding budget decisions, and prioritizing the best use of limited resources.

Beyond the guiding principles, the goals of the center need to be discussed and prioritized. It is important not to raise expectations that the teaching center can do anything and everything. Faculty often offer a range of goals that they desire to see in a center. For example, faculty helped generate the following goals at one state university that I recently visited:

- Offer a variety of faculty opportunities for development in teaching to enable student learning.

- Encourage a focus on who our students are, how they learn, and how different teaching approaches can have an impact on their learning.

- Provide opportunities for faculty to come together across disciplines to share their teaching experiences and expertise.

- Provide orientation, mentoring, and instructional support to new and pretenure faculty.

- Provide opportunities for renewal and growth in teaching to senior faculty.

- Support a campus culture of excellence, recognition, and reward for teaching.

These faculty are now sorting and prioritizing these goals, with a focus on where to get started.

Once started, the faculty developer(s) should think about how to assess effectiveness in accomplishing the goals. Aspects to evaluate could include faculty participation, satisfaction, changes in teaching behaviors, student learning outcomes, and changes in the culture for teaching and learning on campus. Assessing the center's impact is important for several reasons. First, assessment demonstrates to developers that we actually do what we say we do. Evaluations of individual consultations and workshops are a great source of in-process feedback. More comprehensive evaluations of programming are something that one might tackle several years down the line. For example, a faculty associate and doctoral student recently helped our center measure, through surveys and in-depth interviews, the decade-long impact of a pretenure teaching fellows program and individual consultations and workshops (Dale, 1998; List, 1997).

A second reason for doing assessment is that it can satisfy the demand for accountability by the central administration. Each year we prepare an annual report that describes our goals, activities, and outcomes (University of Massachusetts, 1998). We mail it to our central administrators, deans, chairs, and faculty involved in our programs. We see our annual report as a way to solicit peer review and feedback. It also keeps assessment in our hands rather than having someone else doing it for or to us.

Principle 6: Strategically Place the Center within the Organizational Structure

There is no single formula for determining the optimal placement of a teaching center in the organizational structure of an institution. Every program and institution has its unique features. Nonetheless, a number of institutions with successful programs place the director of the teaching center in a direct reporting line to the top—usually the provost or vice provost for academic or faculty affairs (Ambrose, 1995; Nemko & Simpson, 1991; Sorcinelli, 1988). This reporting structure lets faculty know that the staff of the center have a direct line to the academic agenda and financial support of the central academic affairs administration. In addition, proximity to the provost and other academic leaders, particularly deans and chairs, can allow the office to consult readily with and apprise key administrators about developments. Finally, this reporting line can help facilitate the kind of faculty and administrative connections that the program needs to advance the institutional teaching mission.

A related issue that merits discussion is funding for the center. Quite simply, the institution needs to finance core endeavors with hard money. Although external funds can sometimes be found, programs focusing on teaching development are highly competitive and demand that the director or faculty spend considerable time seeking out and writing grants with no guarantee of success (Eison & Sorcinelli, 1999). While centers can get started with modest funding (I opened the Center for Teaching with an operating budget of $5,000), improving teaching costs money. Funds for orientations, conferences, teaching technologies, faculty release time, and outside speakers can quickly add up (our operating budget most recently is close to $200,000). Ironically, we have rarely asked for money. We find that funds readily come our way if we continually build a track record of quality programming in areas that are deemed important by students, faculty, and academic leaders.

A final organizational issue to ponder is the actual physical location of the teaching center. Too often, centers for teaching and learning are perceived as helpful but distant, not well known, hard to find, and on the periphery of campus. While space is often tight at most institutions, it is important that the center develop a presence and identity on campus, that it be accessible, and that it be allocated enough space to allow for individual consultation and group seminars. Negotiations about structural issues such as location, funding, and space may not seem imperative, but together they signal the extent to which a campus-wide center is important.

Principle 7: Offer a Range of Opportunities, but Lead with Strengths

Studies show that faculty have different needs at different stages of their careers (Sorcinelli, 1985). In response, it makes sense that your center create programs to address a range of differing needs and encompass as many faculty as possible. Many centers include orientations for teaching assistants and new faculty, early feedback mechanisms for pretenure teachers, and mentoring opportunities involving senior faculty.

When asked what issues they would most like the center to tackle, faculty often suggest a wide range of programs. Well-regarded activities include the following:

- Individual, confidential consultation services to allow a faculty member to assess what is going well in terms of teaching and student learning and what might merit attention

- Campus-wide workshops or informal seminars on teaching and learning topics

- Special programs for new and pretenure faculty: orientations; mentoring; opportunities to get early, formative, helpful feedback on teaching; and ongoing seminars on teaching

- Special programs to encourage the engagement of senior faculty, such as offering "master teacher" workshops, conducting a set of seminars on teaching and technology, and employing senior colleagues as mentors

- Targeted programs for disciplines, departments, and colleges such as course and program assessment, teaching evaluation (by students, peers, and supervisors), supporting adjunct faculty, and developing leadership skills for department chairs

At the same time, in programs limited by resources, experience suggests that the director would be wise to prioritize commitments carefully, lead with staffing strengths, and insist on quality programming. Credibility with faculty is better fostered by offering a small group of carefully focused, planned, and conducted programs than with a breadth of program offerings which do not maintain distinction.

In fact, I would offer a caution to developers of newly established programs. Do not be dazzled by the number and range of activities an experienced program may offer. At our Center for Teaching, we started with a few projects and spent the next ten years creating a comprehensive program. We now see the need to take stock of each award and opportunity lest we become too stretched—in terms of both staffing and focus. My advice to new developers is to think big but start small.

Principle 8: Encourage Collegiality and Community

Studies confirm that faculty members need each other's support and that many faculty members express the desire to work with colleagues within and outside their disciplines (Eble & McKeachie, 1985; Sorcinelli, 1985). In fact, getting to know other faculty members and sharing ideas about teaching is frequently described as one of the primary benefits of participation in faculty development programs. Faculty conversations about teaching often provide the means for the individual teacher to adapt an idea or strategy for his or her own course. Faculty members also take cues from each other and are more likely to take advantage of faculty development opportunities if based on the personal recommendation of a colleague. The faculty development center can take an important role in convening faculty members so that such discussions can occur. Even small rewards such as a luncheon or refreshments act as a positive motivation and add greatly to creating a congenial setting.

At many institutions that I visit, faculty suggest that there needs to be more good talk about good teaching on campus and that a center could facilitate such discussion. Again, suggestions center on the notion of tapping into the talent of faculty. As one interviewee observed,

> There are great teachers here who could be called on to lead workshops or informal noon-hour sessions. They could provide advice to and facilitate discussions with special groups such as new faculty, faculty who supervise teaching assistants, faculty who involve undergraduates in research projects, faculty who teach large classes or small seminars, faculty who teach freshmen, or faculty interested in different pedagogies such as changing technologies.

Over time, faculty, as well as deans and chairs, become advocates of the center, urging their colleagues to engage voluntarily in activities that support teaching. Our faculty have developed teaching themes within a department, exchanged syllabi and materials, held brown bag lunches to discuss course designs or teaching methods, and worked with new faculty as mentors. A central goal here is to reduce the isolation in which faculty teach their classes and to provide a means of letting colleagues know about useful innovations.

Principle 9: Create Collaborative Systems of Support

Like most teaching centers, our aspirations to serve and influence the institution will never be matched by our levels of staffing and funding. We decided early on that program initiatives would be better accomplished by joining forces with others rather than working alone. In this way, we are doing what we encourage faculty to do—create communities of support. One of our most successful strategies has been to call not only for the approval, but also for the financial support, of key administrative offices on campus. In other words, we have been able to enhance existing faculty development activities and create new ones through a planned strategy of collaboration—of ideas, staff, resources, and funds—with other campus agencies (e.g., Provost's Office, Academic Deans' Council, Writing Program, Office of Academic Computing, Graduate School, Office of Research Affairs, and Office of Academic Planning and Assessment).

One example is our TEACHnology Fellows Program (Shih & Sorcinelli, 2000; Sorcinelli, 1999b). Each year, this fellowship helps ten midcareer and senior faculty apply the capacities of technology to teaching and learning. The year includes a retreat, year-long seminars, consultations, and assessments. We first presented the idea for such a fellowship to our school and college deans, and they agreed to each sponsor one or two fellows by awarding them a high-performance laptop computer. In turn, we agreed to design the program so that it encouraged fellows to return as peer innovators to their home departments and colleges. We then developed partnerships with our Office of Academic Computing and our Center for Computer-Based Instructional Technology. They offered consultation and training not available in the Center for Teaching, and we now work more formally with academic computing to improve teaching technologies on campus. Both the quality of the fellowship and the relationship between our centers have benefited from these partnerships. And much like our other collaborative ventures, this entire fellowship is internally funded—possibly the best indicator of the success of such cooperative alliances.

Principle 10: Provide Measures of Recognition and Rewards

In a number of studies, beyond the specific concerns of faculty members, there is often something vaguely described as a need for recognition and rewards (Eble & McKeachie, 1985; Sorcinelli, 1985). Successful programs use a range of informal and formal means to motivate participation and involvement. Increasingly, faculty with whom I talk give high marks to provisions for class-free time, release time, or other such time-enhancing resources for developing a teaching innovation or for focusing on an especially demanding teaching activity, such as integrating technology into the classroom. Such mechanisms provide faculty with the necessary time for professional development. Others value small teaching grants programs—for books, software, and other teaching materials or travel to a teaching-related conference. Similarly, appreciation and recognition of faculty contributions to the center can be acknowledged through a note, a plaque, a luncheon, a gift certificate for books, or a designation as mentor. These ideas are low cost but high yield in terms of faculty satisfaction. If one were seeking a strategy for faculty development at any institution, such acknowledgment might be a place to begin. It is not, however, the place to end.

CONCLUSION

As the center develops and matures, it can play an important role in creating an institutional structure and culture that values and rewards teaching (Chism, 1998; Sorcinelli & Aitken, 1995). For example, staff in our center now consult on the development of student rating systems and broader teaching evaluation systems, offer programs on the teaching portfolio, help departments design criteria for excellence in teaching, coordinate distinguished teaching awards, and sit on a provost's task force on faculty roles and rewards. These are all potential ways to make the reward structure more responsive to teaching. We have discovered that getting to this point of influence required our recognizing from the start the prime importance of identifying support, crossing boundaries, creating linkages, arranging opportunities for collegiality and community, and providing ways for faculty to develop and receive recognition as teachers.

In other words, when starting or sustaining teaching centers, faculty developers need to live according to the ten principles of good practice.

REFERENCES

Ambrose, S. (1995). Fitting programs to institutional cultures: The founding and evolution of the university teaching center. In P. Seldin & Associates, (Eds.), *Improving college teaching* (pp. 77-90). Stillwater, OK: New Forums Press.

Chism, N. V. N. (1998). The role of educational developers in institutional change: From the basement office to the front office. In M. Kaplan & D. Lieberman (Eds.), *To improve the academy: Vol. 17. Resources for faculty, instructional, and organizational development* (pp. 141-154). Stillwater, OK: New Forums Press.

Cook, C., & Sorcinelli, M. D. (1999, March). Building multiculturalism into teaching development programs. *AAHE Bulletin*, 51 (7), 3-6.

Dale, E. (1998). *An assessment of a faculty development program at a research university.* Unpublished doctoral dissertation, University of Massachusetts at Amherst.

Eble, K., & McKeachie, W. (1985). *Improving undergraduate education through faculty development.* San Francisco, CA: Jossey-Bass.

Eison, J., & Sorcinelli, M. D. (1999, January). *Improving teaching and learning: Academic leaders and faculty developers as partners.* Presentation at the Seventh AAHE Conference on Faculty Roles and Rewards, San Diego, CA.

Green, M. F. (1990). Why good teaching needs active leadership. In P. Seldin & Associates (Eds.), *How administrators can improve teaching* (pp. 45-62). San Francisco, CA: Jossey Bass.

Lindquist, J. (Ed.).(1978). *Designing teaching improvement programs.* Berkeley, CA: Pacific Sounding Press.

List, K. (1997). A continuing conversation on teaching: An evaluation of a decade-long Lilly Teaching Fellows Program 1986-96. In D. Dezure & M. Kaplan (Eds.), *To improve the academy: Vol. 16. Resources for faculty, instructional, and organizational development* (pp. 201-224). Stillwater, OK: New Forums Press.

Nelson, W. C., & Siegel, M. E. (1980). *Effective approaches to faculty development.* Washington, DC: Association of American Colleges.

Nemko, M., & Simpson, R. D. (1991). Nine keys to enhancing campus-wide influence of faculty development centers. In K. J. Zahorski (Ed.), *To improve the academy: Vol. 10. Resources for faculty, instructional, and organizational development* (pp. 83-88). Stillwater, OK: New Forums Press.

Shih, M., & Sorcinelli, M. D. (2000). TEACHnology: Linking teaching and technology in faculty development. In M. Kaplan & D. Lieberman (Eds.), *To improve the academy: Vol. 18. Resources for faculty, instructional, and organizational development* (pp. 151-163). Bolton, MA: Anker.

Sorcinelli, M. D. (1985, April). *Faculty careers: Personal, institutional, and societal dimensions.* Paper presented at the meeting of the American Educational Research Association, Chicago, IL.

Sorcinelli, M. D. (1988). Encouraging excellence: Long-range planning for faculty development. In E. Wadsworth (Ed.), *A handbook for new practitioners* (pp. 27-31). Stillwater, OK: New Forums Press.

Sorcinelli, M. D. (1992). *The career development of pretenure faculty: An institutional study.* Amherst, MA: University of Massachusetts at Amherst.

Sorcinelli, M. D. (1999a). Enhancing department leadership and management. *The Department Chair, 9* (3), 4-6.

Sorcinelli, M.D. (1999b). Post-tenure review through post-tenure development: What linking senior faculty and technology taught us. *Innovative Higher Education, 24,* 61-72.

Sorcinelli, M. D., & Aitken, N. (1995). Improving teaching: Academic leaders and faculty developers as partners. In W. A. Wright & Associates (Ed.), *Teaching improvement practices: Successful strategies for higher education* (pp. 311-323). Bolton, MA: Anker.

University of Massachusetts (1998). *Annual report* (1997-98). University of Massachusetts at Amherst, Center For Teaching.

Wheeler, D. W., & Schuster, J. H. (1990). Building comprehensive programs to enhance faculty development. In J. H. Schuster, D. W. Wheeler, & Associates (Eds.), *Enhancing faculty careers,* (pp. 275-297). San Francisco, CA: Jossey Bass.

Zahorski, K. (1993). Taking the lead: Faculty development as institutional change agent. In D. L. Wright & J. P. Lunde. (Eds.), *To improve the academy: Vol. 12. Resources for faculty, instructional, and organizational development* (pp. 227-245). Stillwater, OK: New Forums Press.

Mary Deane Sorcinelli is Associate Provost for Faculty Development at the University of Massachusetts at Amherst. She has served as a member of the Core Committee and as President Elect (2000-2001) of the POD Network.

Email: msorcinelli@acad.umass.edu

3

Program Types and Prototypes

Delivee L. Wright

Programs for faculty development all have a common theme: improving the quality of education by working with faculty. While this is a shared vision, the services vary greatly, and variations are as numerous as the programs themselves. Indeed, an examination of faculty development programs in different institutions reveals that the one consistency is the variation among them. Early researchers and thinkers in the field of faculty and instructional development, such as Gaff (1975), Lindquist (1978), Eble and McKeachie (1985), and Erickson (1986), established an important basic principle by articulating the need for individualized programs. The innovation must fit the local culture, and the variety in program types is therefore appropriate and proper.

This chapter explores several factors that form the foundation for the design of a faculty development program and describes several types of programs intended to meet differing needs. Although variation occurs, generic program types have emerged for which prototypical programs exist. These program types will be described according to location in the structure of the institution. .

FACTORS OF A PROGRAM

Leadership

A number of contextual factors interact to fashion the specific elements of the program. The leadership of key people such as supportive administrators, faculty leaders, and/or faculty developers is critical for implementation of a program. Their experiences, interests, and areas of expertise influence decisions that shape reasonable and appropriate directions for a program. Each individual also sees a differing kind of potential. This variety of experience and perspective comes into play as needs are assessed, goals are established, and programs are implemented and evaluated. If, for example, the faculty developer's background is in the design of instructional materials and technological innovations and the campus administrators are interested in reviewing the general education curriculum, then the program that evolves will be very different from that of another faculty developer who is experienced in counseling and is charged with duties using student evaluation data to improve teaching.

Institutional Community

Each institutional community has characteristics which influence the needs to be met by faculty development—such as mission, size, student traits, and faculty roles. While contributing to the uniqueness of each institution, these characteristics then establish the limits within which different needs and possibilities may be determined. For instance, a research university with many large classes and graduate teaching assistants will have a very different set of needs from the liberal arts campus which has a smaller student body and prides itself on personalized approaches to learning.

Local Faculty

Local faculty members contribute their own signatures to a program as their sense of ownership and participation influence its development. One of the fundamental conditions of successful activities is that they relate to the needs of the targeted faculty. For example, at one time faculty members may feel pressed to find ways to increase student involvement or critical thinking abilities while at a different time they may be more interested in techniques for testing, grading, or implementing web technologies. The accurate incorporation of the needs of local faculty members is important for the ongoing success and longevity of a program.

Age and Historical Evolution

Age and historical evolution of faculty development in a given institution often affect the elements of a program as they evolve to meet specific goals. A relatively young program may be responding to high visibility, short-term areas of interest, or areas which contribute to building faculty acceptance. A more mature program, which has already gained acceptability, may design in-depth, longer-term activities that address major shifts in the institution's academic perspectives.

Availability of Resources

Availability of resources—financial, human, and informational— place constraints upon every program. Changes that take place are reflections of the interaction of these variables. We are all well aware that the realization of desirable goals and activities is limited by the people and budget required to accomplish them. Therefore, we all prioritize to match these variables to the most valued outcomes.

While the above factors contribute to variation among programs, there are also commonalties which result from location in an institution's structure or from targeting similar functions.

STRUCTURAL VARIATIONS

Structural variations among programs occur both in how and where they are organized:

- A single, campus-wide center is named, staffed, and budgeted within the institution to accomplish targeted development goals. It serves the entire institution or a substantial segment of it, in a variety of ways.

- A multicampus, cooperative program coordinates programs and resources to serve several campuses in meeting their faculty development needs in a number of ways.

- A special purpose center serves a specifically defined audience to accomplish more narrowly defined development goals.

- Development components are a part of a broader academic program. These often occur when resources or numbers to be served are relatively small.

A more complete description of each of these types and current examples follows. However, structures change, and readers should consult the annual directory of the POD Network or the POD web page at [http://www.podweb.org] for more information on specific programs. Increasing numbers of centers and programs have their own web pages which may also be consulted for details.

Campus-Wide Centers

Locus. The typical campus-wide center is organized administratively under the chief academic office of the institution. It has responsibility for designing and implementing developmental program activities which support broad academic goals of quality of instruction in some very specific ways.

Staffing. The leadership to direct the typical center's programs is often selected from the local faculty on the basis of special expertise, demonstrated leadership, or personal interest. Even so, a growing pool of experienced faculty developers can be found nationwide, which increases the availability of external expertise for these positions. Staff in campus-wide centers typically include a director, perhaps an associate director, one or two professional faculty developers, a part-time graduate assistant, and a secretary. Professional staff may hold faculty rank, which is usually negotiated in an appropriate department. In some instances, the director holds faculty rank while other faculty developers are professional staff with no responsibilities in other departments. Both academic year and calendar year appointments are found in these centers.

Budget. Most campus-wide centers are supported by the institution's teaching budget, but some are supplemented by grant funds for special aspects of the program. However, external grant funds for faculty and instructional development efforts have shrunk in recent years, and dependence on such monies for ongoing efforts presents difficulties. Budgets vary greatly in relation to program elements, and amounts depend upon whether they include grants to faculty or other special categories of expenses. Most have adequate funds to support a multifaceted program.

Audience. Campus-wide centers serve faculty in all stages of careers: new, tenure-seeking, and tenured senior faculty. The programs are designed not only for troubled faculty, but for all faculty. Increasingly, part-time faculty needs are being addressed as well.

Programs. In most cases, the activities of campus-wide centers have gone beyond the traditional grants, leaves, and travel for faculty development. They have incorporated innovations to stimulate change for targeted improvements. The programs of the center are designed to utilize a variety of approaches to serve a large audience. Therefore, program offerings are numerous and may include varying combinations of activities. New information or skill-building workshops, seminars, conferences, and individual consultation are found in most program designs. Retreats may be included in the programming as well. Workshops and seminars might be two hours to several days in length and provide an opportunity to stimulate thinking and communication about pertinent topics.

Communication about instruction can also be encouraged with luncheon-discussion or study groups with more informal interaction. Faculty also benefit from programs such as teaching circles to promote networking so that faculty members find others with common interests and needs. Flyers, brochures, electronic notification, and handout materials can be used to announce development activities as well as to maintain visibility of the program. Frequently, newsletters are used for communicating new ideas, event information, or for recognition of contributions. Newsletters have the advantage of reaching people who are reluctant to participate in other ways, especially when a large number of faculty are involved.

One of the most effective modes of development is individual consultation. The skills of the developer are crucial in working in a way that is nonjudgmental, supportive, and knowledgeable, yet can intervene in a way that change occurs. This program element has great potential for promoting change when combined with videotaped analysis of teaching and feedback on student perceptions by questionnaire or by small group techniques.

A resource library of articles, books, and bibliographies can be important in providing information for faculty on instructional topics. At the least, the faculty developer and the center must have a bookshelf of favorite resources to draw upon. Useful materials can also be found in videotapes, computer software, and self-instructional modules. Increasingly, centers are using web pages for the dissemination of resource materials, and features such as the POD listserv provide a responsive resource for consultation with faculty developers in other institutions.

Assisting in curricular review and revision, from single courses to whole programs, is another emphasis the programs of a campus-wide center may take. Well-designed course materials and strategies lead to better instruction. Production of course manuals as well as media materials often result from this approach. In recent years, campus-wide centers have begun to be more involved in partnering relationships with other offices/units within their institutions to enhance the focus on institutional initiatives, examples of which include outcomes assessment, diversity, and writing/speaking across the curriculum.

Recognition and reward elements of a faculty development program can take the form of teaching awards programs or special grants to faculty. Teaching awards are often given with a stipend in special ceremonies in the academic community. Small grants also provide recognition and encouragement, but the funds are awarded to complete an improvement project, travel, or provide a stipend for summer work or leaves. These projects may also include plans for professional or personal development.

Faculty developers often serve on faculty or administrative committees charged with responsibility for instructional quality. Such committees may also be active in seeking external funding for special projects.

Some centers also include an associated program such as student learning skill assistance, examinations and evaluations services, media services, career development, or faculty exchange programs.

While no one program incorporates all of these activities, most campus-wide centers do provide a variety which fit the needs, goals, and resources of their own institution. Within parameters of time and resources, centers will often target a few areas for focused effort, and these can evolve over time into different emphases. While structures may change, a few examples of campus-wide centers that combine media and other faculty and instructional development services include those listed below:

- Center for Teaching and Learning, University of North Carolina at Chapel Hill

- Center for Instructional Development and Research, University of Washington

- Office of Instructional Development and Technology, Dalhousie University

- Office of Instructional Services, Colorado State University

- Office of Instructional Support and Development, The University of Georgia

Centers organized only for teaching/professional development include the following:

- Center for the Enhancement of Teaching, University of Northern Iowa

- Center for Professional Development, Kean University

- Center for Research on Learning and Teaching, University of Michigan

- Center for Teaching, University of Massachusetts at Amherst

- Center for Teaching Effectiveness, University of Delaware

- Center for Teaching Effectiveness, University of Texas, Austin

- Centre for the Support of Teaching, York University

- Faculty Development Center, University of Nebraska, Omaha

- Office of Faculty Development, St. Norbert College

- Program for Excellence in Teaching, University of Missouri, Columbia

- Teaching and Learning Center, University of Nebraska, Lincoln

- University Teaching Services, University of Alberta

Multicampus Cooperative Programs

Locus. Multicampus, cooperative programs usually have a central office which coordinates efforts and administers resources to accomplish goals in faculty development for a number of institutions. In addition, individuals on each campus are charged with local communication and coordination. Such offices and programs may evolve from statewide systems of higher education, or they may be voluntary consortia of colleges in a given geographical region with a similar mission.

Staffing. These programs usually have a central coordinating council composed of academic administrators, faculty, and, occasionally, students from each campus plus one or more central administrators charged with responsibility for managing resources, coordinating the larger group, and developing the program. Central staffing is often quite minimal and is not generally more than three persons. Individual campuses within this type of program may also have faculty committees as well as resource centers and staffs to complement the multicampus resources.

Budget. Budgets tend to be relatively large since they represent the pooling of resources to support development of many faculty members. In some cases, such structures began with funds from grants, and costs were later shifted to support from within the system.

Programs. The unique possibilities for interinstitutional communication are reflected in the activities offered by multicampus cooperative faculty development programs. Often grants are awarded for travel, leaves, research, summer fellowships, and special projects with competition from all campuses. Weekend and summer conferences, workshops, retreats, academies, and institutes frequently are discipline-based and involve faculty from multiple campuses. Communication among institutions is facilitated by newsletters, publications, and other networking devices including electronic bulletin boards. While collaboration among faculty from different campuses is a special opportunity afforded by this structure, the individual consultation approaches to faculty development are seldom available unless campuses provide their own consultants.

Prototypes of multicampus cooperative programs include the following:

- California State University Institute for Teaching and Learning

- The Governor's Teaching Fellows Program, The University of Georgia System

- Faculty Professional Development Council, Pennsylvania State System of Higher Education

- Office of Professional and Instructional Development, University of Wisconsin System

- West Virginia Consortium for Faculty and Course Development in International Studies

Special Purpose Centers

Locus. These centers may be campus-wide and may even serve other colleges and universities. They are designed to target a more limited goal than other campus-wide or multicampus centers, even though they serve a wide range of faculty and, in a number of institutions, graduate teaching assistants.

Staffing. Staff of these centers have special expertise consistent with the goals of the center. Numbers of persons generally range from one to three professionals plus support staff.

Budget. While some of these programs began with grant funds, they are usually either part of the institution's budget or they generate income from services offered to outside clientele.

Programs. Program offerings vary according to the specific topical goals. Newsletters, workshops, publications, and resource materials continue to be a mainstay for communication to audiences. These programs can best be understood by reviewing a few specific examples. The Individual Development and Educational Assessment (IDEA) Center, formerly associated with Kansas State University, is a not-for-profit corporation which provides colleges and universities with regional and national conferences as well as processes for administering and scoring instruments for assessing performance of faculty, department chairs, deans, and administrators. Newsletters and IDEA papers disseminate information on both faculty development and assessment. The Graduate Teacher Program at the University of Colorado, Boulder is specially designed for teaching assistants with workshops, seminars, newsletters, manuals, and videotapes. The Lynchburg College Symposium Readings Program focuses on preparing faculty to teach in this special, interdisciplinary program and has contributed significantly to the overall growth and vitality of faculty members (Pittas, 2000). Computer Training and Support Services at Colorado State University works with faculty, teaching assistants, and staff members to enhance understanding and implementation of computer technologies.

Development Components of Other Academic Programs

Locus. These programs are not essentially different in types of activities or goals from campus-wide centers, but they are organized within the institution under another unit such as a dean's office or a faculty development committee.

Staffing. In these programs, either faculty with release time carry responsibilities for implementation, or an administrator has this assignment as part of his or her workload.

Budget. Allocations depend upon the unit priorities and numbers being served.

Programs. Responsibility for program development usually resides in a faculty committee, with at least some faculty release time. While the goal of instructional improvement is consistent with other types of faculty development programs, the scope may be limited by resources. Examples of these include the following:

- Faculty Development Program, Faculty of Medicine, University of Toronto

- Faculty Professional Development Program, Red Deer College

- Office of Professional and Organizational Development, Institute of Agriculture and Natural Resources, University of Nebraska, Lincoln

- Teaching and Learning Committee, Wabash College

CONCLUSION

This discussion of program types and prototypes provides clear indication that there is indeed a successful variety of structures to promote faculty, instructional, and organizational development. No one way suffices for all institutions of higher education, and there are many ways to accomplish the goal of promoting professional development.

REFERENCES

Eble, K. E., & McKeachie, W. J. (1985). *Improving undergraduate education through faculty development.* San Francisco, CA: Jossey-Bass.

Erickson, B. L. (1986). Faculty development at four-year colleges and universities: Lessons learned. *Proceedings of faculty evaluation and development: Lessons learned* (pp. 33-48). Manhattan, KS: Kansas State University, Center for Faculty Evaluation and Development.

Gaff, J. G. (1975). *Toward faculty renewal.* San Francisco, CA: Jossey-Bass.

Lindquist, J. (Ed.). (1978). *Designing teaching improvement programs.* Berkeley, CA: Pacific Sounding Press.

Pittas, P. (2000). A model program from the perspective of faculty development. *Innovative Higher Education, 25*, 97-110.

Delivee L. Wright is Director of the Teaching and Learning Center at the University of Nebraska, Lincoln. She began as a practitioner in faculty development in the early 1970s, and she has served on the Core Committee of the POD Network. She was the coexecutive director of POD from 1989-1991.

Email: dwright1@unl.edu

4

Establishing an Instructional Development Program: An Example

L. Dee Fink

This chapter describes the ideas and activities that were instrumental in setting up an instructional development program at a moderately large state university. Some of the events and directions of this process were unique to the place and setting, but most have general applicability and can serve as an example of implementation of ideas already discussed in this volume. I will begin with a discussion of the origins of the program, indicate the rationale for the set of program activities that were chosen, and conclude with a set of comments on maintaining the program over time.

ORIGINS

Five important factors contributed to the implementation of our instructional development program:

1) The existence of a support group

2) A low-risk setting for experimenting with new ideas

3) A way of gaining a good understanding of the institution

4) A basis for gaining credibility with the faculty

5) Administrative support

The following narrative explains how these factors helped establish the program.

I first came to the University of Oklahoma in 1976 as an assistant professor, fresh out of graduate school, with interest and a joint appointment in geography and higher education. The dean of education assembled a group of four junior professors, including myself, to see what might be done to promote instructional development on the campus. We met periodically to discuss ideas and possible activities. This small group became a center of support and an action group that kept the impetus going during this formative period.

One of the important contributions of this early group was the initiation of an annual program for new teaching assistants (TAs). Academic departments recognized that graduate students needed help in teaching and encouraged their TAs to attend. This recognition of need gave us as organizers a chance to go public with our ideas on better teaching in a setting where the risks of learning and trying new concepts were relatively low.

A second key factor was my decision to interview a large number of department chairs during that first year about the instructional mission of their units, their instructional needs, and the outside resources that would be most helpful. This activity educated me in two very important ways. First, I became much more familiar with the differences in the instructional programs of departments. For example, some have very heavy service roles while others are primarily focused on their own undergraduate majors and graduate students. Second, I discovered that there were individual professors and departments doing some excellent and/or very innovative teaching. The problem, however, was that nobody knew about it. I took this to mean that there was no significant dialogue and no communication about teaching on campus; hence, there was no sense of a teaching community. This lesson had a major impact on my vision of what an instructional development program could and should try to do.

A third element in the origins of our program grew out of a graduate course I taught for the College of Education in instructional strategies, which focused on course design and involved graduate students who anticipated a career in college teaching. During the course, we visited the classes of several professors who were unusually good and/or innovative teachers. And as a class project, we invited one or two professors to class who had a course they wanted to redesign. We then worked with them on that task.

These contacts with professors had several benefits. First, they put the class and me into a consulting role, which, in turn, created an acceptable image of the role that I eventually was appointed to fulfill on campus. Second, a number of professors who came for design assistance found that the ideas we gave them worked. They were better able to develop their courses in ways that pleased both them and their students.

These two developments, receiving requests for help in the classroom and seeing some professors able to make clear improvement in their teaching, eventually allowed me to present these findings to the provost in the hope that he would be willing to fund a faculty development program. We discussed the costs of running such a program, and the funding was approved.

To summarize this story of origins, I return to the importance of the five factors identified earlier:

1) The existence of some kind of support group. The existence of a support group generated excitement, new ideas, and a readiness to mount trial workshops and retreats.

2) The low-risk setting provided the opportunity to try our ideas. For me, this was the annual TA orientation program. Several of our ideas for session topics worked, and although some did not, those did not create problems.

3) The interviews with department chairs provided an understanding of the details of our institutional situation in terms of instruction and were important in deciding what would and would not be helpful.

4) We gained credibility from the contacts that grew out of the education course and the TA program. This in turn made faculty ready to respond when various activities and services were made available.

5) Administrative support from the provost and the dean of education played a critical role in our acceptance.

ESTABLISHING THE PROGRAM

Funding

Although the costs associated with the implementation of our program are now obsolete, the POD Network has since collected a large amount of program information, including budgets from instructional development programs in the U.S. and Canada. Such information can help institutions decide how much money is needed for the scope of their particular program. More detailed information can be found by visiting the POD web site [www.podweb.org].

Program Activities

In selecting program activities in the formative period, I had two
guiding images of what the program should do. The first, arising from
my interviews with department chairs, was to create mechanisms of
dialogue and communication within the university about teaching. If
professors could talk to each other about their problems, their solutions, and their experiments, a teaching community could develop
that would exert a profound influence on facultys' attitude about and
practice of teaching. Second, as the university's instructional consultant, I needed to provide leadership on ideas for effective teaching.
This would involve reading widely, attending selected professional
meetings, and knowing which professors were valuable local
resources for ideas on teaching.

Given these general goals, I selected six basic program activities
that have worked well over the years. This particular combination has
reached a variety of people and allowed me to be proactive as well as
reactive.

Newsletter. With help from a part-time graduate assistant, I publish a quarterly, four-page newsletter. The most prominent part of the
newsletter is usually a vignette of a faculty member who is doing
something unusual as a teacher or someone who is teaching unusually well. I select the professor who is to be featured, and the graduate
assistant conducts the interview and visits the professor's classes to
gather information for the article. The newsletter, which is sent to all
professors and teaching assistants, is also a good outlet for important
institutional developments on teaching, such as the results of a TA
survey about their training and supervision and the report of a faculty senate committee on the evaluation of teaching.

The newsletter has been an effective mechanism for communicating with the entire teaching faculty. Although it is most likely limited
in its impact on any given faculty member, it is meant to remind them
that they are part of a teaching community. Even though it has the
broadest reach of all the program activities, the cost of the TA and of
printing makes it the single most expensive activity in the program.

Faculty discussion groups. The most exciting part of the program
has been initiating and running a number of faculty discussions for a
year. Faculty members have lunch every two weeks during the year
and engage in a one-hour discussion on an aspect of college teaching.
Some groups are set up to discuss a series of topics, each of which is
selected by the group itself. Others work on larger problems for a

whole semester or year. They have addressed such topics as how to design a course, how to teach creatively, how to write better tests, and how to work with different kinds of students. In these meetings I operate mainly as a discussion moderator and partly as a resource finder; e.g., selecting and distributing a pertinent article or locating and inviting a faculty member who has some expertise on the topic.

These groups have been extraordinarily effective in creating a sense of community. Many participants have said this was the only activity that allowed them to meet and get to know faculty members outside of their own departments. Others have noted that meeting time after time with other professors to talk about teaching renewed their commitment to doing a good job in the classroom. My own observation is that a significant portion of the 50 to 60 people who sign up for these groups each year change what they do in the classroom in some important way.

Compared to the newsletter, the discussion groups reach fewer people, but a high percentage are likely to experience a major impact on their teaching. This activity also allows many individual problems to be addressed in a group format rather than by an individual consultant (Fink, 1984).

Individual consulting. Nonetheless, there are also faculty members who have questions about their teaching that, for one reason or another, are best pursued individually. Each year, 20 to 30 faculty members and some TAs request individualized help. Some are encouraged by their department chairs to seek assistance (usually as the result of student complaints and/or low course evaluations from students), while others decide to come on their own. Some have procedural questions that can be answered by a short discussion, perhaps supplemented by an article or two. Others want a more in-depth analysis of their classroom performance, which requires discussions, classroom observations, and often solicitation of student reactions in the form of written responses and/or interviews. A number of books are now available to help instructional consultants gain proficiency in this process (e.g., Brinko & Menges, 1997; Lewis & Lunde, 2001).

This activity has a high potential for changing the teaching practices of individual professors, but it also requires a fair amount of time and skill. The skills involve knowing how to communicate (including how to listen), knowing what to look for in a course design and/or in a set of classroom events, and identifying activities that help faculty members actually make the changes needed in their teaching.

Special course evaluation questionnaire. One general service I make available through my office each semester is the Individual Development and Education Assessment (IDEA) course evaluation system developed by the Center for Faculty Evaluation and Development at Kansas State University. Our university requires that all courses be evaluated by students each semester, and each college has its own questionnaire for doing this. Many professors, however, feel a need for a more sophisticated approach to this task. I have selected the IDEA form to help professors obtain a more in-depth assessment of their teaching because it has criteria that professors appreciate (e.g., "Did the students learn what the professor was trying to teach?"), a diagnostic section, and national norms.

To promote the use of this course evaluation tool, I send a memo near the end of each semester to all departments for distribution to their faculty members, informing them that materials for the IDEA system are available from my office, without cost to the department, simply by returning the completed form. Typically, 20 to 30 professors avail themselves of this service each semester. When the results come back from the processing center, I strongly encourage each first- or second- time user to come by my office so I can explain the multipage printout. If the results are good, I congratulate them and urge them to keep up the good work. If the results are not flattering, we can begin the process of figuring out what went wrong and identifying possible responses, including, perhaps, their participation in a faculty discussion group or my visiting their classes as an instructional consultant. Hence, this service not only provides useful feedback to professors on their teaching; it also connects faculty members with other program activities.

TA orientation program. Our campus has approximately 600 TAs, and about one-third of these are new each fall. This is a particularly vulnerable group of teachers who are generally new to teaching. We began this program activity with a formal orientation program for all new TAs, which was essentially a one-day intensive course on teaching. I was responsible for organizing the program, but it enlisted the contributions of several faculty members and senior TAs from across campus.

This program operated successfully for some years, but recently our provost provided the funds for a major expansion. As a result, we now have a five-day program for all new international TAs (ITAs) followed by a another four-day program for all TAs. The program for

ITAs includes work on classroom English, an orientation to American higher education, and a preliminary introduction to American culture. The program for all TAs includes sessions on general topics (e.g., the responsibilities of TAs, how to handle cheating, sexual harassment, evaluating your own teaching) and several opportunities for videotaped microteaching on such things as lecturing, leading discussions, and handling classroom problems.

This program activity is a special service for a particular audience. It is one which everyone agrees is needed and the TAs appreciate because it provides them with needed information on their new role and responsibilities.

Program for new faculty members. In 1988, the provost decided to fund a new program activity. As a result, I organized a professional development seminar intended for all new faculty members. It is modeled after our faculty discussion groups in that the group meets for lunch and a learning program. The major difference is that the new faculty group meets only during the fall semester. The purpose of this seminar is to help new faculty get off to a better start and to make them feel a part of the institution (Fink, 1992).

Popularly known as the new faculty seminar, this program has multiple sessions on five general topics:

1) Introduction to the university
   • Organization
   • Policies
   • Procedures
   • Offices

2) Teaching
   • Good teaching
   • Local resources available

3) Research
   • Writing grant proposals
   • Local support programs for finding and administering grants

4) Professional development
   • Ideas and activities that new faculty should keep in mind about their long-term professional growth

5) New location
   • Introduction to the city and state

DISCUSSION

These six activities—newsletter, faculty discussion groups, individual consulting, special course evaluation questionnaire, TA orientation program, and program for new faculty members—described above have turned out to be an effective combination, and they have succeeded in attracting faculty participation since their introduction. Nonetheless, I should also comment on what is not included in the program, and why.

First, our campus does have a program of small grants for instruction-related projects, but they are not handled by my office. These grants are administered by the Vice-Provost for Instructional Services and an ad hoc committee of faculty members. These serve a useful function by supporting experimentation and the professional development of the teaching faculty. They are simply separated organizationally from the activities described above.

Second, I sponsor very few workshops. The main reason is that most topics which might be handled in a workshop are addressed through the faculty discussion groups. In addition, I believe faculty members are more likely to change their attitudes and practices as a result of recurring discussions than as a result of a one-time meeting. The exceptions to this are topics which, by their nature, do not seem to need extended discussions. For example, several requests from faculty members for help in developing the teaching section of their tenure portfolio prompted me to organize a half-day workshop on preparing for the tenure review process. The workshop is now offered every two years and includes presentations by persons from the graduate college, the tenure committee, the counseling center, and the deans of the colleges.

MAINTAINING A PROGRAM

Once a program has been established, I would offer three tips for maintaining the effectiveness over time.

Visit New Chairs

The first is to visit all new chairpersons each fall. As they play a crucial role in supporting, or not supporting, teaching improvement efforts, it is helpful to gain their cooperation. Our campus has a turnover rate of five or six chairs each year. During the first month of the school year, I make an appointment with them to review the list of services from our office and to talk about what this means for them. They are usually delighted to know about the resources we provide. I enjoy being able to sensitize them to issues of instructional development and support, and I also let them know what help I need from them. Additionally these meetings allow us to get to know each other as partners in an organization.

Join Campus Committees

Second, I recommend that the instructional development program staff become members of campus committees when appropriate. This increases the visibility of the program, allows the staff to represent the needs of instructional programs, and educates them about aspects of the university operation that affect instructional programs.

Engage in Professional Development

Finally, staff need to engage in as much professional development as their time and budget allows. For me, in addition to reviewing books and journals, the most important activities have been attending the national meetings of the POD Network and the annual meeting of a regional directors of instructional development programs. These advance my understanding of and skill in dealing with institutional factors, program activities, and specific teaching techniques.

CONCLUSION

This chapter has described the origins of one instructional development program, its substance, and its maintenance. Some general principles can be extracted from this experience and should prove helpful to persons or institutions wishing to establish their own program.

First, the instructional or faculty developer must produce an informed yet creative vision of what is needed and what will be accepted at his or her institution. Second, program activities should meet the needs of local faculty and complement each other in a productive way. Third, one must find ways of connecting and integrating the program with the needs and activities of other persons and units within the institution. Finally, the program staff need to do whatever is necessary to acquire and maintain the skills and knowledge necessary to support the program.

This sounds like common sense, and in a way perhaps it is. To establish a successful and lasting program, however, requires thought and commitment. Having seen some new programs succeed while others floundered, I have learned that there are more effective and less effective ways of starting a program. I hope this chapter offers some worthwhile guidance on the process.

REFERENCES

Brinko, K. T., & Menges, R. J. (Eds.). (1997). *Practically speaking: A sourcebook for instructional consultants in higher education.* Stillwater, OK: New Forums.

Fink, L. D. (1984). Year-long faculty discussion groups: A solution to several instructional development problems. In L. C. Buhl & L. A. Wilson (Eds.), *To improve the academy: Vol. 3. Resources for faculty, instructional, and organizational development* (pp. 90-94). Stillwater, OK: New Forums.

Fink, L. D. (1992). Orientation programs for new faculty members. In M. D. Sorcinelli (Ed.), *New and junior faculty.* New Directions for Teaching and Learning, No. 50. San Francisco, CA: Jossey-Bass.

Lewis, K. G., & Lunde, J. P. (2001). *Face to face: A sourcebook of individual consultation techniques for faculty/instructional developers* (2nd ed.). Stillwater, OK: New Forums.

L. Dee Fink designed and founded the Instructional Development Program at the University of Oklahoma, which he now directs. He has also served on the POD Core Committee.

Email: dfink@ou.edu

Part II
Assessing Teaching Practices

5

Improving the Evaluation of College Teaching

L. Dee Fink

The question of how to evaluate teaching is critical in institutions of higher education. In order to work on improving teaching, individual professors must have some way of knowing whether one way is better or worse than another. If an institution wants to encourage, recognize, and reward excellence in teaching, it must have some reliable means of distinguishing between more effective and less effective teachers. Yet, despite the importance of evaluating teaching, most colleges and universities continue to struggle with the question of how to find a satisfactory system for doing so.

At my university, student evaluations of all courses have been required for several years. This has given administrators a numerical basis for assessing the teaching activities of the faculty in annual performance evaluations. However, many professors are bothered by the idea of having their teaching measured by one number or a set of numbers from student questionnaires. Periodically pressure builds up to find a better solution to the problem. When this happens, a department or college committee often requests that I come in as a consultant on educational evaluation.

In these situations, I share the ideas that have emerged in the published literature on this topic. In 1979, Centra published an influential summary of research and analysis on faculty evaluation, including the evaluation of teaching. Even at this relatively early date, he had separate chapters with comments on the pros and cons of several different modes of evaluation: student ratings, self-assessment, evaluation by colleagues, and assessment of student learning. Later, Seldin (1984) conducted a nationwide survey of prevalent and changing practices in the evaluation of teaching. He noted that from 1978 to 1983, colleges had significantly increased their use of systematic student ratings, assessment of course materials, and self-evaluation. Fink (1995) offered a description of how faculty could do an in-depth assessment of their own teaching using five distinct sources of information. Braskamp and Ory (1994) took a broader view of assessing faculty work in general, by suggesting that faculty members and departments work together to set expectations and then to periodically assess progress. Within this framework, they noted that efforts to assess faculty teaching jointly could use multiple types of evidence—descriptive, student learning outcomes, judgments, eminence indicators, and self-reflection. More recently, several chapters in another book edited by Seldin (1999) on evaluating teaching focused on different sources of information and assessments—student ratings, peer classroom observations, and self-evaluation including the creation of teaching portfolios.

The general conclusion to be drawn from the published literature is that teaching needs to be evaluated using more than student ratings. Hence, whenever I am called on to advise a special committee charged with finding a new and better way of evaluating teaching, I try to persuade the group to change their guiding question. Usually they start with, "How can the student questionnaire be improved?" I try to get their attention focused on the more fundamental question: "How should teaching be evaluated?"

The latter question often points to the need for two essential adjustments. The first is the need to examine multiple dimensions of teaching, rather than just what the teacher does in the classroom. The second is the need for multiple sources of information, rather than an exclusive reliance on student evaluations of their teachers.

This chapter describes the reasons for believing that these two principles are central to effective evaluation. It also presents some guidelines for academic units that wish to establish or revise evaluation procedures to incorporate multiple dimensions of teaching and multiple sources of information.

THE NATURE OF TEACHING

Before evaluating teaching, one must develop a clear concept of what is to be evaluated. For purposes of evaluation, teaching can be defined as helping someone else learn something. To advance this one step further, good teaching can be defined as being effective in the process of helping someone else learn something significant. The two added elements of effectiveness and significance both seem necessary to warrant the label of good teaching.

The act of teaching can also be viewed as an interactive process that involves a teacher and students. This interaction occurs within a context or environment that can influence the success of that interaction. The definition of good teaching and the interactive character of teaching has five of implications for evaluation:

1) The primary purpose of teaching is to generate as much significant learning as possible. Students and teachers may bring additional purposes to the classroom, but for evaluative purposes, the main concern is the amount of significant learning generated.

2) The teacher is an important but indirect factor in the process of learning. This is simply a recognition of the fact that it is the student who does the learning; the teacher's role is to help the student in whatever ways possible.

3) In higher education, the teacher has primary responsibility for key decisions about a course. These decisions include such things as determining the scope of a course, identifying the goals, selecting reading materials, constructing tests, and assigning grades.

4) The quality of the teachers' classroom behaviors also have a major effect on the students' reaction to the course on a day-to-day basis. This refers to characteristics such as the clarity of the teachers' explanations, the enthusiasm they show for the subject, the rapport they develop with students, and the degree to which they are organized and prepared for class on a regular basis.

5) Teaching takes place within several kinds of contexts, all of which can have a significant influence on the quality of the teaching and the learning. Examples of such contexts include the following.

    Physical. This context consists of the characteristics of a classroom and the time at which a course is scheduled.

    Social. The relationship between the teacher and the students is an interactive one; students can inspire or discourage the teacher and vice versa.

    Institutional. The attitudes and actions of the department and the institution as a whole can either encourage or discourage good teaching.

Personal. The situation of the teacher's nonprofessional life; e.g., illness, divorce, or financial problems, can impact attentiveness to teaching.

In summary, teaching can be viewed as an interactive process that takes place within several types of contexts for the purpose of generating as much significant learning as possible.

THE NATURE OF EVALUATION

The type of evaluation appropriate for use in higher education is four dimensional. It calls for an examination of the input, the process, the product, and the context of an event or action. When this general framework is applied to the specific situation of college courses, it results in the six items identified in Figure 5.1.

Input

The first dimension of college teaching is the input, and it consists of two factors: student characteristics and teacher characteristics. Individual students vary considerably in the knowledge, values, and beliefs they bring to the learning situation. In addition, the mix of stu-

Figure 5.1 *Multiple Dimensions of Teaching*

General Dimensions of Evaluation	Specific Aspects of College Teaching to be Examined	
INPUT:	Student Characteristics	Teacher Characteristics
PROCESS:	Course Decisions	Classroom Behaviors
PRODUCT:	Amount and Type of Learning	
CONTEXT:	Multiple Contexts: –Physical –Social –Institutional –Personal	

dent personalities in a particular class can also be a major factor in the success of a course. Similarly, teachers vary in their readiness to teach any given course. Sometimes the subject matter is a topic that has been of interest to a faculty member for many years. However, a faculty member may have to teach a course for which she or he has limited background knowledge and limited motivation. Another important variable for teachers is the degree to which they have learned how to teach in different situations: lower division as well as graduate courses, large classes as well as small classes, or courses that require active learning procedures as well as lecture courses. Teachers who are up-to-date in their fields and have undertaken the necessary research and preparation for a class provide the input essential for significant learning. It follows that any breakdown in either factor of this input component diminishes the learning process.

The Process

The second dimension, the process, involves two separate activities in college teaching: course decisions and classroom behavior. When professors teach courses, they make decisions about the scope of the subject matter, the teaching strategy to be used, the grading system, and course policies. To make such decisions, teachers need to consider factors such as the nature of the curriculum and the characteristics of the students and then design the course accordingly. Also part of the process of teaching, but quite different in nature, is what professors do in the classroom. Once the basic course decisions have been made and professors step into the classroom, they must engage whatever communication and interaction skills they have to deliver lectures, lead discussions, ask questions, motivate students, and generate interest.

Product

The third dimension is concerned with the product of the teaching, which is the amount and type of learning that occurs in a given course. In almost every course, some students are going to learn something. In good courses, a large percentage of the students learn a lot, and they learn things that are significant rather than trite. To draw an example from my own discipline of geography, I would find only limited value in students learning the capitals and products of all the countries of the world. I would feel much better if the majority of the students understood such things as how the human geography of places affects the physical geography and vice versa. Another important part of learning is the students' interest in further learning. If students learn all about the physical and human geography of Europe but also learn that the subject is boring, I have won the battle but lost the war.

Context

The fourth dimension is context. In college teaching, there are several contexts that affect the quality of a given case of teaching: physical (e.g., the characteristics of the classroom), social (e.g., the nature of the students), institutional (e.g., the support given to teaching), and personal (e.g., other events in the life of the teacher).

EVALUATING THE QUALITY OF TEACHING

What then are the questions that have to be answered in order to make confident and valid judgments about the quality of teaching? The five general questions and related subpoints shown below are applicable to all classroom teaching in a higher education setting. The manner in which answers are found to these questions will vary from department to department and from college to college, but the questions themselves are inherent in the nature of teaching and in the nature of evaluation:

1) Does the teacher have adequate and up-to-date knowledge of the subject matter, including academic and/or practical experience and efforts to improve?

2) How good were the teacher's decisions about the course, inclusive of goals, teaching strategies, reading/laboratory/ homework assignments, testing, and grading?

3) How well did the teacher's classroom behavior promote good learning, inclusive of organization and clarity, enthusiasm, interaction with the class as a whole, and relationships with individual students?

4) How good were the educational results of the course, inclusive of the amount of learning, the significance of what was learned, and attitude toward learning more about the subject?

5)   How much was the quality of the teaching and learning
     influenced by contextual factors, inclusive of the physical,
     social, institutional, and personal contexts?

The quality of teaching, therefore, can be conceptualized as consisting of six components—student characteristics, teacher characteristics, the teacher's course decisions, the teacher's classroom behavior,
the amount of significant learning, and the influence of contextual factors. In order to effectively evaluate any particular instance of teaching, one must engage in the task of collecting and analyzing information about each one of these components.

No single source of information, however, is adequate for assessing all six components of teaching. This means that multiple sources
of information are not only advisable but are in fact necessary.
Therefore, different information sources need to be assessed to determine their relative value for answering questions about each of the six
components. A number of different sources of information are available for this particular task:

- Course materials
- Students (current students and alumni)
- The teacher's own comments
- Peers (i.e., other faculty members)
- Administrators
- Observations of an instructional consultant

Types of Evaluation Situations

One further distinction has to be made concerning three types of evaluation situations common in academic settings: annual personnel
decisions, periodic personnel decisions (e.g., tenure, promotion,
teaching award), and diagnostic self-improvement. These three situations have some degree of similarity, but the differences are sufficient
to warrant separate consideration for purposes of evaluation. The primary difference among the situations lies in the nature of the basic
question being asked.

Annual performance review. When teaching is being assessed as
part of an annual performance review, the question is, "How well did

this person teach this year, compared to others in this academic unit?" The only relevant information is the information pertaining to the teacher's performance this year. Hence, information from seniors, unless they were in the instructor's class during the year being assessed, or former students is inherently irrelevant.

Periodic personnel decisions. In the second situation, periodic personnel decisions, a different question is posed, "Does this person generally teach well enough to be worthy of tenure, promotion, or a teaching award?" Hence, information from former students is not only relevant but essential.

Diagnostic self-evaluation. Finally, in the situation of diagnostic self-evaluation, the question becomes, "What aspects of my teaching can most productively be improved?" At this time, all sources of information are relevant to some extent. The major difference is that an instructional consultant is ready to be an important source of information here, something most consultants do not want to be in administrative evaluation situations.

One special evaluation procedure has gained widespread national and international interest in recent years, namely, teaching portfolios. Seldin (1997) has provided the leadership in showing the many uses of teaching portfolios and describing how to create one. Basically a teaching portfolio consists of a brief narrative describing and assessing one's own teaching, plus an appendix containing various supporting documents. Although teaching portfolios are especially valuable for self-evaluation, faculty members can in fact use them in any of the three evaluation situations described.

Recommended Procedures

If one accepts the two principles already explained—multiple dimensions of teaching and multiple sources of information—and also the difference in the three evaluation situations, then two principles of good evaluation become evident:

1) Use different sources of information to assess different aspects of teaching.

2) Use different sources in different evaluation situations.

Figure 5.2 summarizes the sources of information recommended for each of the six dimensions of teaching in each of the three evaluation situations.

Figure 5.2 *Recommended Sources of Information for Evaluating Teaching*

SOURCES OF INFORMATION								
Factors Affecting the Quality of Teaching	Course Materials	Current Semester	Seniors	Alumni	Teacher's Comments	Peers	Administration	Instructional Consultant
Student Characteristics		A	P		A P D	a p	a d	d
Teacher's Knowledge	a				A P D			
Course Decisions	A D	a d	p	P	a P D	a d	a	D
Classroom Behavior		A D	p	P	a p D	a p d	a p	D
Learning		A	p	P	a P D	a p d	a p	D
Context		A D			A P D	a d	a	D

A/P/D = major source
a/p/d = minor source

THREE EVALUATION SITUATIONS
A/a = Annual Personnel Decisions
P/p = Periodic Personnel Decisions
D/d = Diagnostic Self-Evaluation

EVALUATING FOR SELF-IMPROVEMENT

As professionals, all faculty members should be interested in knowing what they can do to improve their teaching. Recently, however, another factor has increased the importance of this activity. As institutions hold faculty members responsible for ever greater levels of performance and accountability, the institutions acquire a parallel obligation to provide resources and information for faculty who are ready to improve their professional performance.

In the area of teaching, the college or university can probably contribute most by supporting a faculty and instructional development program. The academic units, through the office of the chairperson, need to inform their faculty of the availability of support services and to encourage their use.

Faculty members themselves need to use whatever resources are available to better understand their teaching and to improve it.

Possible resources include present students, peers, administrators, and instructional consultants. Of these, a consultant can be an important resource by providing informed, personalized feedback as well as general information about teaching and learning.

The use of an instructional consultant is the primary difference between evaluation for self-improvement and the other two types, both of which relate to personnel decisions. Most consultants work very hard to separate themselves clearly and completely from becoming involved in any evaluation connected with administrative decision-making. They believe that any such involvement would interfere with faculty readiness to contact them for diagnostic evaluation intended for self-improvement, which is the consultant's primary *raison d'etre*. While administrators may and can recommend that particular faculty members with teaching problems consider using the services of an instructional consultant, it is a generally accepted principle that the consultant cannot feed privileged information back to administrators. Such information is only for the faculty member.

EVALUATING FOR PERSONNEL DECISIONS

The two types of evaluation situations for personnel decisions—annual performance decisions and periodic personnel decisions—differ from each other primarily in terms of the question involved. But this creates differences in the appropriate sources of information.

Annual Performance Decisions

Most colleges and universities evaluate faculty performance annually. The evaluator, usually the chairperson or a departmental executive committee, must discern how well each faculty member taught that year when compared with others in the academic unit. Thus the question is that of how well the professor performed this year. Therefore the use of senior students and alumni is not recommended. The main reason for excluding them is that their information is not pertinent to the question at hand. Seniors and alumni are likely to have had a course with a particular teacher at some previous time, but not necessarily this year. This means five of the eight possible sources of information are recommended for annual evaluation: course materials, present students, the individual teacher, peers, and appropriate administrators.

Special note should be taken of the possibility of obtaining information from faculty members about their courses. Although professors, like students, are present in their own classes, academic units seldom ask them for information about their own courses. This could be done by using a simple, one-page questionnaire, which might also be part of a teaching or course portfolio (See Appendix 5.1). By completing a form for each course, professors can comment on such things as the quality of the students, the effect of the classroom, or the scheduled hour of the course. This would be very useful information for those trying to assess the quality of a particular professor's teaching in a particular year.

Periodic Personnel Decisions

Periodically, administrators and faculty colleagues must make more general judgments about a faculty member's teaching. This occurs in decisions about tenure, promotion, and teaching awards. In these cases, the evaluators must answer the question of whether or not the faculty member's teaching performance was adequate during the applicable time period to warrant tenure, promotion, or a teaching award.

In addition to the five sources recommended for annual performance evaluations, this situation allows for senior students and alumni to contacted. This information is now relevant because the period of time being examined is longer.

CONCLUSION

The recommendations of this essay have clear benefits, but they also have clear costs. The main benefit is that this system takes into account much more of the complexity of teaching than does reliance on data from student ratings alone. This broader base of information can give academic units considerably greater confidence when they try to distinguish between above average and below average teaching performance. The main cost is the time involved in collecting and assessing more complex information. Clearly, more time is required to evaluate course materials and information from teachers than to rank student evaluation scores. Yet a recent survey of departments at the University of Oklahoma indicated that at least a dozen departments already collect and assess course materials and/or information from teachers. This means that the work involved is at least within reasonable limits and, to some departments, worthwhile.

Procedures can also be developed to substantially reduce the associated workload. For example, one department has a policy that any professor may submit course materials but that it is mandatory only for those who want to be considered for above average evaluations on their teaching. This has reduced the quantity of course materials submitted by nearly 60%.

Ultimately, the question of whether an institution or department decides to adopt this approach to evaluation will depend on perceived worth. If an academic unit is only mildly uncomfortable with having teaching evaluated by student ratings or some other system, then the cost in time and effort of the procedures described above will probably be too high. On the other hand, if an institution believes that teaching is indeed complex and that it is important to recognize truly high quality teachers, then these procedures are likely to be worth the effort necessary to make them work successfully.

REFERENCES

Braskamp, L. A., & Ory, J. C. (1994). *Assessing faculty work: Enhancing individual and institutional performance.* San Francisco, CA: Jossey-Bass.

Centra, J. (1979). *Determining faculty effectiveness.* San Francisco, CA: Jossey-Bass.

Fink, L. D. (1995). Evaluating your own teaching. In P. Seldin (Ed.), *Improving college teaching* (pp. 191-203). Bolton, MA: Anker.

Seldin, P. (1984). *Changing practices in faculty evaluation.* San Francisco, CA: Jossey-Bass.

Seldin, P. (1997). *The teaching portfolio: A practical guide to improved performance and promotion/tenure decisions* (2nd ed.). Bolton, MA: Anker.

Seldin, P. (1999). *Changing practices in evaluating teaching.* Bolton, MA: Anker.

L. Dee Fink designed and founded the Instructional Development Program at the University of Oklahoma, which he now directs. He has also served on the POD Core Committee.

Email: dfink@ou.edu

58

APPENDIX 5.1
FORM FOR FACULTY REPORT ON TEACHING

Professor: _____   Term: _____

Course: _____   Enrollment: _____

Factors

The quality of the students in this course this semester was:

(Circle one).   Excellent - Good - Fair - Poor

Comments:

What effect did the classroom and the scheduling of the course have on the effectiveness of the course?

What is your honest assessment of your own effectiveness as a teacher in this course? Were there any personal or professional situations that significantly affected your performance this semester?

Were there any other factors, positive or negative, that affected either the effectiveness of the course or your performance as a teacher (e.g., new textbook, new objectives, etc.)?

General Information

My general assessment of this course, compared to other courses I have taught is:

(Circle one).   Excellent - Good - Fair - Poor

Comments:

The grade distribution for this course was:

A ___   B ___   C ___   D ___   F ___   S ___   U ___   I ___

Signed: _____

6

The Process of Individual Consultation

Karron G. Lewis

For a majority of the people in faculty and instructional development, the most time-consuming, yet most rewarding, activity is consulting with faculty members on a one-to-one basis. Through this type of individual work, we are able to focus on each person's strengths and weaknesses and facilitate their discovery of alternative teaching methods, better testing methods, and confidence in themselves as public speakers. We can do whatever will help each one be a more effective faculty member.

As one might expect, there are many different techniques that can be used in the individual consultation process as well as some essential skills which consultants need to cultivate. In this chapter, I will discuss these techniques and skills and provide additional resources to consult when one encounters difficulties.

THE NEED FOR INDIVIDUAL CONSULTATION

One of the primary goals of most faculty and instructional development programs is to help faculty members become happier and more productive members of the higher education community. Though more and more graduate degree programs are providing instruction in how to teach the content (Chism, 1987; Heenan & Jerich, 1995; Lewis, 1993; Nyquist, Abbott, Wulff, & Sprague, 1991), many faculty development programs must still provide information to help those who did not have such training in graduate school learn how to teach more effectively (Erickson, 1986). To do this, most faculty development programs offer periodic workshops during which various teaching skills and techniques are demonstrated and discussed. Over the years, however, I have found that the best way to instill lasting commitment and change is through one-on-one consultation.

Getting Clients

All faculty members in an institution are potential clients for one-on-one consultation, although getting them to contact faculty developers for individual assistance may be difficult until they have a sense of confidence in the development effort. Thus, faculty developers need to prove themselves. This process often begins in institution-wide workshops where one demonstrates competence and gets to know the faculty members. Additional proof comes after one has had a chance to work individually with some faculty members, and they begin to spread the word that the faculty developer can provide useful information and assistance. My individual clients usually come from three sources: 1) university-wide conferences and workshops, 2) former clients telling others about our services, and 3) the student course-instructor evaluations.

Each year in August our center conducts a three-day teaching/orientation seminar for new faculty, and in January we host a two-day experienced faculty teaching conference. Many new clients now say that they feel comfortable asking me for assistance when they run into a teaching problem because they got to know me during these activities.

Other new clients indicate that they decided to contact me because a friend recommended our services. It helps if one's success rate has been high over the years—that is, the clients' student ratings have improved, the clients feel better about themselves and their teaching, and/or the clients have won teaching awards—but former clients are typically one of our best sources of publicity.

On our campus, student evaluation of the course and instructor is mandatory for all courses, with some exceptions. In the past few years, the administration has emphasized that proof of teaching effectiveness must be submitted for tenure and promotion decisions. This expectation has provided the impetus for faculty members with low student ratings to seek our assistance.

Faculty members come if the faculty developers and the programs are visible, and the experience of success with a few faculty members will help to spread the word about the consultation service.

The Many Hats of the Consultant

We all know from learning theory that motivation and relevance are both necessary for effective learning to take place. Thus, the task of the consultant is to help the clients think about what is happening in their teaching and develop alternate strategies for dealing with these problems. In working with each individual, one must wear a number of different hats.

The Consultant as Data Collector

To focus the client's thoughts on what is currently happening in the classroom, one needs to collect data which describe the activities and highlight the effect of these activities on the students. This might consist of the following:

1) Conducting a preobservation interview to determine why the faculty member is seeking assistance and what might be the best course of action to follow. During this interview you will probably collect a variety of data such as:
   - A description of the client's class(es) and review of syllabi
   - The specific types of feedback the faculty member is seeking (for example, "Are my lectures organized?," "Am I responding adequately to student questions?")
   - The faculty member's attitude toward students and teaching
   - Any personal things which may be affecting the client's professional activities (for example, a new baby or overcommitment on committees)
   - Other information which relates to the client's request for assistance

2) Analysis and evaluation of course materials (for example, syllabus, objectives, assignments, exams, texts) to help the consultant and the client determine whether or not the goals for student learning are clearly stated and whether appropriate teaching strategies are being used

3) Sitting in on two or three class sessions to determine the pace, the organization of content, the activities of the students during class, the amount and types of interaction that take place between the teacher and students (through the use of observation instruments such as the Cognitive Interaction Analysis System, Lewis & Johnson, 1986), and attentiveness of students during class

4) Relating previous student evaluation data to the in-class observation

5)   Soliciting early feedback from students through written or verbal evaluations such as the use of small-group feedback (Clark & Bekey, 1979) or TABS (Bergquist & Phillips, 1975)

6)   Videotaping or audiotaping a class session for analysis by both the faculty developer and the client

7)   Anything else which will facilitate the in-depth analysis and evaluation of the course(s) and the way it is being taught

The Consultant as Data Manager

Once the consultant has collected the data perceived as most helpful in addressing clients' concerns, then one must be able to arrange these data in such a way that the faculty members can relate it to what they are currently doing and what they would like to do. Since some educational concepts, which may be familiar to the consultant, are foreign to many faculty members, coming up with ways to make the data seem real may be a challenge. I have found that graphs and other visual presentations of evaluation data and in-class interactions can be grasped much more rapidly than several paragraphs explaining the theory or main ideas behind a particular teaching technique (see Figure 6.1).

Figure 6.1 *Course Instructor Survey (CIS) Means*

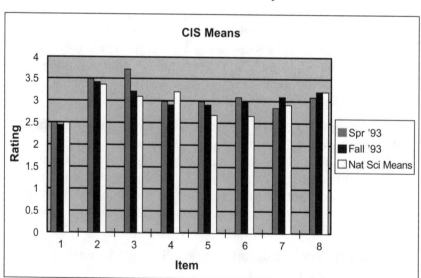

Figure 6.2 *Student Seating Diagram*

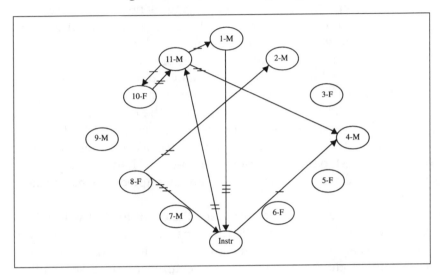

For example, if the instructor is concerned that only a few students are really taking part in the analysis of the cases being studied in class, one might make a diagram of where the students are seated and then place a tally mark in a box each time a particular student speaks. In addition, it is often enlightening to draw arrows to designate the person to whom students are directing their comments. Then tally marks can be made along that arrow when such interactions occur again (see Figure 6.2). Of course, the size of the class is a limiting factor in this type of data collection, but it provides a very clear picture of what is happening. If the data show that there are just a few people participating and that they are always directing their comments back to the teacher, then the teacher, probably with a little assistance from the consultant, can develop strategies for involving a larger number of students in the discussion.

The Consultant as Facilitator

One of the most important hats is that of a facilitator. Once the data have been gathered and arranged in an understandable format, the consultant will probably sit down with the faculty member to discuss the material. At this point, one should try not to make suggestions or judgments about the effectiveness or noneffectiveness of the way things are currently being done. Such restraint is often difficult. Rather, the consultant's role is to encourage clients to talk about what they hoped would happen during the class session, what actually happened, and what might have been done differently to make the students grasp the essence of the lesson more easily.

In order for the instructor to actually do something to change what happened in the classroom, the ownership of the consultation process must be with the client, not with the consultant (Nyquist, 1986; Smith, 1995; Taylor-Way, 1988). Thus, one should facilitate the brainstorming of ideas and alternative techniques, not present a ready-made list to the client. However, the consultant can and should help keep the actual changes which are attempted to a manageable number.

The consultant can also encourage the client to start with things which require the fewest drastic revisions and then progress to more radical ideas. For example, one can try to discourage completely changing a course from straight lecture to all case studies. Incorporating one or two case studies to illustrate concepts discussed in the lecture would probably be more reasonable. Then, if those case studies go well, the client can add additional case studies and maybe other types of group work to help the students relate the material to real problems.

The Consultant as Support System

Once the instructor has, with the consultant's assistance, determined what needs to be done to enhance teaching effectiveness, then the consultant becomes the client's support system. Often, the first attempt to incorporate something new into one's teaching winds up not changing anything or, even more traumatic, making things worse. At this point, the consultant needs to help the client analyze what parts of the change actually did go well and why the new technique did not bring all of the expected results. One should always be as positive as possible.

It is often helpful if the consultant can be in the class when new techniques are being tried. This provides direct knowledge of what the instructor actually did, not reliance on the memory of what took place. Frequently, things are much worse in our memory than they were in reality. An audiotape or videotape of the class session might also be very helpful if it would not be distracting to the instructor.

Some instructors prefer to try out a new technique privately and then, when they feel comfortable, request that an observation or videotape be made. The consultant has to judge what is most appropriate for each particular client.

The Consultant as Counselor

Often, problems which faculty members are having in their classrooms stem from personal or professional stresses. Because being a faculty member takes so much of one's time and energy, it is not uncommon for family problems to arise. If a faculty member is going through a divorce or has a child who is having problems in school or is rebellious, these stresses affect the ability to concentrate on teaching. This is not to say that the consultant should try to solve these problems unless, of course, one has training in counseling. However, one needs to be alert to the possibility of these influences on the performance of a client. In some instances, it is advisable to consult a professional who may help decide whether or not professional expertise is needed.

As an example of this difficult situation, I had a client—a third-year faculty member—who had become overcommitted in the department and was in charge of a major committee in his professional organization. In addition, his wife, who was also working, was expecting their second child. On top of this, he was teaching three courses with extensive labs. Needless to say, his student evaluations plummeted, and he was frantic when he called me. In this case, we were able to determine that his problem was an inability to be assertive and to say no. There was not much we could do about that particular semester, but we talked about assertiveness and roleplayed some typical situations in which he found himself. Then, to manage the rest of that semester, we worked on some time management and relaxation techniques which might help him cope with the tension and stress he was continually feeling. Happily, he made it through that semester. The next semester he had managed to reduce his departmental committee commitments, and he was no longer chairing the committee in his professional organization. Consequently, his student evaluations returned to their previous highs, and he was able to enjoy life—and the new addition to his family—a little more.

The Consultant as Information Source

If the consultant and client have decided to incorporate a new technique into the teaching repertoire, it is useful to provide articles or chapters which describe the technique and give case studies showing how it has been used. If possible, one should provide copies of the actual articles, not just a reference for the client. One must remember that time is a valuable commodity for a faculty member. In fact, if the articles are extremely long, the inclusion of a brief abstract is almost essential. Otherwise, the client will not be enthusiastic about wading through many pages. After these have been read, one should sit down with the client and discuss the articles, clarifying unclear words or concepts and relating how the ideas can be adapted for use in the client's classroom.

Most of the time my own awareness of new techniques come from keeping up with the current teaching literature, from trying new things myself, or from observing someone else use a particular technique. Because most faculty members tend to teach as they were taught, the lecture mode predominates. However, the learning literature shows that active students learn more and retain what they learn longer, so one of my main objectives is to encourage more student participation. Suggestions for specific resources are provided at the end of this chapter.

Thus, it is evident that the role of the consultant in the individual consultation process is constantly changing. In order for us to provide this service to our clients, we need to be flexible and willing to let the client make most of the decisions. A wonderful resource for persons just getting started in individual consultations is the book edited by Brinko and Menges (1996), titled *Practically Speaking: A Sourcebook for Instructional Consultants in Higher Education.*

SKILLS NEEDED

As with any profession, there are skills which will make one effective in the job. Faculty development and the individual consultation process is no different. Those skills which seem to be most essential in our profession are as follows:

- Listening skills
- Data collection skills

- In-class observation skills
- The ability to facilitate data analysis by the faculty member
- The ability to provide positive reinforcement
- A feeling of empathy
- Knowledge of the literature of faculty development and teaching

Listening

Listening is perhaps the most important skill because one does a lot of it—when talking to clients, when observing classes, and when obtaining verbal student evaluations. The consultant who has trouble listening and concentrating on what is being said needs to develop that skill.

Data Collection

Some procedures for data collection have already been discussed. The person getting started in faculty development is likely to have already done quite a bit of data collection in pursuing one's own educational goals. However, collecting qualitative rather than quantitative data is new to many. Suggestions for additional readings on this topic are provided at the end of this chapter.

In-Class Observation

What kinds of things are important to student learning in a class of 500? Are these drastically different from the things which are important in a class of 50 or 15? Learning to attend to the important factors in an in-class observation and leaving out that which is unimportant is also a skill. During my first in-class observation for a client, I try to be a typical student: I take notes, may or may not read/do the assignment prior to class, try to make sense of the lecture, and write down questions which came to mind. However, I seldom ask questions in a class because it usually makes the teacher nervous. In addition, if obvious problems are noticed (for example, the writing on the overhead transparency is too small to read), I make note of them. It is also helpful to have determined beforehand one or two things the client would like the consultant to look for during the observation. This helps focus the observation as well as the later discussions about that class session. Use of check sheets, evaluation forms, or an objective observation system are also helpful in this respect (Bergquist & Phillips, 1975, 1977, 1987).

Facilitate Analysis of Data

The ability to facilitate analysis of data by the faculty member is critical. Just as the consultant may be unfamiliar with the techniques and results of collecting qualitative data, clients may also have difficulty understanding anything without definite numbers attached. The key to facilitating this understanding is in being as objective as possible when collecting the data. Use of observation systems such as the Cognitive Interaction Analysis System (Lewis & Johnson, 1986) can help make the explanation of the interactions which took place in the class much easier to understand. Such instruments provide a concrete means for assessing change. (See the additional readings section for more information.)

Provide Positive Reinforcement

The ability to provide positive reinforcement is often difficult for persons in higher education because they have spent so much time criticizing journal articles, others' research studies, and their own writing. Consequently, it can be hard to focus on the positive aspects of a client's teaching and written output. In addition, one may sometimes get a client who is really bad, and finding something good to say to get things started may take a lot of skill in this area. It is helpful to practice by first writing down all of the words and phrases which you consider reinforcing (for example; good job, excellent, you're on the right track). Then one can audiotape one's own classes in order to discern the kinds of reinforcement provided for correct answers, good questions, or good behavior. If the reinforcement vocabulary identified is limited, one should try to expand it. If the consultant has a tendency to criticize more often than reinforce, one should try looking for positive things first and then move to constructive criticism.

Empathy

Empathy is an important feeling to have. If the consultant has been a faculty member, this should not be a problem although one cannot, of course, identify with every situation. However, by pooling resources with the client and by using the POD Network listserv or specific people one may have met, most problems will be able to be resolved. One's feeling of empathy can be heightened, even lacking direct experience.

Knowledge of the Faculty Development and Teaching Literature

Knowledge of the literature of faculty development and teaching is a foundation stone for the consultation process, and for any kind of work in faculty development. If one plans to succeed as a consultant, one should be familiar with learning theory, motivation theory, teaching techniques for a variety of classes and situations, data collection instruments, questioning skills, and much more.

Success

Although this may seem like a lot to keep up with, beginning and experienced faculty developers probably already have many of these skills at some proficiency level. Once one has consulted with a few clients, the satisfaction with the process will emerge. Any specific knowledge one needs to help a client can usually be acquired with a trip to the library or by calling or emailing one of your POD colleagues.

The real key to a successful instructional consultation is the consultant's desire to help a fellow faculty member find enrichment and fulfillment in becoming a more effective instructor.

REFERENCES

Bergquist, W. H., & Phillips, S. R. (1975). *A handbook for faculty development (Vol. 1)*. Washington, DC: Council for the Advancement of Small Colleges.

Bergquist, W. H., & Phillips, S. R. (1977). *A handbook for faculty development (Vol. 2)*. Washington, DC: Council for the Advancement of Small Colleges.

Bergquist, W. H., & Phillips, S. R. (1987). *A handbook for faculty development (Vol. 3)*. Washington, DC: Council for the Advancement of Small Colleges.

Brinko, K. T., & Menges, R. J. (1996). *Practically speaking: A sourcebook for instructional consultants in higher education*. Stillwater, OK: New Forums Press.

Chism, N. V. N. (Ed.). (1987). *Institutional responsibilities and responses in the employment and education of teaching assistants*. Columbus, OH: The Ohio State University, Center for Teaching Excellence.

Clark, J., & Bekey, J. (1979). Use of small groups in instructional evaluation. *POD Quarterly, 1*, 87-95.

Erickson, G. (1986). A survey of faculty development practices. In M. Svinicki, J. Kurfiss, & J. Stone (Eds.), *To improve the academy: Vol. 5. Resources for faculty, instructional, and organizational development* (pp. 182-196). Stillwater, OK: New Forums Press.

Heenan, T. A., & Jerich, K. F. (Eds.). (1995). *Teaching graduate students to teach: Engaging the disciplines.* Urbana-Champaign, IL: University of Illinois at Urbana-Champaign, Office of Instructional Resources and the Office of Conferences and Institutes.

Lewis, K. G. (1993). Section II: Development programs for TAs. In K.G. Lewis (Ed.), *The TA experience: Preparing for multiple roles* (pp. 95-137). Stillwater, OK: New Forums Press.

Lewis, K., & Johnson, G. R. (1986). *Monitoring your classroom communication skills: A programmed workbook for developing coding skills using Johnson's Cognitive Interaction Analysis System (CIAS) and Expanded CIAS.* Unpublished programmed workbook and audiotape for skill training in CIAS. Available from Center for Teaching Effectiveness, Main Building 2200 (G2100), The University of Texas at Austin, Austin, TX 78712-1111.

Nyquist, J. D. (1986). CIDR: A small service firm within a research university. In M. Svinicki (Ed.), *To improve the academy: Vol. 5. Resources for faculty, instructional, and organizational development* (pp. 66-83). Stillwater, OK: New Forums Press.

Nyquist, J. D., Abbott, R. D., Wulff, D. H., & Sprague, J. (Eds.) (1991). *Preparing the professoriate of tomorrow to teach.* Dubuque, IA: Kendall/Hunt.

Smith, R. A. (1995). Reflecting critically on our efforts to improve teaching and learning. In E. Neal & L. Echlin (Eds.), *To improve the academy: Vol. 14. Resources for faculty, instructional, and organizational development* (pp. 5-25). Stillwater, OK: New Forums Press.

Taylor-Way, D. (1988). Consultation with video: Memory management through stimulated recall. In K. G. Lewis & J. T. Povlacs (Eds.), *Face to face: A sourcebook of individual consultation techniques for faculty development personnel* (pp. 159-191). Stillwater, OK: New Forums Press.

SUGGESTED ADDITIONAL READINGS

General Readings

Boice, R. (1996). *First-order principles for college teachers: Ten basic ways to improve the teaching process.* Bolton, MA: Anker.

Erickson, F. (1986). Qualitative methods in research on teaching. In M. C. Wittrock (Ed.), *Handbook of research on teaching* (3rd ed.). (pp. 119-161). New York, NY: Macmillan.

Flanders, N. A. (1970). *Analyzing teaching behavior.* Reading, MA: Addison-Wesley.

Seldin, P. (1999). *Changing practices in evaluating teaching: A practical guide to improved faculty performance and promotion/tenure decisions.* Bolton, MA: Anker.

Seldin, P., & Associates. (1995). *Improving college teaching.* Bolton, MA: Anker.

Sorenson, D. L. (1994). Valuing the student voice: Student observer/consultant programs. In E. C. Wadsworth (Ed.), *To improve the academy: Vol. 13. Resources for faculty, instructional, and organizational development* (pp. 97-108). Stillwater, OK: New Forums Press.

Lecture/Discussion Techniques

Davis, B. G. (1993). *Tools for teaching.* San Francisco, CA: Jossey-Bass.

Ekler, W. J. (1994). The lecture method. In K. W. Prichard & R. M. Sawyer (Eds.), *Handbook of college teaching: Theory and applications* (pp. 85-89). Westport, CT: Greenwood Press.

Frederick, P. J. (1994). Classroom discussions. In K. W. Prichard & R. M. Sawyer (Eds.), *Handbook of college teaching: Theory and applications* (pp. 99-110). Westport, CT: Greenwood.

Nilson, L. (1998). *Teaching at its best: A research-based resource for college instructors.* Bolton, MA: Anker.

Osterman, D., Christiansen, M., & Coffey, B. (1985). *The feedback lecture* (Idea Paper, No. 13). Manhattan, KS: Kansas State University, Center for Faculty Evaluation and Development.

Small-Group Techniques

Bouton, C., & Garth, R. (Eds.). (1983). Learning in groups. *New Directions for Teaching and Learning, No. 14.* San Francisco, CA: Jossey-Bass.

Michaelsen, L. K. (1994). Team learning: Making a case for the small-group option. In K. W. Prichard & R. M. Sawyer (Eds.), *Handbook of college teaching: Theory and applications* (pp. 139-154). Westport, CT: Greenwood.

Miller, J. E., Groccia, J. E., & Miller, M. S. (Eds.). (2001). *Student-assisted teaching: A guide to faculty-student teamwork.* Bolton, MA: Anker.

Stein, R. F., & Hurd, S. (2000). *Using student teams in the classroom: A faculty guide.* Bolton, MA: Anker.

Effective Questioning Strategies for Discussions and Case Studies

Hoover, K. (1980). Questioning strategies. In *College teaching today: A handbook for postsecondary instruction* (pp. 120-149). Boston, MA: Allyn and Bacon. (See also chapters on Discussion Methods, pp. 120-149, and Analyzing Reality: The Case Method, pp. 199-223).

Lewis, K. G. *Developing questioning skills.* An unpublished handout available from the Center for Teaching Effectiveness, Main Building 2200 (G2100), The University of Texas at Austin, Austin, TX 78712-1111.

Lewis, K. G. *Evaluating discussion.* An unpublished handout available from the Center for Teaching Effectiveness, Main Building 2200 (G2100), The University of Texas at Austin, Austin, TX 78712-1111.

Watkins, K. (1983). *Handling difficult questions and situations. Innovation Abstracts, 5* (24). Available from National Institute for Staff and Organizational Development, SZB 348, Austin, TX 78712-1293.

Active Learning/Getting Students Involved

Kolb, D. A. (1984). Experiential learning: *Experiences as the source of learning and development.* Englewood Cliffs, NJ: Prentice-Hall.

Svinicki, M. D. *Some applied learning theory.* An unpublished handout available from the Center for Teaching Effectiveness, Main Building 2200 (G2100), The University of Texas at Austin, Austin, TX 78712-1111.

Svinicki, M. D., & Dixon, N. M. (1987). Kolb model modified for classroom activities. *College Teaching, 35,* 141-146.

Pintrich, P. R. (1994). Student motivation in the college classroom. In K. W. Prichard & R. M. Sawyer (Eds.), *Handbook of college teaching: Theory and applications* (pp. 23-44). Westport, CT: Greenwood.

RESOURCES TO TAP FOR ADDITIONAL INFORMATION

- POD members. These colleagues are probably your most valuable resource. Call them, email them, and be sure to network with them at the annual conference.

- Newsletters from faculty/instructional development centers. Most centers will exchange newsletters free of charge.

- Other journals and publications:

  To Improve the Academy, annual publication of the POD Network, available to all members free of charge.

  College Teaching (a journal)

  Higher Education Abstracts (a compilation of abstracts of publications dealing with higher education)

  Innovative Higher Education (a journal)
  [http://www.isd.uga.edu/ihe/ihe.htm].

  Journal of Staff, Program, & Organization Development

  Journal of Graduate Teaching Assistant Development

  Teaching journals in various fields (e.g., *Teaching Sociology, Engineering Education,* etc.). See *Idea Paper No. 28, Periodicals Related to College Teaching,* from the Center for Faculty Evaluation & Development, Kansas State University, Manhattan, KS.

  ERIC publications

- Attendance at professional meetings

Karron G. Lewis is the Assistant Director of the Center for Teaching Effectiveness at the University of Texas at Austin. She has served on the POD Core Committee and as the President of POD in 1994-1995.

Email: kglewis@mail.utexas.edu

7

Classroom Observation: The Observer as Collaborator

LuAnn Wilkerson and Karron G. Lewis

It is hard to say how many classrooms we sit in the back of each year, absorbed in following the process of teaching and stimulated by new ideas. As instructional consultants, we have found that feedback to teachers based on the direct observation of classroom process is a powerful and effective faculty development strategy. It enables faculty developers to provide individualized assistance based on the needs and interests of the teacher, whereas workshops—a frequently used approach to faculty development—introduce skills and ideas which may or may not meet individual needs. Videotaping of a class also provides an individualized perspective and more complete record of classroom events. However, it is more obtrusive, with both students and faculty reporting uneasiness and modification of behavior to some extent. The observer, on the other hand, is usually seen as a less disruptive addition to the classroom environment. Additionally, the observer requires no special technological arrangements and can be counted on to function smoothly on almost all occasions.

The process of classroom observation and feedback carries with it the potential for abuse. Many of us can probably remember an occasion when comments made by someone who had just attended a class we were teaching made us feel uncomfortable or even angry. How can we reduce the potential for abuse and enhance the potential for teaching improvement through the use of classroom observation and feedback? Working collaboratively is a cornerstone for doing so.

OBSERVATION FOR IMPROVEMENT OR EVALUATION

The observation of classroom teaching is regularly used in the supervision and evaluation of elementary and secondary school teachers and teacher trainees. Less frequently does it play a role in the evaluation of teacher effectiveness at the college and university level. However, the faculty development movement of the last 30-plus years has adopted classroom observation as a primary tool for the improvement of teaching. The difference between observation for purposes of evaluation and improvement is not so much the method by which they are recorded, but rather the degree to which the teacher participates in the formulation of conclusions about the quality of the teaching observed. When classroom observation is used for the purposes of evaluation, judgments are usually summative, and the teacher plays little, if any, role in making them. On the other hand, when observation is conducted for the purpose of teaching improvement, judgments are formative and the teacher is actively involved in the assessment of teaching quality and needed improvement.

Recognizing the importance of the teacher's ownership of the process of change, we have moved over the years to a more collaborative approach to classroom observation and feedback, seeking to increase the responsibility of instructors for making decisions about their own teaching improvement. Through a process of collaborative observation, we can engage with the teacher in classroom research (Angelo, 1998; Cross, 1998), together determining what questions need to be answered during observation and designing methods of data collection and analysis for answering them. A collaborative approach recognizes the professional status of both the teacher and the observer. It can help to reduce the threat often felt by instructors in being observed, lessen the impact of observer bias, and enhance the instructors' skills in accurately assessing and improving their own teaching.

COLLABORATIVE OBSERVATION

Collaborative observation involves a pre-observation conference, descriptive observation notes, and teacher direction of the post-observation conference.

In order to serve as an effective observer of the teaching behavior of another person, the faculty developer must first carefully examine personal beliefs about effective teaching and learning. We recommend asking oneself the following questions before the observation:

- What do I think is essential in the classroom process for learning to occur?

- Is there anything distinctive about this particular subject or these students that might alter the usual process of learning?

- When I say effective teaching, what standards am I using to determine effectiveness; e.g., student learning, a set of teaching behaviors, student enjoyment?

Since we cannot escape our biases, training, and beliefs, we must recognize that our observations will ultimately represent only one version of the classroom event. The observer's perceptions influence what will be recorded and how it will be analyzed. In addition, Evertson and Green (1986) remind us that "these factors form the 'frame of reference' of the observer and influence the decision-making as well as the observational process" (p. 162). We can reduce the impact of observer bias by consciously recognizing our personal perspectives as just that and not mistaking them for the only reality, by involving the teacher in planning for observation, and by collecting data about the classroom from a number of different sources; i.e., video recording, student evaluations, multiple observers, or observation methods.

The Pre-Observation Conference

The pre-observation conference begins the process of collaboration. As in any research project, the collaborators will need to discuss and agree upon the purpose of the investigation. What questions would the teacher like to answer? Are there others the faculty developer might suggest be added? What special interests, fears, and beliefs does each party bring to the endeavor? The pre-observation conference provides a time for discussing the instructor's beliefs about teaching and learning in general and in relation to the specific class to be observed (Prosser & Trigwell, 1993). Critical decisions need to be made during this meeting:

1) When and where to observe

2) What features of the classroom on which to focus

3) What methods to use in collecting data

4) How to introduce the observer to the students

5) How the data will be analyzed

6) Who will have access to the results of the study

In each of these decisions, the instructor is an active participant. The greater the role of the instructor in making these decisions, the more valid will be the data.

The Observation

An important feature of the collaborative approach to classroom observation is the collection of descriptive, as opposed to evaluative, data which the faculty developer and the teacher can analyze together in seeking to answer the questions posed during the pre-observation conference. Descriptive data provide an account of classroom behavior and interaction without making an effort to judge these events. Description represents, as far as possible, a neutral stance on the part of the observer. It avoids pejorative language and inferences. Judgments which are eventually made will be reached in collaboration with the teacher. For example, if the faculty developer observes the instructor as a discussion leader asking long, tortuous questions which elicit little if any student response, this is a judgment. Operating within a descriptive framework, one might instead create a list of instructor questions—verbatim—and describe associated student responses. The descriptive approach leaves instructors free to discover the patterns in their own behaviors and to assess, with the assistance of the faculty developer, the effectiveness of those behaviors, or lack thereof.

Observation methods. Observations can be collected in any number of ways and numerous observation instruments and methods are described in the literature (Brinko & Menges, 1996; Hoge, 1985; Lewis, 1991; Lewis & Lunde, 2001; Simon & Boyer, 1970). In a review of observational methodologies in the *Handbook of Research on Teaching,* Evertson and Green (1986) describe four broad types of observations from which we might select, depending on the particular goals of our study. Each of the following is capable of being used to produce either descriptive or evaluative data:

- Category systems contain closed, preset categories which are used to tally (descriptive) or rate (evaluative) samples of behavior; e.g., Flanders Interaction Analysis, Cognitive Interaction Analysis System, rating forms.

- Descriptive systems usually have preset categories but call for the collection of detailed description within each category with attention to the context and multiple aspects of the behaviors observed; e.g., incident technique.

- Narrative systems contain no preset categories. An attempt is made to record broad segments of behavior using the syntax of those being observed; e.g., anthropological field notes, diaries.

- Technological systems can be used to record events verbatim; e.g., videotape, audiotape, photographs.

In general, we favor a narrative system, attempting to record as much as possible of the verbal and nonverbal behaviors of the teacher and the students during the class period. Arriving a few minutes before the beginning of class, we note the physical environment of the classroom; e.g., size of room, type and arrangement of chairs, and audiovisual and board facilities. Notetaking is done in a way that allows documentation of the flow of student-teacher interaction by dividing the page lengthwise to create two columns, one labeled "teacher" and one, "students." (see Table 7.1). In a discussion class, these columns might be of equal width. In a lecture class, the teacher's column would be much wider than that of the students. Some portion of the verbal interaction using verbatim narrative and/or summaries of the content of the discussion is then recorded. In parentheses, we describe nonverbal events or comment on the group process and also keep track of the passage of time.

A more focused descriptive or category system might be appropriate when the purpose of the study is more narrowly defined; i.e., the faculty developer and the instructor have agreed to study the nature of questions and responses. Rarely do we elect to use a category system because of the narrow vision of classroom events that can

Table 7.1 *Classroom Environment*

	TEACHER	STUDENTS
Time Notation	transcription of verbal with nonverbal in ( )	student is identified with verbal response described and nonverbal in ( )
8:45	What do you think of that? (nods head at John)	John: I think there should be a lot of dialogue to clear things up. (gestures with hands)

be captured with quantitative ratings. However, with appropriate training, an observer can use a category system to provide a detailed record of classroom events. For example, the Cognitive Interaction Analysis System results in a numerical record of the occurrences of selected teacher and student behaviors, maintaining the interactive pattern by coding classroom activity at three-second intervals (Johnson, 1987; Lewis, 1986).

Whichever observational system is chosen, the major criterion should be that the approach provides for the fullest description possible of the classroom events with the least amount of observer inference and judgment required. It should also be appropriate for the type of class and the preference of the faculty member for numerical versus verbal versus visual data.

Post-Observation Conference

Once observational data have been collected, the faculty developer then meets with the instructor to analyze the results and reach a collaborative judgment about what action might be taken in response to the data. It is generally good practice to send a copy of the observation notes to the teacher for consideration prior to this meeting. To begin the discussion, one can first ask the teacher to reflect on the class session itself—Was this typical or atypical? How did it match with the plans he or she had made before class? The teacher's self-assessment introduces the issues which form the focus of the collaborative work.

Second, the instructor reacts to the observation data. Has the observation instrument used generated an accurate picture of the class? The instructor usually responds by reflecting on that portion of the data which is of most personal interest, perhaps the most surprising, or that which confirms his or her own views most strongly. Working together, one then can determine answers to the questions posed during the pre-observation conference, sharing perspectives and interpretations.

The collaborative mode does not suggest that the observer avoids making judgments or never offers advice, but rather that the discussion entails the mutual definition and resolution of problems. We try to withhold judgment until the teacher has analyzed the data and reached his or her own conclusions as to their meaning. Judgments offered too quickly may destroy the collaborative nature of the work or discourage the instructor from developing skills in reflective self-assessment essential to the ongoing improvement of teaching. After encouraging the instructor to select the initial focus of the discussion and to take the lead in interpreting the data, the faculty developer can then indicate topics of concern and share interpretation of the data collected. The issue is not one of directive versus nondirective consultation, but of the sharing of direction with an attitude of mutual respect.

LIMITATIONS TO CLASSROOM OBSERVATION

We have already discussed the limitations posed by the bias of the observer and the tools chosen for data collection. There is an additional limitation to classroom observation as an approach to teaching improvement. When used as the single source of data on teaching effectiveness, classroom observation produces an incomplete picture of the teaching and learning that is occurring: Are students accomplishing intended learning outcomes? What do students perceive to be promoting or discouraging their achievement? How do course assignments and examinations relate to the stated objectives of the course?

In order to more completely depict the full range of teaching variables, we need additional data such as student performance results, student evaluations of teaching, observations by others or on other occasions, videotaping of classroom sequences, and review of teacher-prepared materials including the course syllabus. Such information, when coupled with the faculty developer's observation(s), can provide the broadest possible base for interpreting the events of the classroom. By reinforcing observational data with information collected from a variety of other sources, we can more accurately collaborate with instructors in identifying, assessing, and improving their teaching skills.

REFERENCES

Angelo, T. A. (Ed.).(1998). *Classroom assessment and research: An update on uses, approaches and research findings.* New Directions for Teaching and Learning, No. 75. San Francisco, CA: Jossey-Bass.

Brinko, K. T., & Menges, R. J. (Eds.). (1996). *Practically speaking: A sourcebook for instructional consultants in higher education.* Stillwater, OK: New Forums Press.

Chism, N. V. N. (1999). *Peer review of teaching: A sourcebook.* Bolton, MA: Anker.

Cross, K. P. (1998). Classroom research: Implementing the scholarship of teaching. In T. A. Angelo (Ed.), *Classroom assessment and research: An update on uses, approaches, and research findings.* New Directions for Teaching & Learning, No. 75, (pp. 5-12). San Francisco, CA: Jossey-Bass.

Evertson, C. M., & Green, J. L. (1986). Observation as inquiry and method. In M. C. Wittrock (Ed.), *Handbook of research on teaching* (3rd ed.) (pp. 162-213). New York, NY: Macmillan.

Hoge, R. D. (1985). The validity of direct observation measures of pupil classroom behavior. *Review of Educational Research, 55,* 469-483.

Johnson, G. R. (1987). Changing the verbal behavior of teachers. *Journal of Staff, Program & Organization Development, 5,* 155-158.

Lewis, K. G. (1986). Using an objective observation system to diagnose teaching problems. *Journal of Staff, Program & Organization Development, 4,* 81-90.

Lewis, K. G. (1991). Gathering data for the improvement of teaching: What do I need and how do I get it? In M. Theall & J. Franklin (Eds.), *Effective practices for improving teaching* (pp. 65- 82). New Directions for Teaching and Learning, No. 48. San Francisco, CA: Jossey-Bass.

Lewis, K. G. (1996). Collecting information via class observation. In K. T. Brinko & R. J. Menges (Eds.), *Practically speaking: A sourcebook for instructional consultants in higher education* (pp. 29-51). Stillwater, OK: New Forums Press.

Lewis, K. G., & Lunde, J. P. (Eds.). (2001). *Face to Face: A sourcebook of individual consultation techniques for faculty/instructional developers* (2nd ed.). Stillwater, OK: New Forums Press.

Prosser, M., & Trigwell, K. (1993). Development of an approach to teaching questionnaires. *Research and Development in Higher Education, 15,* 468-473.

Simon, A., & Boyer, E. G. (Eds.). (1970). *Mirrors for behavior: An anthology of classroom observation instruments.* Philadelphia, PA: Research for Better Schools. (ERIC Document Reproduction Service No. ED 031 613)

Karron G. Lewis is the Associate Director of the Center for Teaching Effectiveness at the University of Texas at Austin. She has served on the POD Core Committee and as the President of POD in 1994-95.

LuAnn Wilkerson is the Senior Associate Dean for Medical Education at the School of Medicine, University of California, Los Angeles. She has served on the POD Core Committee and was Executive Director in 1984-85.

Email: kglewis@mail.utexas.edu
          lwilker@deans.medsch.ucla.edu

8

Small Group Instructional Diagnosis: Tapping Student Perceptions of Teaching

Nancy A. Diamond

Six weeks into a new academic year...
On Thursday I received a call from the head of the economics department. He recommended the services of our office to a fourth-year assistant professor who is having trouble with the only section of a required course for majors. The instructor called and made an appointment stating that he goes forward for tenure in two years, needs some good student ratings, and wants advice.

Later I had coffee with Professor Geddy. We had worked together a few years ago, and he has won an outstanding teaching award. He talked about his nine o'clock English history class, a section of 220 students. This is his first experience teaching a large class. They seem apathetic, and Geddy feels out of his element.

Friday I met with the sophomore medicine course leader and instructors in the College of Medicine. The course had been revised drastically and taught in the new version for the first time last year. Additional changes were made, and now the instructors want to hear student reactions. The course head suggests we interview the students after each of the five instructors completes a section.

In the afternoon Arlene stopped by on her way home. She is a teaching assistant (TA) for a perspective drawing class and has full responsibility for the course. We had met several times last summer to discuss her course plans for this fall. She said things are okay although she has not been able to keep up with the outlines. I wonder what else is wrong since TAs won't say directly that there is a problem with a class. I volunteered to provide feedback on the pace but she thought the students would feel that an observer was intrusive in such a small class.

These notes describe real, but disguised, encounters with instructors. Each individual had noted a teaching problem in an ongoing class and wanted assistance from the instructional development office. Thus began, and begins, the instructional consultation process. As is often the case, there was a definite expectation on the part of these instructors that results occur during the current term; i.e., the course runs more smoothly, the instructor feels better, the students are happier with the course, or the department head smiles.

Let us assume that three to five weeks have elapsed since the beginning of the term. Students and instructor are now used to one another. The instructor and I, the faculty/instructional developer, have talked and looked at the available course artifacts such as the syllabus, assignments, grading plans, early informal feedback, and a possible classroom visit. I am now at a point of introducing another consultation strategy, the Small Group Instructional Diagnosis (SGID), which will bring perspectives that help create a more balanced view of the course and its immediate effects.

THE SGID PROCESS:
A GROUP INTERVIEWING TECHNIQUE

There are several types of group interviews (Dawson & Caulley, 1981; Powney & Watts, 1987), but our office uses and recommends the whole-class interviewing technique of Small Group Instructional Diagnosis. It is taken, with little variation, from a detailed description written by Dr. Joseph Clark when he was project director of a Fund for the Improvement of Secondary Education (FIPSE) grant to the Biology Learning Resource Center at the University of Washington, Seattle. The purpose of the grant was to investigate and disseminate the SGID method. It is a well thought out process that was initially used in over 100 classes and with over 10,000 students (Clark & Redmond, 1982).

Step 1: Setting the Stage for the Interview

Early meetings between the consultant and client focus on the value of student perceptions. If the instructor feels student views are important, the consultant describes the SGID process and the three very general questions asked of the students:

- What do you like about the course as taught by Instructor X?

- What would you like changed about the course as currently taught?

- What suggestions do you have?

Instructor-generated questions. In addition to the questions above, the instructor is encouraged to suggest others of special interest. Instructor-generated focus questions often tap areas students may not think of but to which they readily react. As the consultant, I have already reviewed course and class materials in order to understand the course structure. This way, less time is needed for clarification during the class interview.

Student feedback. The instructor also decides who will see the student feedback. Generally only the instructor and the faculty developer review the feedback. At no time are interview results supplied for use in personnel decisions. If instructors want those results to go to the department, they must provide them.

Instructor reaction. The interviewer must judge how sensitive the instructor will be to student feedback. This judgment will later affect which verbatim student remarks to include in the feedback report. Since several student groups typically offer the same idea, albeit couched in different words, it is possible to select the phrasing that may best speak to the instructor.

Necessary details. The place and date of the interview, number of students involved, and a time to discuss interview results are established during these meetings with the instructor. A half-hour of class time is the minimum needed for the interview. Occasionally, despite one's best persuasive efforts, an instructor balks at the thought of giving up half an hour of lecturing time. That much time is needed to do the job; however, one might be forced to use other methods.

Discussing the interview with students. Many instructors do not feel comfortable telling students that an interview about the course will take place. However, there are a few points to be made. First, it is important for students to know that the instructor is in charge of initiating the interview. Any good will that accrues from students' interest in the process belongs to the instructor. Secondly, students should not infer from the interview process that the instructor is in trouble. The latter might result in an increasing lack of confidence in the instructor's ability to help them learn.

Before the interview takes place, the instructor should briefly tell students that she or he would like information from them about the course before the end of the marking period and that interview arrangements have been made. Students' cooperation should be encouraged; however, it is not always wise to give students the exact date of the interview since some may not show up.

Realistically, huge course changes will not be made during the term of the interview. It is therefore helpful for instructors to say that they will seriously consider all remarks but that students should not expect major course revisions overnight.

Students will expect some reaction from the instructor to the interview comments. If, at the first class after the interview, the feedback session between the instructor and interviewer has not been held, the instructor can thank the class for their cooperation, letting them know that she or he has not yet seen the comments and that the debriefing will be at a later date.

Step 2: Conducting the Interview

After the instructor introduces me and leaves the room, I tell the students that she or he is interested in teaching and wants to know their honest views of the course. I then briefly describe the following process to them.

Student groups. Students form groups of six to eight persons and choose a recorder. The recorder receives three separate pages, each in a different color and each with one of the three basic questions: What do you like about the course, what would you like changed in the course, and what suggestions do you have for improving the course? The recorder writes student comments on the papers, which are collected at the end of the interview. I also write down on a chalkboard or overhead any questions the instructor would like answered.

Occasionally students start to leave. To prevent an exodus, one can close the door and casually stand in front of it. If it still looks like some students might exit, I remind them of the importance of improving courses and the value of their cooperation. Most do remain.

Seeking consensus. Seeking consensus, although a critical part of the SGID process as originally conceived, has been augmented by including student minority comments. First, each group discusses the three questions, and the student recorders write down the comments with which all in the group agree.

Clark's rationale for stressing consensus is as follows. Instructors often have difficulty knowing how to use feedback from an entire class. When different students make conflicting remarks, instructors feel all the comments are worthless and tend to ignore all student remarks. In addition, if instructors are to make changes based on student feedback, it is important to know what segment of the class to target. Many instructors do recognize those comments that are particularly unusual. However, others are less skilled at reading student reactions, and they may not know when they are receiving important but biased information. They may make changes based upon perceptions shared by only a few students, wonder why the class is still not going well, and reject student feedback entirely.

With increasing knowledge of different student learning styles, with the variety of classroom student profiles, and with the commitment to educating nontraditional students, Clark's emphasis on including only consensus comments has become problematic. In order to be most effective, faculty need information from all segments of a class. Therefore, small group recorders should be asked to include nonconsensus remarks, indicating the number of students agreeing with each such remark.

About 12 minutes is allocated for the small group part of the interview if class size is under 100 students. For larger classes, less time (eight to ten minutes) is allocated. I usually tell the students when two minutes are left. Neither bolted-to-the-floor seating nor tiered auditorium settings inhibit the small-group discussion.

Understanding the comments and establishing whole-class consensus. At the end of the small group discussion, students are asked to return to their seats and face front. In order to put the remarks in perspective for the instructor, I ask students to indicate by a quick show of hands, on a scale of one to five, with five being the highest, how they would rate the course in general. It makes a difference, given the same number and kinds of comments, whether students think the course is one of the best or one of the worst they have taken.

Then each group recorder, in round-robin fashion, reads to the entire class one answer to each of the three general questions. All students indicate whether they agree or disagree with a particular comment by raising their hands. In classes of more than 100 students, having another person along to distribute and collect papers and take notes during this part of the interview is very valuable. It is helpful in large classes to count beforehand the number of seats in given areas of the room so that one can later note with a fair degree of accuracy the percentage of raised hands. Otherwise you cannot be confident that your reports are reasonably accurate. Time often runs out before all unique comments are brought before the entire class. Therefore, collecting the written remarks is extremely important.

Step 3: Organizing the Information

Working from the written remarks, it is not difficult to analyze and group comments under three headings: 1) likes, 2) like changed, 3) suggestions. Under each, arrange comments in order of frequency. Whenever available, a subset of verbatim student remarks, copied from the collected small group papers, is included to provide flavor and illustration.

There is always the question of which student comments to include, especially when the most vivid ones may contain personal crudely phrased attacks. Such comments command immediate instructor attention. Their longer range effects, however, can be counterproductive by increasing hostility toward students and lowering the value of students and student feedback in the mind of the instructor. Comments should be written down in sufficient detail so that the instructor can understand them without a consultant present since the written feedback is usually read and reread several times.

Step 4: Conducting the Feedback Session

Although the character of the feedback session is influenced by many factors, it contains certain constant elements (Clark & Redmond, 1982). Factors influencing the session are the goals for the SGID, the interaction between consultant and instructor, and the time available for the session.

Review of the interview. A brief review of the SGID, the students' reactions, and the organization of the feedback is helpful for instructors who are not familiar with the method or have not used it recently.

Review and analysis of comments. During a review of the comments, we try to make sure that the instructor and interviewer share the same general interpretation of each comment and that the interpretations closely reflect students' views. Instructors can shed light on comments you, as the interviewer, might not have fully understood.

At some point in the session, the instructor may feel somewhat defensive about negative student comments. In this instance, empathy is in order. It is not always profitable to review every topic orally. Highlighting those most important to learning and those about which something can be done may ultimately result in more change than an oral laundry list of everything. All written comments are available for later reading.

As the instructor identifies the major student themes, another goal for the feedback session is that the instructor realize that student comments are true from the students' viewpoints and that they have to be evaluated from the instructor's perspective as well. This is important since some instructors accept students' remarks at face value without further thought. Other instructors might tend to reject students' comments out of hand. Questions which instructors find useful in dealing with students' comments are as follows:

- What happened in class to elicit this comment?

- Is X within my control?

- Is X important to student learning?

- Can I reasonably change in regard to X?

- Do I want to change in regard to X?

- What action can I take now or the next time I teach the class?

Step 5: Instructor Plan for Responding to Students

The SGID process raises students' expectations that changes for the better will occur. Instructors, however, do not always know how to respond to the class after a group interview, so we talk about what the instructor plans to say. If that seems vague, we work out a short response together. This response usually includes a thank-you and references to some positive student comments, suggestions which the instructor has found helpful, and any changes which may be implemented. It may be worthwhile to point out that a litany of instructor excuses or statements of disappointment in the student comments is counterproductive.

EFFECTIVENESS OF SGIDS

Let us refer back to the scenarios at the beginning of this chapter and ask whether or not the student interviews contributed to more effective instruction in those instances.

Although the assistant professor sent to our office by the head of the economics department was eventually tenured and promoted, he still has more than the usual trouble teaching. He returns to the office periodically and has worked with three different consultants. He always asks that we speak with his students. Since the comments are usually the same, we use paper-and-pencil measures instead of SGID. Because the instructor seems firmly lodged at the "tell me what to do and I'll do it" stage of instructor development, he cannot generalize beyond the current course he is teaching. Initially, detailed student feedback was very motivating; currently, its helpfulness is limited.

The large-class instructor, Professor Geddy, took off with the student comments. After noting the similarities and differences in his teaching in large and small-class settings, he introduced elements into the large class which had been successful for him in smaller classes. He also developed other activities suitable for large group teaching. Subsequent SGIDs showed that students liked the course better. Geddy is more satisfied, too, although he still prefers small classes. The SGID process worked very well in this consultation.

The medicine scenario of complete course revision presented unusual problems. SGIDs use a lot of class and consultant time. Interviewing for each of five instructors would have required $2\frac{1}{2}$ hours of class time, five analysis/write-up hours, and six feedback hours. Although the course leader did not object, several of the other instructors were reluctant to give up so much course time. We also anticipated that students would find five interviews excessive. Consequently, several questions were developed to focus student memories on specific parts of the course, and only two interviews were conducted. The medicine team instructors found the student comments confirmed their expectations that the course was much improved overall. Comments about individual faculty were written up separately from the course comments and given only to the instructor involved. The course leader, however, wanted all information since it affected the success of the course. As a result of renegotiation, everyone agreed that the interviewer could make general oral remarks to the course leader about the strengths and weaknesses of each instructor. He, in return, would try to help them individually. Another set of SGIDs is planned for the next year.

Arlene, the teaching assistant in art, did think some kind of student feedback would be useful (Bordonaro, 1995-96) although she was not willing to let a consultant or another TA into her classroom.

After listening to several alternative data collection suggestions, she decided to have the students individually respond to the three SGID questions and mail the results to me to analyze and type so that students' handwriting would not be recognized. This procedure took more consultant time than a regular SGID, there was no check on consensus, and we did not have control over data gathering. However, we did learn in great detail what Arlene undoubtedly had already felt, that the students were very hostile toward her. I gave her a gentle but true picture of the student comments. She said little and left. The following semester she came around again and asked that the procedure be repeated. Nothing else would do. This time, the students' reactions to her personally were better, and there were specific suggestions about improving the course. Again she said little and disappeared. The following semester she sent a note asking me to expect student comments through campus mail and to please look them over. This time two groups of students thought she and the course were very good. This interview procedure certainly resulted in instructional improvement, and it serves as an illustration of the flexibility of modified SGIDs.

CONCLUSION

Judging by student and instructor satisfaction, SGID is an effective strategy for faculty and instructional development. Instructors and students like the midcourse timing since feedback can result in more immediate change than feedback at the end of a term. Instructors are impressed by the richness resulting from interview data. They trust the data, comparing them favorably with data from student rating forms (Brinko, 1993; Diamond & Smock, 1985). Instructors also say that SGID feedback contains very specific information which makes it easier for them to know where and how to implement changes. In the interaction between consultant and instructor lies one probable source of improved teaching (Brinko, 1993). Since SGIDs require more consultant time, however, than do paper-and-pencil evaluations, other sources of student evaluation are necessary (Braskamp & Ory, 1994). In summary, when representative, detailed student feedback, including a clear picture of effective class dynamics, is important to instructional improvement, the SGID process is available and effective.

REFERENCES

Bordonaro, T. (1995-96). Improving the performance of teaching assistants through the development and interpretation of informal early evaluations. *The Journal of Graduate Teaching Assistant Development, 3*, 21-26.

Braskamp, L. A., & Ory, J. C. (1994). *Assessing faculty work.* San Francisco, CA: Jossey Bass.

Brinko, K. T. (1993). The practice of giving feedback to improve teaching: What is effective?" *Journal of Higher Education, 64* (5), 54-68.

Clark, D. J., & Bekey, J. (1979). Use of small groups in instructional evaluation. *Insight to teaching excellence,* VII.I. Arlington, TX: The University of Texas at Arlington.

Clark, D. J., & Redmond, M. (1982). *Small group instructional diagnosis: Final report.* (ERIC Document Reproduction Service No. ED 217954)

Dawson, J., & Caulley, D. (1981). The group interview as an evaluation technique in higher education. *Educational Evaluation and Policy Analysis, 11,* 4.

Diamond, N., & Smock, R. (1985, October). *Description and evaluation of the senior clinical interview process.* Paper presented at the tenth annual conference of the Professional and Organizational Development Network in Higher Education, Somerset, PA.

Powney, J., & Watts, M. (1987). *Interviewing in educational research.* London, England: Routledge & Kegan Paul.

Nancy A. Diamond is a specialist in education in the Division of Instructional Development, Office of Instructional Resources at the University of Illinois at Urbana-Champaign. She is a longtime POD member and a frequent presenter at POD conferences.

Email: ndiamond@uiuc.edu

9

If I Knew Then What I Know Now: A First-Year Faculty Consultant s Top Ten List

Jill D. Jenson

A new school year was about to begin, and I was anticipating another year of doing something I truly enjoy—teaching writing to juniors and seniors about to embark on their own career paths. So when I was offered a part-time position as a faculty consultant, I must admit that I had never given the role much thought. Nevertheless, the prospect of doing something new, particularly working with faculty to improve teaching, was inviting.

As soon as the funding was approved, I found myself agreeing to start immediately in a position I was not at all convinced I was qualified to hold. Still, I trusted the other two faculty consultants at our university, both of whom thought I was the person for the job. The situation under which I was hired did not allow for a thorough training before I began, but with the guidance and patience of the seasoned consultants as well as access to the resources housed in our Instructional Development Service library, I quickly learned what makes for a successful experience for the consultant and client alike.

THE TOP TEN

I have developed a list of the top ten tips I wish I had had the day I began as a faculty consultant. These helpful tips are listed in descending order with the most important lesson learned listed last.

10) Know the Limits of Your Position

Begin by learning what the consultants at your college or university have typically done and are authorized to do. For example, some faculty look to this program not so much as a service but as a stamp of approval for their teaching. They want letters of recommendation from the consultant that will verify their abilities for promotion, tenure, or other rewards. However, this practice may put the consultant and the entire program at risk by creating a situation for which either becomes liable. Therefore, while such letters are not written for our clients, any materials generated during the consulting process are the property of the faculty member and may be used for evaluation procedures. That is the client's choice. Knowing what the consultants at your institution are hired to do and what they must avoid doing is a crucial first step.

9) Prepare to Work with Each Client and Each Situation Individually

In one-on-one situations, several decisions need to be made prior to the time a consultant actually attends any classes. While being in class the first day that a group of students gathers is vital, meeting with the instructor before that happens is equally important. During that initial meeting, decide how the consultant's presence in class will be handled. In the case of a planned long-term observational process, although students may initially think that the consultant is also a student, it will become obvious as the term continues that this person's role is different from their own. Therefore, it is often wise to introduce the consultant, in most cases as someone who was invited into the classroom to partner with the instructor about ways to make the class more effective. This not only explains the person's presence, but also indicates to the students this faculty member's dedication to improving teaching. Ultimately, though, the decision as to how to handle the consultant's presence is the instructor's. Each situation and client is unique.

Another important step to take prior to the first day of class is to determine the goals for the consultation process. Discuss with the instructor what is to be accomplished by having a consultant visit the class. Be careful to avoid putting too much on this agenda. Stick to one or two main objectives. Only so much can be accomplished in a few weeks, and you both need to focus on what that is. Once the goals have been determined, seek out the most pertinent literature on the subject(s). It is your job, however, to find the most helpful material. Make sure both you and your client have copies of the materials so that you can study and learn together; the client does not have time to sift through everything available on any one topic. Read as extensively as possible and then provide only that material which is directly relevant and highly effective in meeting the established goals. This is an excellent time to seek advice from other faculty consultants or other faculty you know who have worked on a similar topic.

8) Learn What to Observe in Class and How to Take Consultant Notes

As a consultant you will want to experience the class in much the same way the students experience it. But you also need to pay attention to those habits or practices of which the teacher may be unaware but that potentially inhibit learning, such as:

- How often does the instructor call on male versus female students?

- Who asks questions in class?

- What time did particular events occur?

- When did the students appear bored, restless, or inattentive?

- Where did the instructor stand during the class period?

Noting all of this is difficult, especially when trying to also capture the notes students would normally be taking, so creating a method for yourself before you actually do it is important. I drew a line down the notebook page and used one-half for notes I thought the students would be taking and the other half for my observations. Whatever method you choose, remember that being able to quote the instructor with a high degree of accuracy is often vital when trying to determine what happened and why. Using specific examples of what occurred at a particular moment is an effective way to help the faculty member actually visualize the point you are trying to make. As a result, the instructor will be more conscious of that particular point in the future as well.

7) Be Aware of the Client's Expectations for Conferring with You

Some instructors will want to speak with you after every class session if you are doing observations over an extended period of time. Others prefer to meet once a week or less. Most often, the frequency of your meetings will vary, depending on the situation. In any case, verbalize your intentions to avoid confusion. I learned that I had unwittingly created an expectation to visit with one client after each class period. One day, however, I had to leave immediately in order to keep another appointment, but I failed to tell the instructor that. The result was an upset client who thought something had gone terribly wrong in class because of my hurried exit. Simple communication easily avoids such mishaps.

Moreover, when someone does want to speak with you after each class, those conversations are best kept positive and light. A simple comment referring to how much you enjoyed being there or how much you learned about whatever subject matter was being taught that day is a better choice than giving immediate, extensive feedback. You need some time to process what happens in the classroom, and offering quick assessments and judgments is usually not helpful. Taking the time to strategize the most effective way to share what you see happening between the instructor and students pays large dividends in the long run.

6) Conduct a Midterm Course Evaluation

Whether done formally or informally, verbally or in writing, conducting a course evaluation midway through the term allows you to verify and/or clarify your observations. It also exposes issues that neither you nor the client may know exist (something that is also accomplished by some indiscriminate eavesdropping on students' conversations before and after class). Encourage honest feedback by reminding the students of their instructor's sincere desire to make the class effective, evidenced by your presence, and by offering suggestions as to what type of comments you seek. Although you do not want to put words in their mouths, using examples that relate to the goals that were established for the consultation and observation process will provide the most helpful feedback. When assessing the evaluations and discussing them with your client, remain focused on the objectives. Students' remarks vary widely and provide many, often conflicting, suggestions. Avoid fixating on one or two comments of any kind; instead, search for themes, particularly those that relate to what you and your client set out to accomplish.

5) Celebrate Successes, However Small They May Be

No matter how dire the circumstance of your client, always find something to celebrate. These celebrations may or may not relate to

the objectives you both set out to accomplish; the point is to be dili-
gent at reminding the person of what is going well. I make a deliberate effort to begin and end each meeting with a client on a positive
note. Granted, the point is to improve the teaching and the course, but
hammering away at problems relentlessly only serves to wear a person down. Also keep in mind that the client has been developing a
personality and teaching style for years, perhaps decades. Be realistic
in the amount of change you can expect over a few weeks and channel that pragmatism to the client as well by praising all steps taken in
the right direction—even baby steps.

4) Let the Client Tell You What Needs to Be Improved, Rather Than Vice Versa

In our eagerness and haste to help, faculty consultants sometimes
come on too strongly. After only one hour in the classroom, we can
usually create a lengthy list of what can and should be done differently to improve the teaching and learning environment. Avoid that
temptation. Instead, guide the client to discovery. Ask probing questions that eventually lead the instructor to a personal awareness of
what did and did not go well such as:

- How did you think class went?

- What were your goals for the students?

- How well were they met?

- How did you feel at the end of the class period?

- What, if anything, would you do differently?

Of course self-awareness is difficult for all of us, so where the instructor is blind to the reality of what happened in the classroom, an extra
effort to uncover that reality must be made.

3) Retain Confidentiality at All Times

This tip may seem to be self-evident, but for those inexperienced at
consultant work, it is anything but that. Hallway and office conversations about other faculty members flow all too easily for most of us
involved in higher education. Guard against slips in confidentiality
by reminding yourself every day of its importance. Do not tell other
faculty members or your friends the name of the person with whom

you are working. If the client chooses to tell others, that is the client's business. Furthermore, no matter how amusing you might find what happened in a classroom, resist the temptation to tell the story around campus. You may think you are taking precautions against anyone discovering who you are talking about but more often than not, the faculty member's name is eventually determined. If you must talk to someone, talk to other faculty consultants; they will understand both your need for sharing and the client's need for privacy.

2) Know This: It's Not about You

Because faculty consultants are also teachers themselves, there is a tendency to approach the one-on-one consultation from the perspective of one's own academic discipline and experience. Therefore, one of the most difficult, yet valuable, lessons I learned was this—it wasn't about me. The issue was not what I wanted the students to learn or how I thought they should learn it. The issue was determining what the client set out to do and then helping that person succeed at doing it, all for the betterment of the students. For example, my personal opinion about the content of a final exam was unimportant. What was important was to make sure that the instructor had thought about the goal of that exam and then developed a test that would meet that goal. By the same token, what was taken for granted in my own discipline may or may not be pertinent in another discipline. As a writing instructor, holding regularly scheduled office hours and keeping them at all costs is a given. In contrast, faculty in the fine arts may be expected to be any number of places other than their offices— the studio, the stage, the control booth, or the box office. In other words, the written and unwritten rules of one academic area may not pertain to another. Be careful not to assume that they do. Ask questions, especially of faculty members who work in fields with which you are unfamiliar. Expand your range of vision and view the teaching and learning experience through different lenses.

1) Build a Relationship, Not a Case

By far the most important lesson I learned during that first year as a faculty consultant was that—more than anything else—this is really about relationships. As a consultant you are not a detective gathering evidence to convict a person of having poor teaching practices. The goal is to work collaboratively with the client to make the teacher and the course the absolute best they can be. However, this is most effectively done by remembering that your client is a person who has feelings and an ego that needs to be protected. Your client, whatever degree of talent he or she displays in the classroom, is someone who is teaching for the joy of seeing others learn. Nothing is accomplished by taking the pleasure out of the experience. Avoid setting yourself up as an expert whose job it is to correct and change. Ask yourself how you would want to be approached about issues in your classroom. Learn how to read your clients. Know when to gently push and when to back off. Remind yourself regularly of why you're there:

- Not to torture, but to nurture

- Not to disparage, but to encourage

- Not to command, but to coach

- Not to correct, but to suggest

- Not to clone, but to hone

I would be less than honest not to admit that I learned many of these lessons the hard way. Nevertheless, my first year as a consultant was highly rewarding, not so much for what I taught others, but for what they taught me.

Jill D. Jenson has taught writing courses at the University of Minnesota, Duluth since 1987. In addition, she is a member of POD and works for UMD's Instructional Development Service as a one-on-one consultant and workshop presenter.

Email: jjenson@d.umn.edu

Part III

Practical Strategies

10

Promoting Your Professional Development Program

Susan A Holton

Everything is ready. Your needs assessment told you what programs and services your faculty want. You're very excited about a speaker you heard at a national conference. You booked the best room on campus, the coffee and danish have been ordered. Your faculty development field of dreams is ready. But in order to reach your audience, you must actively and continuously promote your professional development program to make faculty aware of it.

MARKETING CALENDAR

Faculty have busy schedules, and you will want to get events on their calendar as soon as possible. Fortunately for the purposes of promotion, academic institutions have natural timelines that can be used to develop a calendar and publicize planned faculty development events. In early May, before the academic year is over, mail out a flyer of programs for the next academic year. Even if you do not have the complete program planned, let faculty know of upcoming major events. This first promotional step, the marketing calendar, is a general one sent to the entire potential audience on campus. By sending out this announcement, you offer an open invitation for every program.

This calendar can also be posted on your web site and sent electronically to everyone on campus, depending on your system's capabilities. Also be sure that your events are included in any calendar that the college prints for the academic year.

REMINDERS

By the end of August, even those faculty who have let their minds wander for the summer are refocusing on the academic year ahead.

Send a brochure about your faculty development program, and a calendar of events for the year to every faculty member.

If there is an all-faculty meeting before classes resume, include the events calendar in the packet of materials faculty will receive. Yes, you're giving them the same information now three times. And yes, it often takes that much to register an event in people's minds. But this overload is necessary since faculty lives and priorities change. The first time you sent the announcement, the topic may not have been important to some faculty, but it may now prove to be quite useful.

Two weeks before the event send out a flyer that is specific to the upcoming program and geared to the potential audience. For example, if you are conducting a workshop on preparing for tenure and promotion, your target audience is not those who already have it but those still seeking tenure and promotion. This information, along with mailing labels, should be available through your human resources office.

There may be other means at your institution to get the word out. If there is a new faculty packet, for example, be sure that information about your programs and services is included. If there is a faculty handbook, offer to write the section describing your program or to revise it annually if a section already exists.

The week before the program, place an announcement on the institution's electronic bulletin board and in a prominent section on the web page that serves as a home page for faculty computers. It might also be possible to have your message stream across the machines of every person on campus, depending on your technology system and culture. Make use of the technology available to you. If your center or program has a web page, be sure to update it frequently to include a feature on the next program. You may also be able to include a link on the institution's home page to your article about the featured speaker. Use electronic mail and voicemails as you can and as appropriate. Your audience members use these modes of communication and it only makes sense for you to use them, too.

Although email systems differ, it is an easy way to publicize your programs. Email is an efficient and effective way to get the word out, and faculty who do not wish to read your message can simply delete it. Sending out an email message one week prior to the program, and another a few days before the program, is a good reminder for those faculty who forgot to put the event on their calendar and who need that last minute impetus to attend.

Do not assume that your potential audience knows—or remembers—that you exist. If they have been on campus for a while, they may forget about what you do. If they are new, they may not know at all. All faculty need to be regularly (at least once a year) reminded of what you do, and how you might help them be more effective in their professional lives.

Tips on Promotion

Visibility is the key to promotion, and several strategies can make your program(s) more visible.

Making Friends

Assuming that your programs and services are geared to faculty in your own institution, campus-wide newsletters and/or newspapers which go to all campus employees can serve as an excellent promotional tool.

The head of the internal publicity/public relations department can be a valuable ally in helping you promote your programs. If you have never met with him or her, do so immediately. Due to the nature of her position, she will know what works and what doesn't with this particular campus. She may have valuable ideas on how to promote your activities and she will be the person who ultimately decides who gets the space, whose programs will be featured, and what information to send to the campus community. If you have established a relationship with her, she will look more favorably on your programs and your work.

Going the Extra Mile

When you want an article about your program to be considered for publication, provide the public relations director with complete information. If you can, write the article yourself, and submit an article about each program and event you sponsor. Send biographical data about speakers, including a picture, if available, and the time and place of the events. Stress the unique angle to each program or service. The more professional your article, the more likely it will be included in the internal publication. Not every story can have, or will warrant, a feature, but be sure that at least one paragraph about the upcoming program appears in each issue of the publication. At the beginning of the year, submit a feature article on the overall program and services offered.

Use the student newspaper as well. Students like to know what the professors are doing, and professors also read those papers. Submitting articles that are geared specifically to the students may draw their interest in your program. For example, if you have a workshop on learning communities, focus your article on how students' lives are changed by learning communities. Also, remember that many student newspapers do not have enough staff, so you may need to write the article yourself.

Think about how you can involve the students on campus. Some of your programs may be enriched by having student speakers or student participants. Their thoughts and opinions can contribute significantly to the program.

Targeting the Audience

You have already alerted the entire institution to faculty development activities for the term through the general publicity flyer. You sent the brochure and schedule to every faculty member and distributed bulletins at the beginning of the term. Now you need to target the audience for each specific program.

First, this requires that you know your faculty. Demographic and psychographic information about the people at your institution will be invaluable. It is helpful to have demographics of faculty members:

- Sex
- Age
- Courses taught
- Size of classes taught (i.e., seminar, large lecture)
- Work with TAs
- Current research projects
- Areas of specialization

If the size of your institution allows, it can also be beneficial to have psychographics on individuals:

- Special interests

- Hobbies, special contributions to the institution
- Community service involvement and interests

A computerized database could be constructed and maintained within the faculty development office. With this psychographic and demographic data in hand, it is easier to target your programs.

You should also regularly conduct a needs assessment survey to determine what your faculty want. Vary the survey to elicit different information and lessen faculty complaints that you are always asking the same questions.

You can assume that if you are giving a program on the special problems inherent in teaching an introductory course, faculty who only teach senior seminars are not likely to be interested. Mail and time will be wasted by notifying them again (remember, you have already made them aware of the program through the general notice in your earlier mailing). If your program concerns preparing for retirement, you will want to target that special audience.

Targeting the potential audience for your programs in this way will let them know that you have taken the time to be selective and they will more carefully read your mail, knowing that the featured program pertains specifically to them.

READ ME

Of the dozens of pieces of paper that come in campus mail, most are boring. Some are visually appealing, but most are either white or color with black words (usually too many), and almost none grab my attention. Most end up in my circular file, unread.

Academics are not likely to take the time to read something that has no appeal. So how do you get your potential audience to read the mail you have so carefully chosen for them?

To encourage your potential audience to attend your event, I recommend the motivated sequence, a standard organizational format used by communication professors to teach persuasive speaking. It involves five simple steps that, if followed carefully, will spark faculty interest in your programs.

Step One: Attention

What grabs your attention as you read through the myriad of flyers that sneak onto your desk? Usually, it is clever graphics, good use of color, and clean copy.

For a workshop on critical thinking, what graphic comes to mind? Perhaps it is Rodin's "The Thinker." For a recent program on critical thinking at my institution, "The Thinker" was featured prominently as the graphic on the initial announcement flyer, the follow-up flyer, and the evaluation form to the participants.

What graphic will suit your program? Search through your paper or electronic graphics files or look through art books for graphics in the public domain. (Remember to always keep copyright issues in mind.) For example, when a highly successful speaker returned for another event, I used a theater marquee and the words "Back by popular demand." A picture of an old movie camera accompanied a program on videotaping of faculty. For meeting announcements, I always use a clever graphic or cartoon. Not only does it invite attention, but I have been told by some people that they look forward to my flyers and their graphics. When I once sent out a meeting announcement with no graphic because I was in a hurry, numerous people on the committee voiced their disappointment.

As I noted earlier, almost all of the paper announcements that come across my desk are on white paper. Anything in color will draw attention, although you may be limited by what is available at your copy center. However, if you have the opportunity, order any color you want. Get a variety of colors so that you can use a different one every time. If that is not possible, then rotate your colors. And just as you keep the graphics consistent throughout all handouts of a particular program, you want to keep the color consistent as well.

Be aware of the psychology of color. While gold and bright colors will grab the reader's attention, pinks and pastels will soothe the reader. Use a color appropriate to your program but do not hesitate to experiment. Your audience will pay attention to your flyer if it stands out from the rest of their mail.

After getting your faculty's attention, you want to be sure that you keep it. Don't have so much copy on your flyer that it is impossible to read. Keep it simple. Include necessary information, but be sure to leave space without words or graphics. This makes your flyer more readable.

There are also ways to grab faculty members' attention as they scroll through their daily email. Use a clever headline, a catchy phrase, a promise of rewards. Which message are you more likely to open, one that says, "program on community service," or "show your stuff?"

Step Two: Need

You are competing for faculty members' most scarce resource—time. So once you have their attention, you have to give them a reason to come. Since you have already carefully selected your target audience, this should be an easy step for you. Why did you choose this audience for this program? What is in it for them? What particular skills are they going to learn? What new information are they going to take away to make them more effective or more satisfied? You need to make the audience aware of what this program will give them.

Some faculty development programs provide certificates for faculty who attend a series of workshops. That may entice junior faculty who want to include that certificate in their folder, or others who like that sort of recognition.

Step Three: Satisfaction

Now that you have established the need, how are you going to satisfy it? In this section of your flyer, tell the audience about your featured speaker(s). Avoid the temptation to oversell the person. There is no need to give the speaker's entire pedigree, only the salient credentials. You can refer the audience to the speaker's web site or to web links which will give them more information about the topic or the speaker. It is a good idea to photocopy some articles by the speaker and have them on reserve in the library. I also give faculty a brief bibliography on the particular topic so they can read more about it if they choose.

Step Four: Visualization

In the visualization step, the audience should be able to determine the specific results they will glean from the program:

- Will they be able to use a computer in writing tests?
- Will they be able to implement web technology?
- Will they learn principles of effective lecturing?
- Will they learn how to reduce the stress in their lives?
- Will they be able to handle their income tax?

Tell them, as clearly as possible, what they are going to learn.

Step Five: Action

Because your flyer is so persuasive, they're ready to sign up immediately! Include a registration form or registration instructions on your flyer, and be sure no pertinent information is on the back of that registration form. Give your name, telephone number, email, and the best time to call if someone has a question or needs more information. Provide all relevant data, including the time and place of the program, the cost (if any), and any other information that will prepare the person for that program.

CONCLUSION

It sounds trite to say that no program or event is going to be a success unless you have an audience. And yet, we frequently forget the promotional aspect of our programs and hope that by some miracle the word will get out.

By planning ahead, using all available means of publicity on campus, targeting your audience, and following the steps of the motivated sequence, you will not only alert your faculty to your program, but will make them realize that they want to be a part of it.

Effective promotion of your program will change your problem from "Will we have enough people?" to "Where are we going to put them all?"

Merely building the field of dreams for your faculty development program is not enough. You have to let others know that the field has been built and get them to want to be a part of your dream as well.

Susan A Holton is Professor of Communication Studies and the Coordinator of the Bridgewater Institute at Bridgewater State College. She was the founder of the college's faculty development program and the founder and coordinator of the Massachusetts Faculty Development Consortium (now the New England Faculty Development Consortium). She has served as a member of the POD Core Committee.

Email: sholton@bridgew.edu

11

Staging Successful Workshops

Linda R. Hilsen and Emily C. (Rusty) Wadsworth

Workshops are an accepted and stable component of many, if not most, faculty development programs. In this chapter we share what we, and others, have learned from our successes and failures in conducting workshops for faculty members. Although our two programs are quite differently funded and focused, the reasons for our workshop triumphs and defeats are common. At the end of this chapter, we include an appendix that provides a checklist of things to consider to as you go through the process of planning and implementing workshops.

Often, people in nonprofit organizations feel they must educate their target market about the services the organization offers. In our experience, workshops are most likely to succeed when they meet a targeted and perceived need. Thus, responsiveness to faculty and administrative needs is the starting point for selling the product (i.e., workshops).

IDENTIFYING NEEDS AND CHOOSING TOPICS

Great food and a world famous presenter are liabilities if no one comes to the workshop. Therefore, it is essential to know what faculty members want and need before choosing a topic. To identify these areas among the full constituency, formal research methods, either qualitative or quantitative, should be used. Whichever method is implemented, it is important to sample a cross-section of the constituency to learn about the silent majority persons who have not actively participated in workshops before and/or have not volunteered their workshop interests. It is also important to note that the collection of data on interests and needs is an ongoing activity.

At one of our institutions, we conducted a qualitative needs assessment during the first year of the faculty development program.

We first identified a random, stratified sample of the population. The members of the professional development advisory committee then interviewed the sample using the focused interview technique, whereby the individuals identified for participation respond to relatively open-ended questions relating to a specific topic, in this instance their workshop interests and perceived needs. Our aim was to identify the basic needs and values of our professional employees. We asked questions about how and why they chose academic careers, how the institution was different from what they had expected, and whether or not they wished they were in some other career or institution. We then sought to assure that our workshop topics were appropriate to the values identified by the research and to address the gap between the reality of academic work at the institution and the ideal as expressed by the interviewees. Instead of conducting a paper and pencil survey, we used quantitative data gathered by other institutional units and continued to conduct interviews.

When the Instructional Development Office was started at the University of Minnesota, Duluth, we sent a survey to the faculty inquiring about professional needs and interests. We then generated a list of potential workshop topics from this data. We supported and added to the survey data by talking with other institutions, faculty, and instructional developers about their experiences with particular workshop topics. Informal feedback also can help to identify topics of interest, and we routinely invite suggestions for future workshop topics on evaluation forms. Thus, most of our workshops have been initiated in response to faculty request.

In addition to using surveys, evaluation form suggestions, previously identified interests, and faculty requests, we keep up on current educational issues on both national and institutional levels. Possible topics surface when faculty developers listen to constituents. We also find it useful to be among and with the faculty—we teach, we lunch, we coffee. Checking these informal data against our hard data gives us additional ideas for workshop topics.

PLANNING

Having identified needs and chosen a topic or topics, the planning process now begins. Good advance planning is critical for workshop success. It also lowers the stress level for the faculty developer(s).

Choosing a Presenter

Presenters can be nationally known individuals, peers from within the institution, colleagues from other campuses, or yourself. All can turn out an audience if the topic has been thoughtfully chosen and you correctly coordinate the workshop from beginning until end.

Whether you use someone from inside or outside may depend to a large extent on budget, but selecting the person with appropriate expertise for the topic and conduct of a workshop is critical. Of course, a presenter from within the institution is cheaper, probably even free. Although some may be inclined to believe that insiders may not attract as large an audience as outsiders, this has not been our experience. For example, if respected campus presenters are chosen and publicity is handled well, the audience may be even larger than for a national expert who is not well known to the faculty. If you are tuned to the institutional grapevine, you will have an idea of persons who could present a good workshop on particular topics. Moreover, you can add to the list of potential presenters by posing your topic to others at the institution such as department chairs, deans, student affairs personnel, and your speaker's bureau or public relations people.

If you decide to look outside for a presenter, you may be able to find a reasonably priced expert nearby. Doing so saves on travel, housing, and other costs. Occasionally, you can even barter a workshop trade with an institution close to you. Unless the trades can occur virtually simultaneously, however, problems might arise. Institutional budgets tend to fluctuate, frequently in a downward fashion, so that one of the two parties might be denied the opportunity to present elsewhere or suddenly might be a workshop short.

We have had tremendous good fortune in selecting effective presenters from outside our universities by attending conference programs of professional organizations such as the Professional and Organizational Development Network (POD), the American Association for Higher Education (AAHE), and various disciplinary associations. You can also ask your own network of professional colleagues if they know anyone who might fit your needs.

However, we urge extreme caution in accepting anyone else's suggestion. If at all possible, only engage someone whom you have actually seen do a presentation. Even hiring pleasant conversationalists whom you have met can be a mistake. Chatting casually and organizing an interactive, structured presentation require different skills. Hiring presenters who sound good on paper or over the phone or who worked for someone else may result in disaster for you and your faculty. Thus, we strongly recommend attending an individual's workshop, if possible, before having the person come to your institution to conduct one.

If your budget is low, or you need to conserve funds, splitting the costs of a presenter with another department or service organization within your institution can result in savings. Another way to share costs is to work with other institutions in your area. Two universities can split airfare and housing costs while each pays the consulting fee for the work performed on site. You might also consider a consortium arrangement in which each of the members selects workshop topics and presenters well in advance and exchanges their plans so that these resources and costs can be shared.

Preparing the Presenter

Except for minor variations, both internal and external presenters need the same kind of preparation for the workshop. Send external presenters information about your institution so that they know the important demographics, and the major current campus issues. For both internal and external presenters, identify those campus issues that may affect the success of the workshop. Use the issues to get the presenter to tailor the workshop to your institution's needs. For example, if your institution is in the middle of a major retrenchment which will affect faculty positions, the presenter of your career development workshop needs to know this.

In addition to issues, identify the kinds of activities the audience will expect. What works? What does not work? At both our institutions, the audience will expect to do something rather than just sit there. On the other hand, faculty members at one of our institutions dislike activities that are personally revealing. Be sure that the presenter works in some kind of networking activity to get participants acquainted with each other. One should not assume that all presenters are skilled at conducting effective workshops; therefore, this kind of preparation is necessary. As soon as possible, send the presenter the names of the people attending, their departments, and any other pertinent information.

On a more mundane level, set deadlines for having the presenter's handouts to you for reproduction, or agree that the presenter will provide the handouts. Prior to the workshop, discuss audiovisual needs and room arrangement. If computers or computer projection are to be used, make certain that your hardware and the presenter's software are compatible. It is wise to have the presenter talk directly with your computer people; check to make certain this has occurred before the presentation day.

If you are working with a consultant who is charging a fee, be certain you understand exactly what you are paying for. Have a clearly negotiated fee set well in advance. Are expenses included in the fee or added to it? If a presenter is doing a workshop one afternoon and repeating it the next morning, are you paying for two days' time? Can you expect that person to meet with other special interest groups or your staff while on campus? Settle these matters before the person arrives on campus.

Negotiating fees clearly is crucial. Ordinarily, the presenter has a set fee per workshop, and such fees vary greatly depending upon expertise and national or international status. A word from the now wise: Any portion of a day's work is counted as a day's pay, which is why you need to maximize the impact of the presenter by planning meetings with appropriate groups or administrators during available times. Repeating the workshop on a different day means you pay another day's fee. Be aware that federal grants may have maximum amounts for daily consulting fees. You may also have to include costs for preparation days in your budget.

Collect any information required by the institution to establish a contract, such as the address and the social security number of the presenter. Being prepared with this information as well as having all of the appropriate paperwork correctly done will allow the presenter to be paid as quickly as possible given the idiosyncrasies of your institution. Both you and the presenter must keep receipts for any allowable expense.

For most external presenters, you need to make arrangements for a place to stay and transportation to and from the airport and around campus. Some people like to be alone the evening before they present; others do not enjoy solitude in a strange place and prefer to be entertained. Ask about your presenter's preferences and try to accommodate them. Send maps of the campus and city, enclose parking permits, or arrange to meet the presenter at the airport. Be certain your consultant knows where to park as institutions are often reluctant to pay parking tickets.

If your workshop involves a panel of speakers, you face additional organizational responsibility in coordinating the preparations of several people. Begin working with the panel two months before the program. Make certain panelists have a fairly clear idea of their roles by the end of the first brainstorming session. Give specific work assignments with due dates. Deadlines for materials to include in a workshop packet need to be set well ahead of the workshop date; one polished procrastinator can cause havoc in your busy preworkshop life. As workshop time draws near, it might be advisable to have a practice session with all present. As a courtesy and as a tranquilizer for yourself, talk to every presenter the day before the session to check last-minute needs.

Choosing a Format, Length, and Date

As you choose your presenter, you must also determine the time format to fit the participants' needs and the presenter's abilities and time schedule. You must decide with the presenter how much time is needed to address the topic. Be sure that the presenter includes networking activities and uses an interactive style. A workshop is meant to be participatory; it is not a lecture. Workshops geared for a certain audience have a specific set of demands. Hands-on experience may be a priority. In how-to workshops, participants benefit more if time is allocated for practicing the skill. Once your presenter understands the audience, the two of you will be able to determine the time needed to cover the topic and to propose potentially effective formats.

You know your audience better than anyone else. How much time can you expect them to commit for any single session: a full day, half day, one hour? Will they come if the weather is bad, good? Spend some time with the room and those in charge of class scheduling to determine the times during the week when the fewest classes are being offered. It may be advisable to repeat the workshop on a different day and time to attempt to reach as many faculty as possible. We have had success offering the same workshop on a midweek afternoon and then repeating it the following morning. We have not had success with workshops in the evenings, on weekends, or on Mondays or Fridays. However, programs with budgets sufficient to offer weekend retreats are able to host successful workshops in that time frame.

Time of the term and academic year are other concerns. Scheduling a workshop for the first week of classes is not recommended. Every institution has its own rhythms, to which faculty developers need to be attuned. Surprisingly, faculty at the University of Minnesota, Duluth are very willing to attend workshops at the end of the winter quarter, which is probably directly related to the accumulation of snow. However, the last week of classes in spring is filled with year-end activities, and such times should be avoided.

You also must take your presenter's schedule into consideration when determining the dates and length of the workshop. If you are using external consultants, how long can they be away from their own classes, campus, job, and family? Each topic, each presenter, and each faculty group must be considered carefully as decisions are made about format, length of presentation, and dates.

Promoting the Workshop

Promotional efforts for your workshop include, at a minimum, listing the event in a newsletter or schedule for the term; individual flyers two to three weeks before the workshop, including a registration form; electronic announcements, depending on how your institution conducts its business; and perhaps also personal phone calls and notes.

At the University of Minnesota, Duluth we use the same color and format for all print workshop flyers; it is a yellow Professional Development Opportunity flyer. Another idea is to color coordinate flyers with the evaluation forms and packet covers for each workshop to facilitate record keeping. Because you have been listening to your constituents, you can begin your publicity with, "in response to your request" or "returning by popular demand." In addition to your own flyers, advertise in in-house publications, faculty/student newspapers, and media when appropriate. While you are out listening to your faculty, you can also promote your next workshop. Make a special point to run into a person who you think might be interested in attending once you have made a personal invitation.

Creating a coordinated series of workshops is a good way to keep regulars returning and to increase the number of participants. Word travels fast about quality presentations, so your audience builds with each additional member to your series. Such topics as "Cooperative Learning," "Support for Computer-Based Instruction," and "Successful Instruction with Students (Learning Disabled, International, Older-than-Average, etc.)" have all worked for us as a workshop series. Although it is usually the topic which causes a faculty member to sign up and attend, some off-campus presenters can establish a following of their own based on previous presentations and will increase your attendance.

Selecting a Place

The choice of the workshop site depends on the requirements of the workshop itself. As soon as you know your presenter's plans and topic, you can determine your room needs. The anticipated number of participants will determine room size. The workshop activities will determine the kind of seating needed; moveable chairs facilitate group functioning. If the presenter wants an overhead projector, you also need a screen, a blackboard, chalk, an easel, newsprint, and markers. If the presenter is using PowerPoint, you need a computer and a screen. Try to find a room that is away from students passing to classes and other distractions.

As soon as you know your room needs, explore your campus for one that will best suit your workshop. Inspect the room thoroughly, making certain that it will accommodate the physical setup and audiovisual needs. Just because the room has a phone, do not assume it is a live line. A dead phone can put a real damper on a computer workshop using modems; check the line ahead of time. On your equipment list, type the phone number of the people who supply equipment. Make friends with the janitor. Find out where the dollies are. Schedule the room for one-half hour before and after the presentation.

If your budget allows, order food and drink for workshop participants. There are also some little things to keep in mind. Standard fare for either morning or afternoon should include coffee, tea, cold soda, and some kind of juice. When it is hot, you can safely eliminate hot drinks for afternoon sessions. The food should be "silent;" avoid loud crunching carrots and celery during a presentation. Sweet rolls, cream cheese and bagels, or cream cheese and nutbreads work well in the morning with the addition of "quiet" but firm fruits and cheese or soft cookies for the afternoons. Participants sincerely appreciate being treated in this fashion. In fact, food is a big budget item in many programs because it draws people and helps them socialize, which promotes your program. To entice preregistrants, list the menu on the flyer and the reminder memo which participants receive a day or two before the workshop.

This reminder should also include a "looking forward to seeing you at time in room on day" statement. The reminder truly helps keep attendance equal to the number of preregistrants.

IMPLEMENTING THE WORKSHOP

Now that you have everything planned, it is time to execute your plans. On the day before the workshop, have a list of everything that you will need the next day. Put the extension numbers of the janitors, food service, and audiovisual center on the checklist. Gather all of the workshop materials, and have them ready to go. Prepare a tote bag with workshop supplies such as extra markers, a nail file, a projector bulb, extra nametags, chalk, a stapler, pencils, paper, and anything else that you think might be necessary in an emergency. You will be amazed at how well a fingernail file can fix a faulty computer connection!

If you have preregistered your participants, try to learn something about each one before the workshop, information which you can then use in conversation. Of course, attempt to learn their names, departments, and faces so you can greet and introduce people on the big day.

Clear your schedule so that you are free for at least an hour before the workshop and afterward so you are able to stay and speak to the participants. Have someone available to run errands—perhaps a student or staff assistant.

Get to the room early and check that everything is in order:

- Set up a registration table.

- Arrange preprinted nametags in alphabetical order (unclaimed preprinted nametags will tell you which preregistants did not attend).

- Neatly display any materials that you are giving to participants before the workshop begins. Do not include the evaluation form in the packet of materials; have it separate so people can fill it out before they leave.

- Have a sign-in sheet for everyone, but especially for a record of those who arrive but did not reserve space.

- Verify that the food is there, that it is what you ordered, and that it is attractively arranged.

- Have a waste container available for refuse.

- Make sure the phone works.

- Survey the audiovisual equipment to assure yourself that what you ordered is there and functioning.

- Provide water for the presenter during the workshop.

- Make certain your presenter has no obligations for at least an hour before the workshop for last minute prep time.

- Provide a secluded spot such as your office for the presenter to review notes.

Be sure to have someone else stationed at the registration table so you can greet people as they arrive and introduce participants to each other. This is a good time to help people network. Helping the presenter connect names with faces will promote participation during the workshop. Welcome those who have not preregistered with open arms. Always have extra nametags available.

After people have had a chance to socialize, call the group together and begin on time. In your introduction, you have an opportunity to promote your program. Explain the services offered: publications, workshops, and opportunities for individual and group consultations. Thank the participants for attending and encourage them to help themselves to refreshments. When you introduce the presenter, say something that indicates that you have some sort of relationship with this person; e.g., "In our discussion last evening." If the presenter is from your campus, mention times that you have worked together before. Provide a brief introduction to the material the presenter will cover, build participants' anticipation, and turn it over to the person they are there to hear.

Your job is by no means done at this point. You must stay in the room to assist the presenter and participants in any way you can. Participate only if you do not detract from your registrants' experiences. Help circulate materials. Pass refreshment trays when appropriate. If the presenter breaks attendees into groups, assist in facilitating the groups whenever possible. If you run out of beverages, call food services immediately. Have extra pens and paper available for those who need them.

Have your campus photographer snap a few pictures during an interactive section of the workshop. These photographs can be put on display in a case or on a bulletin board. They will make those who

118 A Guide to Faculty Development

attended feel important, make those who did not wish they had, and act as a publicity base for future endeavors.

When the presentation is finished, formally thank the presenter and the participants. Remind them to complete the evaluation form. Mingle with those who are left discussing the workshop. Offer the presenter a cold beverage and congratulations.

Leave the facility in order. Take the time to thank all who helped you, from the janitors to the faculty person who helps you lug extra materials and equipment back to your office. As soon as you return to your office, jot reminder notes for yourself. If workshop participants became interested in materials not available at the workshop, write this down so you can circulate copies of the article, book, video, or software. Before the presenter leaves campus, check with your secretary one more time to be certain financial forms have all the needed signatures and information.

EVALUATING THE WORKSHOP AND FOLLOWING UP

The most basic information to gather is level of attendance. Our records allow us to identify how many faculty have attended and who they are. With this information we can gather further data on colleges or departments represented and this is useful for the overall assessment of our programs.

Gather more in-depth data with an evaluation form designed for each workshop. This allows you to include workshop-specific questions to determine if cognitive and affective goals were met. You can also gather information needed for evaluating the effectiveness of your program. Always leave space for workshop topic suggestions and additional comments. The evaluation stage is both the official completion of the workshop and the beginning of new workshop activities. Take the time to record original sign-ups, actual attendance, and returns of evaluation forms in your database. Summarize evaluations and send the results to the presenter with a letter of appreciation. In the letter be certain to ask if all financial commitments have been met. At University of Minnesota, Duluth, we now include a parchment recognition award for the presenter. Also, certificates of participation are appreciated by faithful attendees.

If participants expressed interest in follow-up groups or activities, conscientiously address their requests. Circulate materials of interest. Convene a follow-up discussion. Create a listserv. Such groups encourage networking, promote your services, and make faculty feel their needs are being met. Publish faculty reactions to workshops, and provide the opportunity for major points to be shared by all faculty via your newsletter.

CONCLUSION

All of these suggestions arise from our experiences as well as those of other faculty developers. However, we cannot neglect to mention the most important key to success: politeness. Remember every rule of courtesy your parents ever taught you because you will need to put them all to use to manage a workshop effectively. Without support, your workshop can fall apart before your very eyes. Be especially supportive of your secretary, the food service people, the room scheduler, the printer, the janitors, your presenter, and anyone you may have to call upon for help. If it is possible for anything to go wrong, it very well may. But following these guidelines and tips has proven to be quite a good recipe for workshop success.

RESOURCES

The following four web sites and organizations will put you in touch with virtually every other organization and publication about faculty, instructional, and organizational development.

American Association of Higher Education: www.aahe.org

Professional and Organizational Development Network in Higher Education: www.podnetwork.org

Association of American Colleges and Universities: www.aacu-edu.org

Dalhousie University's Instructional Development and Technology Sites Worldwide: www.dal.cal~oidt/ids.html

Linda R. Hilsen is the Director of the Instructional Development Service at the University of Minnesota, Duluth, where she also teaches writing. She has served two terms on the POD Core Committee.

Emily C. (Rusty) Wadsworth is Dean Emerita at McHenry County College and was coexecutive director of POD in 1989-1991.

(Samples of the "Faculty Needs Assessment Survey" and promotional materials may be requested from the authors.)

Email: lhisen@d.umn.edu
           ewadswor@pobox.mchenry.cc.il.us

APPENDIX 11.1

A WORKSHOP CHECKLIST

PLANNING

____ **Collect Suggestions for Workshops**

__Qualitative needs assessment

__Survey

__Grapevine

__Important issues

____ **Pick a Topic**

____ **Find a Presenter**

__On-campus experts

__Off-campus experts

____ **Determine Dates and Times**

____ **Establish Contract with Presenter**

__Fee per day

__Travel costs

__Housing costs

__Duplication costs

__ *presenter bringing materials*

__ *materials duplicated on campus*

__Note arrival and departure times

__Housing reservations made

____ **Determine Format**

____ **Publicity for the Term**

__Newsletter ad

__Flyer listing activities

__Electronic communication

____ **Workshop Flyer with Registration Form**

____ **Personal Invitations Via Phone Chat**

____ **Prepare Presenter**

__Send information about institution

__Identify major current issues on campus

__Describe audience

__Provide list of participants and departments

__Discuss audience's preference for activities

__Set a handout deadline

__Determine audiovisual needs

__Decide room set-up

__Make certain contracts are ready

__Facilitate payment on site

__Plan entertainment activities

__Send maps of campus and city

__Enclose parking permits if needed (For on-campus individuals or panel)

__Begin working with panel early

__Establish part each member will play

__Allocate time

__Give specific assignment with due dates

__Set deadline for materials/ duplication

__Have a dress rehearsal

__Check with each presenter the day before the workshop

__Check audiovisual/room needs

____ **Schedule Room (½ hour before and after)**

____ **Arrange for Photographer, if desired**

____ **Carry an Equipment List with Phone Numbers of Providers**

__Overhead projector

__Screen

__Blackboard/chalk

__Easel/newsprint/markers

__Live phone line

__Computer

__Computer projection equipment

____ **Place Equipment Order**

__Determine if equipment will

be delivered or picked up

_Find dollies if necessary

___ **Order Food and Drink**

___ **Send Confirmation of Registration Memos Two Days Prior to Workshop with Reminder of Time, Room, Day, and Refreshments Provided**

___ **Have Checklist for the Day Before the Workshop**

_Extension numbers of janitors, food services, media center

_Workshop materials

_Tote bag

___ *extra markers*   ___ *chalk*

___ *nail file*   ___ *stapler*

___ *projector bulb*   ___ *scissors*

___ *name tags*   ___ *pencils*

___ *paper*

___ **Prepare Evaluation Forms**

_Cognitive goals

_Affective goals

_Workshop topic suggestions

_Additional comments

___ **Familiarize Yourself with Preregistrants**

_Names

_Faces

IMPLEMENTING

___ **Clear Schedule on Both Sides of the Workshop**

___ **Have an Errand Runner on Standby**

___ **Get to the Room Early**

___ **Set Up Registration Table**

_Arrange preprinted nametags alphabetically

_Display materials

_Keep evaluation form separate

_Greet participants, introduce them to each other and to the presenter

_Do the introduction

_Explain your services

_Thank-you's

_Introduce the presenter

___ *career comments*

___ *introduction to the materials*

___ *build anticipation*

___ **Remain in Room**

_Participate only if you do not distract from participants' experience

_Help distribute materials

_Facilitate groups

_Provide supplies

_Circulate food

___ **Thank Presenter and Participants at Conclusion**

___ **Mention any Follow-up Activities**

___ **Have Participants Complete Evaluation Forms**

___ **Mingle, Helping to Problem Solve**

___ **Leave the Facility in Order**

EVALUATING AND FOLLOWING-UP

___ **Record Information in Data Base**

_Original sign-ups

_Actual attendees

_Returns of evaluation forms

___ **Summarize Evaluation Forms**

___ **Send Results to Presenter with Letter of Appreciation**

___ **Meet all Financial Commitments**

___ **Plan Follow-up Groups or Activities**

___ **Circulate Materials**

___ **Publish Faculty Reaction to Workshops in Newsletter**

___ **Thank your Assistant(s)!**

12

Ideas for Campus Newsletters

Laura Border, Linc. Fisch, and Maryellen Weimer

Newsletters are a frequent service of faculty and instructional development offices, and the key to successful writing of newsletters for faculty lies in the name newsletter. The most fundamental and certainly most important purpose of the newsletter is that it brings to its readers news, that is, information that they may not have heard, or in the case of teaching and learning, information they may have forgotten or only know vaguely. This need not be news in the late-breaking-development sense. If you are writing about teaching and learning, you will soon run out of that kind of information. However, the newsletter does need to provide information of interest and value to readers.

Information, especially if it contains research results or other educational material, must be presented in readable form. The word "letter" says a lot about the tone and style newsletter writers should assume. The letter summarizes activities and events. It does not contain every detail of how it transpired. The newsletter format presents information succinctly so that it can be read and digested quickly and easily. Letters should not be composed of obscure and complicated prose. Rather, they should read easily.

Newsletters must have substance. If part of their purpose is to encourage readers that there may be more to learn about an issue, then they must include references and follow-up information. This is especially true when readers are faculty members who take pride in scholarship and their ability to judge it. To the extent that we want them to take teaching and learning seriously, the publication must reflect the complexity of the phenomena about which we write and convey that these issues have been the objects of sustained and concerted attention. Put simply, although letters do not include footnotes and references, newsletters written for faculty audiences should.

The newsletter is a curious blend of objectivity and personal involvement. It must report in a good, clear, and objective way. On the other hand, the format makes the personal involvement of the author or editor acceptable. If, in your judgment, something qualifies as a good idea, say so. The key is balance—a delicate mix of facts and feelings. Finding that balance comes with experience and listening closely to the feedback of your readers.

This chapter focuses on newsletters distributed in the print medium, not posted on web pages, as a few faculty development offices have begun to do. However, many of the same principles of preparation and design apply to both media.

THE PURPOSE OF A NEWSLETTER

While the general purpose of a faculty development newsletter is to provide faculty, administrators, and graduate teaching assistants (TAs) with support and information to improve teaching and learning, it can also help the faculty developer address several audiences and achieve goals important to each one.

A Newsletter for Instructors

A newsletter for instructors can serve the following purposes:

- Present information about effective teaching, stimulate discussion, and promote the sharing of good ideas on teaching
- Encourage further exploration of the topics presented
- Discuss teaching and learning styles
- Provide instructional support by presenting helpful hints
- Showcase award-winning faculty and TAs
- Serve as a forum for the presentation of local faculty members' and TAs' innovative ideas on teaching and learning

A Newsletter for Administrators

A newsletter for administrators can serve the following purposes:

- Outline faculty activities and the importance of teaching
- Serve as a public relations vehicle when recruiting students, soliciting funds, and hiring new faculty

A Newsletter for the Public

A newsletter for the public can serve the following purposes:

- Signal that good teaching is honored and rewarded
- Emphasize that the quality of undergraduate education is a high priority

In addition, a newsletter serves as a vehicle for a faculty development center to advertise, market, and feature its services, resources, and staff, as well as those of other service units on campus.

EDITORS' MUSINGS

When the assignment of writing a chapter for current and prospective editors of faculty newsletters came upon us, two things became immediately clear. First, we recognized that we could not present everything that a fledgling editor would need to know. Therefore, we tried to anticipate any questions and focus on the essentials. We also tried to suggest things that are relatively easy to carry out and which bring significant dividends. Second, we realized that a number of other people around the country could handle the assignment at least as well as we could. That was a sobering thought. We considered asking each of them to contribute a segment, and then recognized what a logistical nightmare that could turn into. Consequently, we settled for tapping the ideas of a sample of editors and including them in this chapter. The rest of the material we decided to write ourselves. (That kind of decision is often a sound one for editors.) We encourage you to communicate with us and other colleagues in editorship. By sharing ideas and experiences with each other, we all enhance our efforts.

We posed only one question to a handful of successful editors, those among the best in the faculty development newsletter business. Their institutions range from the Atlantic to the Pacific, from Alberta to Texas, from community college to complex university. This question was this: What are the five best pieces of advice you could give to fledgling college and university newsletter editors?

The majority advised to keep the newsletter short, simple, and sweet as faculty members have many things competing for their attention. Other suggestions included editing all unnecessary and redundant words then repeating the process, and constructing short paragraphs that aim for an ideal length of sentences.

Additionally, there is agreement on the need for carefully defining newsletter objectives and then designing a format for achieving them. While newsletters can serve a multitude of purposes, they cannot be all things to all people. Once you have a clear sense of purpose, style, and presentation, announce it and stick to it. Then, as the newsletter is accepted, move slowly in making changes.

Quality

Many editors stress the critical importance of quality content. You may have to do a lot of writing yourself in order to control both style and quality. Don't be afraid to edit submissions constructively, but remember that you are an editor first, an author second.

The newsletter can be a collaborative effort by and/or about faculty members. Working drafts can be sent to faculty to edit, correct, and supplement. Remember to always give a deadline for return. While many good editors may exercise a heavy editorial hand at times, rarely is it obvious and rarely do they seek credit for their background efforts. As part of quality control, heed the warning to proof carefully.

Topics

How do you find quality material? Much of it can come from faculty, particularly if you view your newsletter as a medium of communication among teaching colleagues. Soliciting material to help match the content to faculty needs and tastes shares ownership of the newsletter with faculty. Including coverage of legislation and other topics of state, regional, or national interest in higher education is also worthwhile as the newsletter may be the only place where faculty can read about such issues. Over time, you may develop a cadre of writers to do reviews and regular features.

Occasionally interviewing a faculty member about activities and then writing it up yourself is an efficient way to produce a concise, effective article. This can include interviewing faculty members who have received teaching or other awards. Maintaining an exchange of newsletters with other institutions is another source of content ideas. If you run across a particularly good article, you will more than likely be able to obtain permission to reprint it or to quote from it in your own publication.

Additionally, surveying faculty for topic suggestions and inviting the sharing of teaching tips can be a rich source of short items or longer articles. Some editors find it helpful to solicit ideas from a faculty advisory committee. Most editors find getting feedback from faculty directly and personally, formally and informally, to be worthwhile.

The POD network began an annual publication series in 1989 entitled *Essays on Teaching Excellence*, and many faculty/instructional developers include these essays as features in their newsletters. The pieces are intentionally short and succinct, and authors are chosen to represent the best in thought and practice. An institutionally licensed subscription allows unlimited reproduction within the institution. The essays are also available in electronic format so that they can be posted on web pages, provided access is restricted through firewalling.

Sometimes a newsletter may focus on a single topic or theme, and this can even be done for a year or for a series of issues. A good mix of articles serves a diversified readership. Quality content helps market institutional faculty development opportunities, and some use insert sheets and tear-offs that facilitate replying to announcements of faculty development events.

Experience indicates that pertinent, current information seems to motivate faculty more than reports of past happenings. The most important articles should be placed on page one and the back page, keeping the newsletter to four pages, if possible. Anything more than eight pages becomes something to be read later (if read at all). Teaser material; i.e., quotations from articles and books, can motivate readers to delve further into the sources.

Appearance

Although quality content is essential, quality appearance is also important in the presentation of your newsletter, which should be attractive to both the eye and the mind. Make it handsome but not slick. There is a fine line between producing an attractive, professional publication and wasting the institution's money on yet another glossy piece of trash can fodder.

The first issue of a new publication is critical because it sets the tone and pattern for the entire endeavor. If at all possible, use a graphic artist for at least this issue and then copy the format yourself in subsequent issues. Allow ample time for the design as things tend to take longer than anticipated. If you are just starting, it is helpful to read one or two texts on publishing, study other newsletters, and then do the entire first newsletter from start to finish, including layout. Those who have regular access to a designer for layout and graphics have a valuable luxury. Even a small college probably has one person who is versed in these areas and can function as a consultant.

Visual variety attracts readers. Effective devices for this are boxes, screened sections, cartoons, graphic elements, photos, clip art, and even just plain white space. Fillers should be tasteful, relevant, and not too cute. Most editors find that a two- or three-column format is more easily read than a single column stretching across a page.

Select a good type font and stick with it, providing variety and emphasis through different type sizes, italics, and bold face. Do not be tempted by your computer to mix several different fonts. Ten-point type is a commonly used size for text; headlines can be set in 12- or 15-point. Also remember that the "greying of faculty" calls for easily read print.

A general rule of thumb for visual variety is one illustration or photo for every two pages, and photos turn out best when there is high contrast between ink color and page color. Be sure to consider pull-out quotes, both to provide variety and to draw readers into the articles.

Final Suggestions

Additional suggestions from our survey include 1) selling your newsletter to faculty and administration and linking it to a clear pattern of support and development services and activities and 2) overdistributing the newsletter to administration, staff, boards, and anyone whose support would be strengthened by knowing more about your institution's endeavors.

Much more could be said about publishing effective newsletters given the additional suggestions from editors. However, perhaps all this advice can be summed up by asking ourselves whether we would read our newsletter if we received it in the mail. If the answer is no, modify, adjust, and delete accordingly.

NAMING THE NEWSLETTER

Initiating a newsletter requires you to title the publication and to design its nameplate or banner. Naming a newsletter brings with it a variety of possibilities. Search for something catchy that reflects your goal and can also carry over into some interesting graphics.

Reviewing newsletters from other institutions gives a sense of the great variety in names and may help to provide you with some ideas.

Frequently, the initials of the institution and the word "teaching" are included in the name: Teaching at UNL, VCU Teaching. Graphic elements can also enter into the name itself, for example an apple for the letter "o". The nameplate conveys the purpose and character of the publication. Whatever is selected should be considered carefully; the name truly sets the tone for the entire publication, and it is likely to remain fixed for a long time.

DESKTOP PUBLISHING

Many faculty developers need a way to communicate directly with faculty or TAs on a regular, though relatively formal, basis and the faculty development or TA newsletter can be a useful vehicle for accomplishing this task. Fortunately, the recent advances in computer technology now allow us to produce a professional-looking newsletter in-house by doing our own desktop publishing.

An individual with word processing skills and the proper computer equipment can produce an electronic layout easily. Desktop publishing means that we can produce print material using computer equipment and software to design pages electronically, to set up columns, to specify typefaces and type, and to insert images. Thoroughly investigating the variety of hardware and software can seem overwhelming but it pays to be patient and to choose equipment that does what you need and that you can learn to operate. The final output or camera-ready copy may be photocopied or sent to a conventional printer.

You need to budget for training workshops for yourself and/or for staff members as well as for hardware and software. If your office has a low budget, computer equipment may be available in another office on campus or at a local print or photocopying shop. Training in the use of the equipment is essential and can save you frustration and time. Most computer stores provide some level of training, as do most campus media/computer centers. Computerized tutorial programs may be purchased for some desktop publishing software.

If you are already familiar with the traditional publishing process, you will enjoy having more control over editing, design, layout, paste-up, turnaround times, and deadlines. Additionally, you will save money formerly spent on outside typesetting and design services. If the job is done right, the end result will be a professional looking product.

Desktop publishing is very enjoyable and satisfying. It is rewarding to look at the final, printed version of your newsletter, knowing that you and your colleagues created it.

Tricks of the Layout Trade

As we began our newsletters, we found ourselves filled with desire and motivation, but rather low on knowledge and techniques. Talking to experienced persons at our institutions was most helpful, and we have acquired an understanding about what constitutes a good layout for a newsletter:

- Compose the newsletter from the outside to the inside. Lay out the front page first, then the back page (think of this as the second front page). Then adjust continuations of articles (if any) and remaining items on the inside pages.

- Strive for a modular or block format. Avoid "doglegs" caused in an article by columns of unequal length.

- Limit continuation of articles from one page to another as much as you can. Each "jump" loses a significant number of readers.

- Compose headlines that attract readers. Avoid "label" heads except for standing columns (e.g., Book Review). Extend heads over two columns when possible; one-column heads are hard to set and often bump other one-column heads. Avoid setting heads in all capitals; use lower case whenever possible.

- Use teaser and "reefer" lines on the front page to direct readers to interesting material on inside pages.

- Use break-out or pull-out quotations from articles to draw reader interest and to break up solid copy; all-gray pages can bore readers.

- Use graphic elements to provide variety and interest (and as attractive fillers) but do not use so many that the publication looks choppy.

- Do not disdain white space; it provides relief from solid copy. However, do not trap white space in the interior of a page; arrange copy so that it can flow out easily.

- Orient photographs appropriately. The persons in them should be looking toward the interior of the page. If a photograph is within a column, place it on the right, starting copy on the left.

Most importantly, remember that all these tips and all these pieces of advice are guidelines, rather than rigid rules. Good judgment and quality of the content and its presentation should always prevail over sheer mechanics.

CONCLUSION

Serving as editor of a newsletter takes much more time and effort than one anticipates. Such an effort is loaded with frustrations, from scratching for material and tightening up loose copy, to racing for deadlines and combing for typos. It is a certainty that you will never quite get a perfect issue, no matter how hard you try.

Why, then, do individuals take on this task? Because it can bring the pride of accomplishment, the satisfaction of sharing good things with colleagues, and the joy of a challenge well met. Whether the benefits outweigh the tribulations is sometimes hard to determine, but the call is close enough for most of us to forge forward.

If you are presented with the opportunity to produce a newsletter, first ask yourself these questions:

- Are there clear and worthy purposes for the publication?

- Is there faculty and administrative support for the effort?

- Are there sufficient funds to do a good job?

- Can I squeeze out the time?

- Do I have the courage?

If your answers are affirmative, particularly with regard to courage, then our advice to you is this: If you are a creative, responsible, involved, sensitive, and patient risk-taker, then you will be a good editor.

ACKNOWLEDGEMENTS

The following editors kindly provided us with a wonderful variety of advice and are to be thanked: Judith Chandler, Furman University; Loren Eckroth, University of Hawaii; Jim Eison, University of South Florida; Bob Flager, University of Minnesota, Duluth; Clem Gruens, Appalachian State University; Edwina Hertzberg, Augsburg College; Lee Humphreys, University of Tennessee, Knoxville; Glen Ross Johnson, Texas A & M University; Ed Kamso, Red Deer College; Susan Kahn, Indiana University, Purdue University at Indianapolis; Christopher Knapper, Queen's University; Ann Lucas, Fairleigh Dickinson University; Delivee Wright, University of Nebraska, Lincoln; and Kenneth Zahorski, St. Norbert College.

Laura Border is Director of the Graduate Teaching Program at the University of Colorado, Boulder. She has served on the POD Core Committee and also as coordinator of the POD annual conference in 1999.

Linc. Fisch is an independent consultant and writer. He resides in Lexington, Kentucky.

Maryellen Weimer is Associate Professor of Teaching and Learning at Berks Leigh Valley College of Penn State and is also editor of *The Teaching Professor*.

Email: border@spot.colorado.edu
          Lincfisch@aol.com
          grg@psu.edu

13

Factoring Out Fear: Making Technology into Child s Play with Fundamentals

LeAne H. Rutherford

Risk and change are a growing part of the lives of postsecondary faculty—particularly in light of technological advances. Many instructors rise to the challenge; others respond with fear—fear of time commitment, fear of appearing incompetent, fear of technolingo, fear of technological failure, fear of not knowing where to start and whom to ask, and fear of making the wrong choices.

Part of a faculty developer's job, however, is persuading faculty members of the need to change—helping them to change and to adapt; aiding them in adopting new strategies and techniques; working with them to design instruction appropriate to the plethora of new platforms; and training them to manage the mechanics of the new instructional platforms such as multimedia, the World Wide Web, asynchronous individual learning programs, interactive television (ITV), and presentational software.

Unfortunately, faculty development is not linear and one-dimensional. Rather, it is dynamic. The transformations which faculty or instructional development efforts attempt to promote or enable occur rather like demonstrations of computer morphing. Viewers start by looking at a person's picture and continue watching as change after change happens until the similarity to the original is almost gone. Thus, an instructor who comes to a faculty development center to inquire about encouraging more class discussion may move into some cooperative learning activities and then into some student peer projects followed by case studies which might lead to simulations. All the while, in another dimension, the platforms for student learning are changing, and so is the instructor's role. Now overlay these morphings with new technological features, and a whole new face to teaching and learning is created. Each new face, in turn, begets a fresh set of questions and puzzlements.

How can faculty developers meet the challenges, answer the questions, and solve the conundrums caused by putting technology and teaching together? First, they have to recognize that there are two sides to faculty—the expected intellectual side and the less frequently mentioned emotional side. Secondly, faculty must recognize that technology is here to stay by taking charge of technology and its uses by deciding who is boss; easing into the technological flow little by little; understanding that technology is not monolithic, but many-faceted; and becoming familiar with technoculture by immersion. These pieces of information are all valuable, but they are also intellectual or rational in nature. Although prescriptive, they do little to touch the fearful child in most people, faculty members included.

It is through an instructor's emotional or affective side, however, that most risk will be assumed and most change accepted. For faculty, several entry points into mental attitudes which accept the changes that technology presents include play, partnering, and reversing roles with students.

WANTS TO PLAY

To illustrate the concept of play, let us consider training faculty to teach on interactive television (ITV) as an example. Initially on my campus, we held half-day workshops called Tuning in to Teaching on ITV to prepare a fairly large cohort of faculty to teach on interactive TV for the first time. The workshops covered a wide range of topics meant to create confidence and comfort for novice ITV instructors as they began to teach on this exotic new medium.

How to perform proactive planning was the central issue in the workshop. After all, anticipation is the name of the game in the ITV business. Usually, instructors assume a certain level of support for on-campus, everyday teaching. That support, however, may be lacking, different, or less immediate in a distance education/ITV framework. Therefore, faculty need to stop assuming that ITV support is the same as the support to which they are accustomed in conventional teaching settings. They need to start asking the right questions—questions which would allow them to foresee problems. Supposing that they could frame the question, they could identify a potential problem before it emerged and possibly avoid it. Some participants' questions are listed below to illustrate their concerns.

- How will students at different sites get to know each other, and how will I get to know them?

- Whom do I call in case of broadcast troubles?

- How does teaching on ITV differ from same-room teaching?

- Where should I look to make eye contact?

- What do I do about monitoring my tests if there is no assistant at distant sites?

- How will I learn to run the equipment?

Sometimes these questions were answered during the early workshops and sometimes not. Frequently, though, faculty participants left the workshops with a larger set of concerns than they had before they came. They were more enlightened about the potential pitfalls than they had been when they arrived, but that enlightenment did little to assuage their fears. What they were concerned about was handling the controls and the mechanics of transmission, such matters as selecting cameras, handling switches, zooming, and panning. They told us that the thought of teaching on ITV left them feeling out of control because there was too much to attend to simultaneously—the content, the students here, the mechanics, and the seeming lack of flexibility in the way the classroom was physically set up. They felt they were expected to be television performers without preparation, training, or practice. Generally speaking, their immediate reaction was to cling to the familiar; i.e., the lecture, with a death grip. Although we incorporated exercises to engage them in active learning while they were learning about active ITV teaching and demonstrations of alternatives to lecturing, they were not persuaded that they could do it. As trainers, we concluded that we had tried to do too much, too soon. For the workshop planners, it was back to the drawing board. These workshops were good, but they were not yet good enough.

Consequently, to determine what ITV sessions should follow these initial offerings, we sent out a questionnaire to ITV-targeted faculty. We attempted to find a common denominator as well as the areas in which faculty desired more training. The questionnaire asked about their previous experience with ITV, their plans to teach with it in the future, their greatest challenges with or concerns about it, and it listed 13 items with which they might like to have hands-on help.

These items included:

- Console controls, FAX machine
- Videotape (play and/or record)
- Presentation software
- Session design
- Course design
- Analysis of student mix
- Site-to-site interactivity
- Speaker phone
- Elmo visualizer
- Email
- Slides
- Others

Survey responses were spread across the board but seemed not too subtly to suggest that the mechanics (controlling the dials, switches, and peripherals) still perplexed the majority of respondents the most. Consequently, we offered another set of workshops: *Using ITV with Grace and Ease: Flipping the Switches*, and *Part II: Using ITV with Grace and Ease: Launching the Class*. We were heading in the right direction by separating the manual from the more conceptual or instructional issues and by putting the equipment in the hands of the instructors. However, in retrospect the workshops were flawed in two critical ways. They asked busy faculty to spend precious hours on two workshops. And to make matters worse, the workshops were "just in case" as responsibility for ITV courses had not been definitively assigned at that point. Without the passion for learning (or the panic) that immediate need inspires, intense attention to ITV was not apparent.

Factoring in time and necessity, we were beginning to zero in on the answer. Analyzing these rather sober and caveat-filled sessions, we began to look for newer, more engaging ways to connect faculty to ITV teaching. It was quite apparent that the starting point for the workshops had been at the level of abstract conceptualization on

Kolb's learning cycle (Svinicki & Dixon, 1987). Faculty participants, on the other hand, had concrete, experiential concerns which needed to be addressed first—before theory and before application to serious instruction. We needed to create workshops based on entering the learning cycle from the concrete, experiential side, putting a hands-on, microteaching experience on a nonthreatening topic foremost in the session. This could then be followed by reflection on the micro-cosmic (capsule) teaching experience and conclude with a discussion of theory.

Concrete Experience

To accomplish what we now see as a better solution, providing a con-crete experience, we offered yet another workshop advertised as an ITV Play Day. The approach met with success.

Workshop participants were asked to come prepared to teach a familiar, nonthreatening topic. They chose such things as properly waxing a crosscountry ski, learning how to juggle with scarves, build-ing a toy airplane with Duplos, giftwrapping an elegant package, doing the Highland Fling, learning how to play video poker, appliquéing a design on a sweatshirt the simple way, or other such rather lighthearted topics.

They were divided into two groups. One group was deployed to the broadcast site; the other was sent to an on-campus receiving site. Midway through the workshop, participants changed locations so they could experience and empathize with what their students would encounter either on- or off-campus. That empathy would help them to anticipate students' instructional needs and to plan accordingly. After a few, brief welcoming remarks, acknowledgment of their per-sonal levels of tele-experience, and a quick lesson on basic control handling, the workshops moved directly into the microteaching seg-ments.

Reflective Observation

On completion of a lesson, it was immediately critiqued—not for the merit of its content, but for what was learned about ITV instruction. For example, in the juggling lesson, the question arose of how and when the juggling equipment would be sent to the distant sites. After the appliquéing lesson, we discussed what colors transmit well. To demonstrate Highland dancing adequately, camera angles and zooming needed to be adjusted. Playing video poker illustrated having props ready and the potential for scripting in audience responses. All of the capsule lessons showed the necessity for large visuals, moderate pacing, and precise timing.

Abstract Conceptualization

Discussion moved naturally to how this playful, trial run on ITV would apply to the more serious endeavor of actually teaching a class and a whole course. Where were there analogies between microteaching and macroteaching a course on ITV? What learning concepts were in place when faculty were microteaching? Where were pedagogical theories transferable? Why were they transferable?

Active Experimentation

An important part of our workshop agenda was to get the point across about teaching interactively with ITV. To help faculty leave the familiar and venture into the unknown, we wanted to reach them before they became lecture entrenched. Many of the workshops training faculty to teach on ITV tell participants to teach actively; yet many workshops do not model active learning.

Ideally, a large segment in the second half of a workshop should be slotted for a second microteaching for each participant, this time on teaching course content. Although participants needed to experience the fun and exhilaration of active learning first, their ultimate aim would be to experiment actively with ideas which they actually teach. However, because of time constraints we are planning to produce a videotape modeling active teaching on ITV and illustrating the many ways teaching methods can be varied with success. The video will show actual clips of simulations, intersite group work, cooperative learning techniques, case studies, presentations, and even the use of break time for building relationships across the miles.

In summary, the ITV Play Day format was a successful way to simultaneously introduce one type of technological platform for teaching as well as active learning. The first half of the Play Day—microteaching—epitomized active learning. By working from the playful to the purposeful in a supportive atmosphere, everyone was involved in playing the game that ITV teaching presented. The tension in the task was erased, and participants chatted site-to-site, side-by-side; they laughed and coached each other when they forgot to change cameras. They even started to see the advantages of teaching in a broadcast studio over a technically plain classroom. As they empathized with students' needs to engage in the learning process in significantly captivating ways, they confessed to delight most in those minilessons which let them participate. In short, they had fun with the fundamentals, and they had an immediate opportunity to try out ITV teaching. By starting out simply, they thought about the implications of what they did and began to apply them to a larger learning scenario. They saw interactive teaching on ITV modeled as it applied to college teaching, and they were in company of other learners (see Appendix 13.1 for an ITV Play Day agenda).

PLAYS WELL WITH OTHERS

Companionship of others on the isolated, uneven, and erratic road to using technology effectively is a powerful antidote to fear and stimulant to success. While some faculty members have worked independently to learn about incorporating technology into their teaching, there has been no "planned community of technology travelers" ("To dance with change", 1994, p. A11). Whatever has happened has occurred, for the most part, in isolation. A few fortunate instructors have accidentally found another tech pioneer in a neighboring office to assist them when they become mired. That serendipity, however, depends more on luck than on planning.

Furthermore, because the technology topics were chosen by the pioneering faculty according to personal need or personal inclination, the distribution of skills is quite random. Everyone has a piece of the puzzle, but few have a sense of the full picture, which, of course, is changing every moment. Some are versed in elementary email; others transfer files across platforms with aplomb. Skill levels range from those who eschew overhead projectors as too technical to those who put their syllabus or course on the World Wide Web. Progress along the tech road is controlled by speed bumps—other work, prior commitments, finding development time while everything else is going on. It is quite easy to break an appointment with oneself to learn how use PowerPoint or the interaction in ITV. Technological development goes in fits and starts when individuals depend on themselves for motivation.

Creating community to learn technology is appealing to faculty who are frequently isolated in their own fields, departments, and offices, unaware of the available technology from which to choose and unable to sustain a steady enough pace to maintain forward momentum. It is appealing not because misery loves company, but because company defangs misery.

On my campus, as at many institutions, a technological initiative is underway. As part of that initiative, the Instructional Development Service under a Bush Foundation grant gathered a group of 35 faculty who have invested in the idea of investigating technology's many options for enhancing instruction. Meeting quite regularly, they have laid out a map of the territory they want to survey together. They have offered to share what they know with others in the group. They have empathized with each other, reassured each other, supported each other, and most importantly, laughed with each other. By having meetings set up for them, they are propelled forward with some comfort and greater predictability.

Over a period of 20 weeks, for instance, they engaged in the following:

- Investigated the need for shifting paradigms

- Inventoried their skills and goals for learning TECHniques

- Connected with what is available online in library resources and learned how to access them

- Viewed, played, and discussed a computerized Jeopardy game created by one of the group members

- Explored the Web together in a lab using URLs

- Connected with computer design teams from another campus

- Examined a fully-activated, expandable syllabus on the web and discussed its merits

- Experimented with teaching on ITV

- Learned to put their own syllabi on the web using modified HTML

- Exchanged ideas and feelings about teaching with technological assistance

As important as their tasks, skills, and topics are to these faculty members, of equal importance is the confidence they are building together—the fearless attitude toward meeting and mastering technology. If we can persuade or enable instructors to create a community of technological aspirants, the path is direct. The process for creating almost any faculty group will do. By flyer, email, letter, or other means available, announce the opportunity to participate. Ask for responses and schedules. Set up meeting dates, places, times. Reserve rooms and order refreshments. It is crucial, though, at the first meeting to get a sense of what each individual knows and wants to gain from participating. It is from them that knowledge comes, is dispersed, and is shared. It is critical that everyone brings something to this technological "stew" because that is where the fun lies.

Communication with the group and among the group members is expedited by creating an email alias/listserv for announcing meetings, sending meeting reminders (ticklers), and allowing group members to forward tidbits and passalongs, all the while using a form of technology. For many, email is an entry point and a selling point for other technology applications.

In the facilitative role of faculty developers, we are also assemblers and disseminators of articles and artifacts. Ever watchful, we can be alert for cartoons, games, and language that lighten and brighten the dark moments of technological frustration. For example, since technology has created a linguistic branch to English, have your tech group members each bring a three-by-five card with a technological term to share. Among the more colorful terms that tickled the fancy of our group were "webbot," "alpha geek," "spamming," and "cob web." Share leads to web sites that will help them speak the lingua franca of technology. Baptize them in the river of technological acronyms by starting them with the handy humor of email shorthand: HHOK (haha, only kidding), IMHO (in my humble opinion), F2F (face to face), WRT (with respect to).... Emoticons, can also provide warmth when a human touch is missing in technologically transmitted communication, for example: :=-(for crying, :-& for tongue-tied, or :-@ for laughing. In general, oversee, anticipate, and facilitate, keeping the tone light and the tasks doable.

For those who may drift out of the loop, we can provide networking opportunities which they can pursue independently; e.g., a list of participants, their departments, email addresses, voicemail numbers. Offer catch-up sessions so that absence does not lead to self-exclusion from the group.

If feasible, create an ongoing series with a single focus that is immediately useful. As an example, *How to Teach Your Computer to Fetch: A Five-Week Training Program for Your Computer* drew a large response from faculty and staff with diverse skills who created their own esprit de corps in lively sessions on the new version of WordPerfect for Windows held in a computer lab. Despite their varied experience with the many features of the program, participants helped their neighbors and were in turn helped by them. Reactions to the workshop evaluations ranged from "nonthreatening" to "I learned all sorts of new information and skills. Thanks for the chance to play!"

TAKES TURNS

After being in a conventional instructional role, many faculty find it difficult to return to the rank of novice. It is also true that many college students are more advanced in the use of technology than are faculty. Moreover, it is a fact that, almost uniformly, students are generous with their expertise and help for faculty who ask for it. When this happens, the roles of teacher and learner become reversed. Thus, a way is created not only to learn a specific technical task, but also to start a conversation with students on a nonhierarchical or egalitarian basis.

To use my own experience as an example, I knew I had much to do to be deserving of the term "computer literate." Consequently, I registered to take the course " The Computer in Education," the first in a series for certification in technology. It covered CD-ROMs, digital cameras, scanners, word processing, spreadsheets, graphics, databases, desktop publishing, presentation software, and multimedia in addition to identifying their instructional applications. Meeting only three hours per week in a lab with the instructor, the class members worked on their own to complete the assignments. Taking the class was further complicated by the fact that the Macintosh platform selected for the class was totally foreign to me, a PC DOS user. If it were not for the gracious student lab attendants and the other students taking the course with me, I would not have known any success in that class. Clustering around one computer screen, several of the other students and I put our bits of knowledge together to master Excel or to learn to drag those stubborn, slippery shapes around the graphics program. In collaborating with them, I was once again reminded of how capable students are and how much fun it is to drift in the wake of their energy. Shoulder-to-shoulder with them, I could not help but deepen my understanding of how they learned and processed information. This opportunity allowed me to use my metacognitive skills to help them learn, and they used their computer skills to help me understand how I best learn technology and where to go for the assistance I needed (how-to books, on-screen tutorials, personal assistance, instruction manuals). By gladly relinquishing any pretext to expertise, I was allowed into the circle of learners.

CONCLUSION

"Oh, to be a kid again," doesn't have to be a lament. It can be a prescription and a celebration. It is the daring attitude of play, of romping with pals, and of taking turns on the swing that factors out the fear of technology and turns it into child's play. Human warmth does indeed take the chill off technology. Play is the work of children, but it can foster the work of adults as well.

REFERENCES

Pew Foundation. (1994, April). To dance with change. *Policy Perspectives, 5* (3), A1-A12.

Svinicki, M. D., & Dixon, N. (1987). The Kolb model modified for classroom activities. *College Teaching, 35,* 141-146.

Verduin, J. R., Jr., & Clark, T. A. (1991). *Distance education: The foundations of effective practice.* San Francisco, CA: Jossey-Bass.

RESOURCES

Albright, M., & Graf, D. (Eds.), (1992). *Teaching in the information age: The role of educational technology.* New Directions for Teaching and Learning, No. 51. San Francisco, CA: Jossey-Bass.

Austin, A., & Baldwin, R. G. (1991). *Faculty collaboration: Enhancing the quality of scholarship and teaching.* (ASHE-ERIC Higher Education Report No. 7)

Bates, A. W. (1996). *Technology, open learning & distance education.* Madison, WI: Magna.

Bonwell, C., & Eison, J. (1991). *Active learning: Creating excitement in the classroom.* (ASHE-ERIC Higher Education Report No. 1)

Brown, D. G. (1999). *Always in touch: A practical guide to ubiquitous computing.* Winston-Salem, NC: Wake Forest University Press. Distributed by Anker Publishing.

Brown, D. G. (Ed.). (2000). *Interactive Learning: Vignettes from America's most wired campuses.* Bolton, MA: Anker.

Brown, D. G. (Ed.). (2000). *Teaching with technology: Seventy-five professors from eight universities tell their stories.* Bolton, MA: Anker.

Cyrs, T. E., Smith, F. A., & Conway, E. D. (1994). *Essential skills for television teaching.* Las Cruces, NM: New Mexico State University.

Duning, B. S., Van Kekerix, M. J., & Zaborowski, L. M. (1993). *Reaching learners through telecommunications.* San Francisco, CA: Jossey Bass.

Falk, D., & Carlson, H. (1995). *Multimedia in higher education.* Medford, NJ: Information Today.

Johnson, D. W., Johnson, R. T., & Smith, K. (1991). *Cooperative learning: Increasing college faculty instructional productivity.* (ASHE-ERIC Higher Education Report No 4)

Meyers, C., & Jones, T. B. (1993). *Promoting active learning strategies for the college classroom.* San Francisco, CA: Jossey-Bass.

Oblinger, D. G. & Rush, S. C. (Eds.). (1997). *The learning revolution: The challenge of information technology in the academy.* Bolton, MA: Anker.

Rossman, M. H., & Rossman, M. E. (Eds.). (1995). *Facilitating distance education.* New Directions for Adult and Continuing Education, No. 67. San Francisco, CA: Jossey-Bass.

Rutherford, L. H., & Grana, S. (1994). Fully activating interactive TV: Creating a blended family. *T.H.E. Journal, 22* (3), 86-90.

Rutherford, L. H., & Grana, S. (1995). Retrofitting academe: Adapting faculty attitudes and practices to technology. *T.H.E. Journal, 23* (2), 82-86.

Silberman, M. (1996). *101 strategies to teach any subject.* Boston, MA: Allyn and Bacon.

LeAne H. Rutherford teaches writing at the University of Minnesota, Duluth, but her concentration for a number of years has been faculty development. She is the editor of *Instructional Development*, a one-on-one consultant to faculty, and works to integrate technology into teaching.

Email: lrutherf@d.umn.edu

APPENDIX 13.1
AGENDA FOR AN ITV PLAY DAY

Context
Ask participants to introduce themselves by name and by experience with and interest in ITV. Ask them what they teach and how they teach now (in anticipation of talking later about how teaching on ITV is both different and similar to same-room teaching).

Concerns
Have participants write down a question they have about teaching on ITV. Quickly hear the questions but without attempting to answer them at this time.

Controls
Give each person a map of the controls. Show how the map can be simplified to its most basic elements. Have each person practice on the controls. Mention the peripherals, but do not attempt to deal with them.

Capsule Teach
Each participant has five minutes (more or less) to present a short lesson on a topic of choice.

Critique
Directly after the capsule teaching, everyone discusses the microteaching experience for themselves as students (at whatever site), as potential ITV teachers, and as ITV performers.

What worked, what didn't work, what will be done differently next time. (The content is not in question, only the process as it relates to the medium.)

Connection
Connect the microteaching to teaching a course. View a videotape of classes being taught interactively on ITV, or if time allows, have participants plan to teach a segment of a real course on ITV with attention being paid to active learning and site-to-site association.

Close
Return to the participants' initial questions about ITV. Let the group help to answer them. Point to resources which might help expand the answers.

14

A Helpful Handout: Establishing and Maintaining a Positive Classroom Climate

Linda R. Hilsen

The purpose of this chapter is to share a handout designed to help those working with faculty one-on-one, in small groups, or in a workshop setting. By sharing this, I am only emulating what I have seen in action since I became involved with the POD organization: If I have something you can make use of, share. The actual handout is an appendix to this chapter so that it can be easily reproduced.

The ideas in "Suggestions for Establishing a Positive Classroom Climate" (Appendix 14.1) have been gathered over the years by watching other faculty teach, by discussing teaching with colleagues, and by reading whatever I could get my hands on. If I have ever talked to you, attended one of your presentations, or read anything you have written, you may recognize an idea. This handout is a synthesis of helpful hints for those who either need to work on developing better rapport with students or who just want to try something new. Not every technique listed will work for every instructor—have your faculty attempt only those suggestions and fit their personalities, which feel comfortable for them.

EFFECTIVE WAYS TO USE THE HANDOUT

I have used this handout in numerous ways. For example, I have sent it to faculty who have discussed classroom climate with me but who have been reluctant to appear in the office and as a basis for a small group discussion with a given department or an interested mix of faculty. When I do this, I always give the participants the assignment of coming to the group ready to share one strength they have as teachers. I model how I want the faculty to do this, using no more than two minutes. If you let them, they could easily fill the entire time you have allotted to discussing themselves without ever getting to the handout.

Once the participants have shared their strengths as teachers, I break them up into small groups, assigning each group a segment of the handout, depending on the total number of participants. Their job is to read the segment, discuss the techniques listed, and come to consensus on one idea—either listed on their reading assignment or suggested by a participant—to share with the large group. Great discussion ensues. Using this format takes approximately one to one and a half hours.

I have also used this handout as the core of a two- to three-hour workshop that I have done around the country and on my own campus. Even when this workshop is full, I still begin by having each participant discuss a teaching strength. I feel this is crucial for networking. Ideas such as exploration of Kolb's Experiential Learning Cycle (Svinicki & Dixon, 1987), Maslow's Hierarchy of Needs (Atkinson, 1981), the various learning modes, a "Visualization Exercise: Classroom Climate" (Hilsen, 1988), "Suggestions for Establishing a Positive Classroom Climate" (Hilsen, 1988), sample icebreakers, and ways to collect information about students (in particular, TABS, Form B by Erikson, 1974) lead to a discussion of academic bonding (Fisch, 1988), the coaching concept (Fisch, 1983), qualities of good teachers (Gabriel, 1987), and how to put all of this together to make a meaningful impression on students' lives. Teaching tips on lecture, discussion, and group use are also shared as length permits. Participants are encouraged to bring examples of their syllabi, icebreakers, and student information-gathering instruments or techniques. And, of course, hearty hors d'oeuvres and helpful handouts are provided. Participants are required to preregister so that small group sizes can be determined in advance.

Connecting learning and living is the purpose of education. Establishing and sustaining a positive classroom climate will result in more effective teaching and learning, greater rapport, increased student retention, more satisfying experiences for both students and teachers, and, possibly, even better teaching evaluations.

Therefore, I suggest you give this handout a try. Please contact me if you have additional suggestions to add to the list, or if you are curious about trying the "Visualization Exercise: Classroom Climate"; it truly sets the stage for using the handout around which this chapter revolves.

Some of the techniques listed in Appendix 14.1, "Suggestions for Establishing a Positive Classroom Climate" may help your faculty and students to enjoy the networking and sharing that leads to productive education, which is what the POD organization is all about.

ACKNOWLEDGMENTS

In the early years, Rusty Wadsworth, Lynn Mortensen, Linc. Fisch, Marilla Svinicki, Karron Lewis, LuAnn Wilkerson, Dean Osterman, Joyce Povlacs-Lunde, Bob Young, Del Wright, Jody Nyquist, Don Wulff, Glenn Ross Johnson, Libby Gardner, Bette Erickson, John Anderson, Bob Pierleoni, Sheryl Riechmann Hruska, Elizabeth Moran, and Bobbie Helling, to mention a few, took me under their pragmatic wings. Without the time they gave me, without the materials they shared with me, I would have had no idea how to be an instructional development consultant.

REFERENCES

Atkinson, L. et al. (1981). *Introduction to psychology*. New York, NY: Harcourt Brace Jovanovich.

Erikson, E. H (1974). *Dimensions of a new identity*. New York, NY: Norton.

Fisch, L. (1983). Coaching mathematics and other academic sports. In M. David, M. Fisher, S. C. Inglis, S. Scholl (Eds.). *To improve the academy: Vol. 2. Resources for student, faculty and institutional development:* (pp. 3-6). Orinda, CA: John Kennedy University.

Fisch, L. (1988). *On academic bonding*. Unpublished manuscript.

Gabriel, D. (1987). Characteristics of successful developmental educators. *Review of Research in Developmental Education, 5* (1), 1-5.

Hilsen, L. (1988). Some possible suggestions for establishing a positive classroom climate. In L. Hilsen (Ed.), *Establishing and maintaining a positive classroom climate* (pp. 9-14). Duluth, MN: Instructional Development Service, University of Minnesota, Duluth.

Hilsen, L. (1988). Visualization exercise: Classroom climate. In L. Hilsen (Ed.), *Establishing and maintaining a positive classroom climate* (p. 8). Duluth, MN: Instructional Development Service, University of Minnesota, Duluth.

Lewis, K. (1987). *Taming the pedagogical monster: A handbook for large-class instructors*. Austin, TX: Center for Teaching Effectiveness, University of Texas at Austin.

McKeachie, W. (1998). Teaching tips: *A guidebook for the beginning college teacher* (10th ed.). Lexington, MA: D.C. Heath.

Povlacs, J. (1985, March). More than facts. *University of Minnesota, Duluth Instructional Development*, 1-2, 4.

Svinicki, M., & Dixon, N. (1987). The Kolb model modified for classroom activities. *College Teaching, 35,* 141-146.

Linda R. Hilsen is the Director of the Instructional Development Service at the University of Minnesota, Duluth, where she also teaches writing. She has served two terms on the POD Core Committee.

Email: lhilsen@d.umn.edu.

Appendix 14.1. Suggestions for Establishing a Positive Classroom Climate

Tips for the First Day and Beyond

1) Get to class early, and chat with students as you set up.

2) Put the class name and number on the board in bold letters so those who are not in your class can leave before you begin.

3) Research shows that students typically decide what kind of teacher you are and what kind of experience they will have being in your class in the first 15 minutes (Povlacs, 1985). Research also shows that instructors who make the most lasting impressions on students are those who possess and generate enthusiasm (McKeachie, 1998). Therefore,

   a)   Be prepared. Carefully structure how you will begin your class. Provide information about yourself and your course that the students need.

   b)   Let the excitement you feel for your field flow to your students. Show some enthusiasm and a little humor.

4) If you take attendance, ask a few questions of students as you go, or ask them to share why they are taking the course. This will help them become individuals in your eyes. Moreover, self-disclose when you discover appropriate opportunities. You, too, can become a person in their eyes without losing any status; as a matter a fact, your personal disclosure will increase your credibility and contribute to a better learning environment by the modeling of openness which is occurring. Let them ask you questions about yourself. This can be an eye-opening experience for you.

5) Stress your availability to students:

   a)   If you want students to come to your office, sincerely state this.

   b)   Give your office hours, email, and telephone numbers at which you are comfortable being reached by students. If there are time limits on when you will accept calls, state them clearly. If you will not accept calls off-campus, state this.

   c)   If there are other occasions when you plan to make yourself available to students, tell them:

   • Some professors have difficulty attracting students to their offices. One such instructor makes contact with students in the student center on a casual basis. The first day of class he states, "I go for coffee at 9:30 every day in the cafeteria. If you want to talk, come sit with me." Not only is this instructor never without students at his table, but he now has more students than he can handle finding their way through a formidable department into his office.

   • Try a voluntary "think and drink" session to discuss course content in the cafeteria or a restaurant near campus. Students sincerely appreciate personal contact, look forward to it, and become more motivated by it (Lewis, 1987).

 • Explain professional commitments you have which make you unavailable at certain periods of time.

6. Directly state your goals for the course and your expectations of the students. Describe what skills a student needs to possess to do well in your course. Give a student-centered overview of the entire course: "When you have completed this course, you will be able to . . ." Write your syllabus so the students can understand what your course is about, not to impress your colleagues with jargon.

7. Establish procedures from day one:

a) Present the major topics to be covered on the board, overhead, handout, or computer projection.

b) Always give an overview of the class which includes what (the material to be covered), why (its relevance to the course), where (this material's importance and placement in the big picture), and how (the methods, exercises, and assignments that will be employed).

c) Consistently introduce, cover, and wrap-up each new segment of material.

d) Always have a summary of the day's events:

 • You can do this, but why not ask a student or two to mention the main points which were covered today? This is not shirking your job; it is helping students internalize information by verbalizing it. The more opportunities you provide for your students to verbalize, the more quickly they will comprehend your process and content.

 • Your summary can be cleverly placed into the final segment of your presentation to avoid the tune-out that many students do when they hear a concluding signal. If you or a student summarizes what has happened before the last major point on your list is covered, the students benefit, frequently without even realizing it.

e) Establish strict rules on packing behavior on the first day. Tell them how long they are expected to participate before getting ready to leave. The following is a short list of techniques I have observed instructors use to signal closure to students:

 • "When the cartoon appears on the overhead, you may go."

 • "After you have posed three good questions about the material covered, you will be dismissed." This works much better than, "Are there any questions?" Instead of students hating those who ask, students appreciate others who will pose good questions.

 • "We will end each class with a short piece representative of the music we are studying."

 • "You belong to me until 10:50!"

f) End each and every class with a hook for the next class period. Give them a good reason to come back.

8) Learn students' names as quickly as possible. One or more of the following could assist you in this task.

a)   Create an icebreaker appropriate for your class so each student will have the opportunity to speak to other students as you circulate. I prefer icebreakers which cause students to talk about their own experiences with course content. In my developmental writing class, for example, much anxiety can be alleviated by having students share their trepidations about the course, and you can learn a great deal about them as you eavesdrop.

b)   Take Polaroid snaps of six students at a time. Have the students write their own names under their picture. This is a great icebreaking technique for the class, too, because six people who may have never seen each other before are getting ready to pose for a family portrait together. Clipping this picture to information sheets you have collected on each student really speeds up your connection of names and faces.

c)   If you have students hand in a schedule, have a place for them to add "What I want you to know about me."

d)   Use information sheets upon which you can collect data on prerequisite courses, hobbies, interests—the possibilities are many.

e)   Have students write their names and concerns about the course on 3"x 5" note cards. Deal with these concerns during the next class period.

9) Ask students what they want, need, and expect to learn in this class. This can be accomplished via discussion, paper and pencil, take-home assignment, or possibly by email. Be certain to take time to address their anxieties.

10) Stay around to answer their questions after class. Talk to students personally. Ask them if your presentation was clear, helpful, and met their needs. Asking your students how you did tells them you respect their opinions.

Tips for Sustaining a Positive Learning Environment

1) Be concerned about the physical setting.

    a)   Check the lighting in the room. Make certain all can see to read the texts, overhead, or large screen projection. On the other hand, there is no good reason why every light has to be on at eight o'clock in the morning.

    b)   Encourage students to inform you about any discomforts. For example, if an open window is causing a chilling draft, tell them to feel free to make needed adjustments.

2) Make the examples you use relevant to your students' lives: "How would you feel if somebody dropped a whole load of oil in Lake Superior?" "How will this current drought affect your food budget?"

3) Do not be so rigidly tied to your syllabus that you do not take the time to capitalize on real life situations. If Jesse Jackson visits your campus, find a way to connect this event with what is going on in your class and your students' lives.

4) Address students by name. Use a seating chart, name tags, the Polaroid technique, or whatever may work for you to learn their names.

5) Remember, not all reasons for incomplete assignments are excuses. Yes, we must establish rules, but there are occasions where the rules need to be broken. Be compassionate, not cynical. Grandmothers really do die.

6) Constantly read your audience's responses:

a) If it is clear from the expressions on their faces they have no idea what you are talking about, be willing to take the time to present the concept in different words, with different illustrations. Expecting their confusion to disappear with time is not good enough.

b) If students are bored or you have just covered an in-depth topic intensively, there is nothing wrong with stopping, allowing them to talk or stretch for a minute or two and then continuing.

c) In long classes, provide a short break to address human comforts. Students have a difficult time following you if they have pressing needs.

7) Provide nonverbal encouragement:

a) Maintain eye contact.

b) Move about the room. Come out from behind that podium. Display your willingness to be a person; sit on a sturdy desk or table. Move into their space.

c) Be animated and expressive, both facially and bodily. Let them see and feel your enthusiasm.

8) Model the thinking processes in your field for your students. Do not just tell them; show them, and then let them practice. If you are not talking, it does not mean you are not teaching.

9) Use positive reinforcement:

a) Give students recognition for contributing to in-class discussions or answering questions. Use positive reinforcement when possible, but if the answer is incorrect, try to lead the student through continued questioning to reach an acceptable position.

b) Use student test answers to review material after a test. Keep track of good answers as you correct the tests, and let the students "star" a bit. This is a lot less boring than you reading all the right answers.

c) After getting permission from the student, share good student work with the rest of the class.

d) Validate student opinions by referring to points students made previously, not always using "as I said last Thursday." Say, "To follow up on John's point Tuesday . . . ."

10) Keep constant tabs on how your students are progressing:

a) Use conferencing outside of class to discuss problems and areas where students are doing well.

b) Be willing to provide review, catch-up, or further explanation sessions.

c) If students are not going to make it, honestly counsel them out before you are forced to fail them.

11) When asking questions, pause. Students need time to process the questions and their answers. Count to 15 before moving on. If you do not, the message you are giving is, "I really don't want to take away from my time to listen to a student." This is not the message you should be sending out if you want your students to learn. Verbalizing information helps students internalize it. We should provide as many occasions as feasible for them to verbalize. Invite responses by pausing for a good length of time. If you wait long enough, you will get an answer if you have not worded the question in an alien language or manner.

12) Do not talk down to students:

a)   Avoid judging behaviors, which cause students to feel inadequate.

b)   Avoid stereotyping. Do not think that females have a certain set of interests and males have another. Do not think that all older students like to talk in class. Do not target examples and questions towards certain groups in your class.

13) Be a facilitator during discussions, not the emcee. You do not have to do all the talking in your classroom. Let the students help each other learn as you guide them. A marvelous peak experience occurs when the students forget you are there and pass right by you in the discussion. It is then you know you are doing your job.

14) Use peer pressure to your advantage on assignments and classroom decorum. Students can motivate and reprimand each other.

15) Give your students possibilities for providing feedback during the course. You might want to try one or two of the following:

a)   At the end of the first week, ask students to take out a piece of paper and anonymously comment on "things I like about this class," "things I dislike," "how I would like to see things change."

b)   Have a suggestion box outside of your classroom or office.

c)   Establish a lecturer's feedback group. Any student can attend to bring up anything about the course. Usually these groups meet in the instructor's office or the cafeteria.

d)   Use a formative evaluation instrument to get a reading early in the course. My favorite happens to be "Teaching Analysis by Students" (TABS).

e)   Have a consultant from your instructional development service discuss the course with the students during part of a class hour.

f)   Have a random sampling of students interviewed by a consultant to answer questions you have composed.

16) The classroom climate is enhanced by out-of-class contact. Recognize students in the halls and malls.

17) Read the deans' lists, the school paper, the sports section of the local paper, etc., to learn about the accomplishments of your students. Mention them in class.

18) The climate in your office is just as important as the one you establish in class.

a)   Let students know where your office is and how to find it.

b)   Make conscious choices about how you arrange your office. When going over papers, have the student sit beside you so you can both see the product being discussed.

c)   If you are located in an inner complex, inform your students that the secretary doesn't bite.

d)   If you are working when a student appears, don't ignore the student. Take a moment to set a meeting time which is mutually agreeable.

e)   Personalize your office. Family photos, rugs, and plants help.

f)   If you make appointments with students, keep them. If you are detained, call someone to post a note for the student.

Part IV

_____
_____

Reaching
Specific Audiences

15

Increase Your Effectiveness in the Organization: Work with Department Chairs

Ann F. Lucas

There is no doubt that higher education is besieged from many quarters and must change. A roundtable convened by the Pew Foundation in collaboration with the American Association for Higher Education deliberated on how colleges and universities can better educate students and meet the needs of a rapidly changing society. In a summary of its work, the Pew Foundation's Policy Perspective on Higher Education (1996) concluded,

> It is no longer a question of whether institutions must change but of who will control that recasting—the nation's colleges and universities, or an increasingly competitive market for postsecondary education that holds little sympathy for institutional tradition (p. 1).

Contained in this perspective is a statement that reflects a beginning consensus that the appropriate agents of change are the academic departments: "A department should be held accountable for the quality of teaching its members deliver, for the coherence of its major, for its contributions to the general education curriculum, and for the supervision and rewarding of its individual members." (p. 2). The statement views the department as "the principal agent for the purposeful recasting of American higher education" (p. 2).

However, if academic departments are to become the agents of change department, chairs must exercise the leadership, knowledge, and skills to motivate faculty to create quality departments. Chairs need to engage in strong leadership behaviors such as convening faculty conversations about teaching, learning, and the curriculum. Based on self-report data from more than 4,500 chair questionnaires, I would argue that most academic chairs do not know how to become change agents, and many lack the knowledge and skills—and even seem to question whether they have the power—to motivate faculty. Less than 30% of these 4,500 chairs report any degree of success in motivating poor teachers, motivating difficult colleagues, or improving the overall quality of teaching in the department. Less than 40% report success in motivating mid-career faculty. The pervasive myths that paralyze chairs are that they are simply peers among equals and have no power. They have "neither carrots nor sticks"; and, therefore, there is nothing they can do to resolve problems in the department (Lucas, 1994).

I would like to see more emphasis on institutions taking the role of the chair seriously by devoting necessary resources to chair training and team building between chairs and departments and between chairs and the dean. I would like to see chairs be given ongoing training in the following areas:

- Building teams

- Creating a supportive communication climate

- Empowering faculty

- Learning how to make quality teaching an ongoing faculty development activity

- Applying the use of goal setting and participative decision-making in ways that ensure faculty commitment to departmental goals

- Learning how to create a climate that enables faculty to engage in scholarship

- Understanding how to manage conflict in departments

Knowing how to keep conflict from going underground, so that the "hollowed collegiality" about which Massy and Wilger (1994) have written does not endanger faculty productivity and the development of community, would also eliminate some of the barriers to building effective teams. Faculty developers can take an important role in making these things happen.

Maximizing Impact on the Institution

Staff in faculty development centers can significantly increase their effectiveness in higher education by gaining access to academic departments and teaching chairs to promote faculty development. For most faculty, the department is the place from which they derive their identification; in good departments, it is also a place of collegiality and support. When chairs are effective leaders, they provide an atmosphere in which it is safe and helpful to discuss what goes on in the classroom. Becoming ever more effective in teaching acts as a stimulant and becomes highly reinforcing simply because faculty members know that they are competent at what they are doing and that student response is increasingly positive. Therefore, working with departments creates a synergy for faculty development staff, and the number of faculty members whose teaching they can impact increases significantly. Because working with chairs affects the institution as a whole, it is regarded as an organizational development strategy.

Organizational development (OD) has been defined as "an emerging discipline aimed at improving the effectiveness of the organization and its members by means of a systematic change program" (Harvey & Brown, 1996, p. 3). In effective organizations, there are two important concerns: productivity is improved through appropriate interventions, and individuals have an opportunity for personal and professional development. OD focuses on planned change so that people will be more effective at what they are already doing. Thus, in higher education, chairs need to learn how to create a climate in the department that makes faculty reflective practitioners, motivating them to read and discuss the literature on effective teaching and decide how they can integrate their reading with feedback and an analysis of their own experience. Ongoing learning about quality teaching becomes a professional development goal. Parker J. Palmer (1993) suggests that each teacher "have a community of honest and open colleagues with whom to explore [his or her] struggles as a teacher" (p. 11). Palmer also makes the point that little talk about teaching will take place if administrators and department chairs do not invite these conversations regularly.

Maximizing successful faculty development interventions results from working closely with academic chairs. Yet because chairs are very busy people who usually feel overwhelmed with paperwork, faculty development staff must have something concrete to offer them, be responsive to their perceived needs, and find a way to make their lives easier rather than harder. Chairs derive satisfaction from learning strategies they can use to achieve departmental goals through faculty development, and this knowledge empowers them to make things happen. The staff of teaching centers must be sensitive to what chairs say they need, not tell them what they need.

But approximately one-quarter of Green's (1988) estimated number of 80,000 chairs rotate into this position each year. Since new chairs do not know what they need and experienced chairs sometimes feel that they do not have anything more to learn, many institutions which have launched chair training focus on new chairs. Yet the training they receive is often on the managerial aspects of their position, rather than on the faculty development and leadership functions they need to perform. How, then, can faculty developers offer a professional training program for chairs that can make a serious impact on the organization?

ALTERNATIVE APPROACHES

The role faculty developers can take to initiate leadership and faculty development programs for chairs will depend upon their current relationship with department chairs, deans, and the vice president for academic affairs (VPAA); the level of confidence they have developed within their own institutions; and their knowledge about leadership development and skills as small group facilitators. Possible approaches, from the simple to fairly sophisticated, include the following:

- Inviting a guest facilitator to conduct a workshop for chairs

- Acting as convener, but not a participant, to a study group of chairs who meet on a monthly basis to discuss chair leadership

- Initiating the structure for a study group and then offering to attend as a resource person, or as a presenter, those meetings at which you have particular expertise; for example, when conducting feedback interviews for classroom teaching or managing conflict are discussed

- Assuming the role of group facilitator on an ongoing basis for a chair study group

Each of these approaches requires working closely with, and being empowered by, higher level academic administrators.

Chair Leadership Development Workshop

Usually chairs are not certain what topics should be included in a leadership workshop. It is helpful to choose a facilitator who will also conduct a needs assessment of chair participants before conducting the workshop. When a facilitator reports, for example, that 60% of the chairs who will participate in the workshop indicated that motivating poor teachers is a topic they would like included, this validates the topic for participants. It also provides a follow-up topic for the faculty development center.

At the end of the workshop, which can be offered on one or two days, chairs should be asked to indicate in writing what other areas they would like to focus on in future professional development work. The workshop should stimulate thinking so that chairs can not only learn some practical skills they can use immediately in the department, but also become more aware of other leadership needs. Analysis of these results provides information to the institution about topics to be covered later.

Initiating and Convening a Chair Study Group

The director of the faculty development center can suggest to the dean or vice president for academic affairs that a study group be formed at which chairs discuss leadership and faculty development skills as an ongoing professional development program. The faculty development center would assume responsibility for arranging the time and space most convenient for chairs and might, with the chairs' permission, conduct an assessment of what the chairs learned from the group. The faculty developer(s) would not be otherwise involved in their regular meetings.

Whether one approaches a dean or the VPAA depends upon the size of the institution. A group of about 12 to 15 chairs allows a range of perspectives with a fair degree of participation. If the number of chairs is much larger than that, it is probably wise to form study groups within each college.

If the institution is large, it is also useful to begin with one group of chairs as a pilot study. In choosing a pilot group, select, if possible, what is perceived to be the most successful college so that other chairs within the institution can understand that the best college is leading the way. When I began my ongoing leadership development program (Lucas, 1986) with a college of science and engineering, perceived to be one of the most successful colleges in a particular university, several chairs from that group, after completion of the program, offered to go with me to speak to chairs from other colleges in the university to tell them how beneficial the experience had been for them. That kind of validation is most helpful.

As a convener, you might also arrange to do an assessment of the program at the end of the year. Simply develop a questionnaire that taps chair responses to the study group. You would want to use the results in discussion with others and include them in your annual report of accomplishments.

Being a Resource for a Chair Study Group

This basic approach is similar to convening a chair study group with the exception that you agree to make a presentation or be there as a resource when topics in which you have specialized knowledge and skills are discussed. For example, at one meeting you might offer a miniworkshop on some aspect of teaching that you would be willing to present to faculty in individual departments. Your goal is to let chairs know that there are many things about teaching that you can share in department workshops and that you have a fair amount of expertise and knowledge of the literature about teaching. You also want to be certain that you are respectful and supportive so that chairs will feel comfortable in consulting with you if they have additional questions about teaching. This kind of contact can establish your credibility and allow you to do further work in departments.

Facilitating a Chair Study Group

Unless you have already had a stint as an academic chair, your expertise will be that of good discussion leader. Come to each meeting armed with questions that flow out of the reading that has been done for this month. The reading list will have been determined in advance by one or two chair leaders, in consultation with the dean, and yourself as resource person. Be very prudent about offering advice, even though you may feel you have answers for the problems chairs raise. You can step out of the role of facilitator when discussions of effective teaching, or other areas of your specialized knowledge, are raised. However, do so with caution. Be certain that what you offer is brief and that you stay within your own area of expertise. Make use of good questions instead of providing answers. Of course, if chairs ask questions of you, or ask that you make a formal presentation about some aspect of teaching or other topic, do so.

CHAIR LEADERSHIP PROGRAM

Once you have given serious consideration to the role you would like to take in originating a chair leadership program, you need a clear sense of the steps you will take to ensure the probability that your suggestions will be implemented. The director of the faculty development center first initiates a conversation with a dean or VPAA indicating that ongoing professional development for faculty members could be increased significantly by teaching leadership and faculty development skills for academic chairs. Suggest that the dean skim one of the books on chair leadership development. Then the dean gives two or three of the most influential chairs copies of the book to read, advising them that a leadership development program is being considered. The dean suggests discussing that possibility with them before the next department chair meeting. Next, the dean meets with those informal leaders to discuss the plan and finally asks them to be prepared to discuss such a program when the topic is introduced at the next department chair meeting. The director of the faculty development office also requests that he or she be present to speak about this topic at the next dean's meeting for department chairs.

All of this takes time. However, deans and VPAAs sometimes tell me that a number of their chairs are not receptive to leadership development programs. When they have tried the approach just presented, chairs are much more willing to support professional development plans. Whenever chairs are actively involved from the outset in the planning of leadership programs, an enthusiastic response is usually generated.

SAMPLE LEADERSHIP AND FACULTY DEVELOPMENT TOPICS

In a study group, chairs usually meet regularly once a month for two or three hours at a time most convenient for the majority. Depending upon the climate of the college, the dean, associate, and assistant deans can also be involved. In some colleges chairs may have a strong preference for including only chairs, feeling that they will be freer to talk about problems with which they are struggling than if the dean were present. In one college with which I worked, the dean actively participated in role plays and discussions, attended all sessions, told stories of mistakes he had made and what he had learned from them, let chairs know he felt the program was important, and generally served as a good model to the chairs in the college.

Chairs usually read a chapter in a book on chair leadership, then come together prepared to discuss that chapter and to relate their own experience to what they have read. A number of good books have been published in the last few years (Bennett & Figuli, 1990; Gmelch & Miskin, 1993; Leaming, 1998; Lucas, 1994; Seagren, Creswell, & Wheeler, 1993; Tucker, 1993; Hecht, Higgerson, Gmelch, & Tucker, 1999), and they offer information on a number of possible topics for discussion, including the following:

- Strategies for conducting meetings

- Leadership versus management

- Motivating and rewarding faculty

- Using performance evaluation as an ongoing tool for faculty development and personnel decision making

- Evaluating teaching performance

- Creating a supportive department climate

- Increasing communication between chairs and deans

When chairs meet on a regular basis to discuss their leadership responsibilities, they feel empowered. Not only can they explore together some of the issues with which they struggle on a daily basis, they also become a support group for one another. When I conducted a leadership development program for 15 chairs, assistant and associate deans, and the dean of a college of science and engineering (Lucas, 1986), I found that the problems brought forward for discussion were usually ones the chairs were facing in their departments; moreover, they often telephoned each other between sessions to get another perspective on some issue. For chairs who often describe themselves as being alone in the trenches, this kind of support network is extremely important. Moreover, when chairs meet on a regular basis to discuss issues and set monthly goals, they try hard to achieve those goals so that they can report back to the group their successes and the problems they encounter. This translation of knowledge to the action level would not necessarily happen if chairs simply read a book about leadership. A subtle, but very real, group pressure becomes a catalyst for continuing professional development.

CONCLUSION

When faculty development centers launch leadership and faculty development programs for department chairs, they increase their impact in colleges and universities. Such programs result in reaching a larger number of faculty, creating synergy in departments so that high quality teaching becomes a goal for ongoing professional development, and expanding departmental awareness that faculty development centers can provide the implementation steps required to achieve these objectives.

REFERENCES

Bennett, J. B., & Figuli, D. J. (1990). *Enhancing departmental leadership.* New York, NY: American Council on Education/Macmillan.

Gmelch, W. H., & Miskin, V. D. (1993). *Leadership skills for department chairs.* Bolton, MA: Anker.

Green, M. F. (Ed.). (1988). *Leaders for a new era.* New York, NY: American Council on Education/Macmillan.

Harvey, D., & Brown, D. R. (1996). *An experiential approach to organization development* (5th ed.). Upper Saddle River, NJ: Prentice Hall.

Hecht, I. W. D., Higgerson, M. L., Gmelch, W. H., & Tucker, A. (1999). *The department chair as academic leader.* Phoenix, AZ: American Council on Education/Oryx.

Leaming, D. R. (1998). *Academic leadership: A practical guide to chairing the department.* Bolton, MA: Anker.

Lucas, A. F. (1986). Effective department chair training on a low-cost budget. *Journal of Staff, Program, and Organization Development, 4* (4), 33-36.

Lucas, A. F. (1994). *Strengthening departmental leadership: A team-building guide for chairs in colleges and universities.* San Francisco, CA: Jossey-Bass.

Massy, W. F., & Wilger, A. K. (1994, January). *Hollowed collegiality: Implications for teaching quality.* Paper presented at the Second AAHE Annual Conference on Faculty Roles and Rewards, New Orleans, LA.

Palmer, P. J. (1993). Good talk about good teaching. *Change, 25,* (6), 8-13.

Pew Foundation. (1996, February). *Policy perspective on higher education* (6: 3). Philadelphia, PA: Pew Foundation.

Seagren, A. T., Creswell, J. W., & Wheeler, D. W. (1993). *The department chair: New roles, responsibilities and challenges.* (ASHE-ERIC Report #1) Washington, DC: George Washington University.

Tucker, A. (1993). *Chairing the academic department.* New York, NY: Macmillan.

Ann F. Lucas is Professor Emerita at Fairleigh Dickinson University, where she served as the Director of the Office of Professional and Organizational Development. She conducts leadership training workshops for department chairpersons, and she has served as a member of the POD Core Committee.

Email: annlucas@aol.com

16

Reaching the Unreachable: Improving the Teaching of Poor Teachers

Ann F. Lucas

When faculty development centers introduce workshops on teaching, they often attract individuals who are already effective college teachers but who are seeking to augment their professional development by becoming reflective practitioners. This development of instructional awareness, or understanding of how they teach, is the first step in instructional improvement, as Weimer (1990) has suggested.

When we design a workshop, we prepare for participants who make up a heterogeneous group: excellent teachers who will communicate their enthusiasm and their experience; new teachers and mid-career faculty members who have the potential to be very effective in the classroom but need to expand their knowledge about teaching and sometimes change their behaviors, attitudes, values, and skills; and poor teachers who may be novices or faculty who have been teaching for many years. At workshops, discussions about teaching and experiential learning segments can address a variety of issues that will improve student learning. Generally, however, poor teachers do not attend workshops on teaching unless they are untenured and their department chairs advise them that their chances of getting tenure will be increased if they improve their teaching.

SOURCES OF FACULTY RESISTANCE

Reaching poor teachers has been a daunting task. In my survey of self-report data (Lucas, 1994), less than one-third of 4,500 chairs who completed questionnaires reported any degree of success in motivating poor teachers. Based on my interviews and workshops with a large number of chairs, it seems they believe that improving teaching effectiveness is not their responsibility; they do not know how to help poor teachers become better; or they feel, sometimes based on painful experience, that any intervention would be resented.

Why is it that faculty who are not effective teachers are so resistant to change? A number of factors from research literature could explain this behavior. In a longitudinal study of 185 new faculty members at several comprehensive universities, Boice (1992) found that when student evaluations were disappointing, faculty explained by externalizing the blame. Poor ratings were seen to be the fault of unmotivated students, heavy teaching loads, and invalid rating systems. When faculty members externalize the blame for poor learning outcomes instead of accepting responsibility, they feel there is no reason to make changes in the ways in which they are teaching.

Based on Boice's findings on the teaching style of faculty in the late 1980s, some inferences can be made about the current teaching methods of the thousands of faculty members who were hired in the 1970s. Colleges and universities seemed to subscribe to the myth that if you knew your subject, you could teach it. This gave new teachers little help in becoming effective teachers. It is probable that, lacking guidance, large numbers of new faculty taught as they had been taught and settled into an approach that depended heavily upon lecture as the only way to teach, with no interaction with students. After becoming accustomed to this content-only approach, most faculty found it comfortable, and the style conformed to student expectations, if not their preferences.

Some of these teachers, although poor lecturers, continued to use a teaching approach that did not work for them or their students, and they have built up defenses to help maintain their self-esteem. They do not want to talk about teaching, except in the most cursory fashion, because such discussions might force them to examine their teaching in ways that would create discomfort (Lucas, 1994). When they receive poor student evaluations, ineffective teachers among senior faculty, like the newer faculty studied by Boice, tend to defend themselves against the need for change by externalizing the reasons for their poor teaching.

Despite student evaluations that might contradict this belief, faculty members feel they are very effective in the classroom. Studies reviewed by Feldman (1989) indicate that faculty tend to rate their teaching higher than do their students or colleagues. K. Patricia Cross (1977), drawing on her survey of self-report data from college teachers, found that "an amazing 94 percent rate themselves as above average teachers, and 68 percent rank themselves in the top quarter in teaching performance" (p. 10). In addition, we know that mediocre and poor teachers are even less accurate in their self-assessments than good teachers (Barber, 1990; Centra, 1993). Therefore, one way of increasing the impact that teaching and learning centers have on teaching is to work directly with academic departments—both chairs and faculty—by initiating difficult conversations about teaching. This can be done not by focusing on poor teachers but by looking at issues such as how all faculty can continue their professional development by becoming even more effective in improving student learning outcomes.

A review of this background information will help you to anticipate the fact that there will be some faculty resistance to any interventions you try to make in the department. This may be expressed by some as, "I've been teaching for 15 years. I know how to teach." Or, worst case, but true scenario, "Students do not have the academic skills to be successful in college, and they are not motivated to learn. My job is to teach, not to motivate them, and any discussions about teaching are a sheer waste of my time." However, what you can look forward to is the energy and enthusiasm of some of the best teachers and the synergy that can be created when you initiate discussions in the department about teaching.

CONDUCTING A NEEDS ASSESSMENT

One of the best approaches to gaining access to the department is to find out what its needs are. Despite feelings some chairs may have that the teaching effectiveness of faculty is not their responsibility, a factor analytic study of 539 questionnaires from chairs in research and doctoral granting universities identified faculty development as one of the four independent roles that chairs perform: leader, faculty developer, scholar, and manager (Carroll & Gmelch, 1992). Nonetheless, to simply go to chairs and tell them that you want to improve the teaching in their departments will immediately raise the question, "Who has told you that our teaching needs to be improved?" While in some cases you may already have a friendly relationship with a department chair that makes access easier, in other instances chairs may be suspicious of any overture you make, be defensive when you talk to them, or be unwilling to spend any reasonable amount of time with you.

In any case, it is better to begin with a visit to the dean who can ease your entry to departments. Since one of the strategic goals of any college should focus on student learning, you can offer deans your services in helping with this responsibility. The dean will then empower you, will be committed to helping you complete your work since this achieves one of his or her goals, will support your work with the departments, and will be interested in what you are doing and the outcomes.

All of this gains visibility for your work in other divisions and colleges in the institution. You can also ask the dean which department has a reputation for excellent teaching, indicating that you want to be perceived as working with a model department to set an example and reduce any faculty anxiety in other departments. If you begin with a department in which teaching is known to be poor, the chair and faculty in that unit might feel as if they have been singled out for poor performance and be unwilling to commit themselves to a change project. A general guideline for intervention is to begin work with the winners.

The next step is for the dean to contact the chair of the department in which you will be doing a pilot study to ask if he or she will volunteer or be willing to be the first department to work with you. Suggest that the dean invite you to attend a department chair meeting which he or she regularly conducts. Student learning and faculty development can be included as items on the agenda. At this meeting, the dean can remind chairs that these items are two of their responsibilities, the outcomes of which will be included in the annual report and monitored, and that he or she has asked the center for teaching and learning to help chairs with this responsibility. Further, since all work done by the center is guaranteed anonymity, no information about specific departments or faculty will be reported back in any way. The dean can then ask one or two chairs to volunteer to involve their departments in a pilot study on improving learning outcomes.

You have now gotten the support of the dean who sees you as helping to achieve a strategic goal, and you have been empowered in the eyes of the chairs who recognize that the dean is supporting you. The dean and chairs will understand that your work can help them achieve both college and department goals and that you can make their job easier by enhancing teaching effectiveness and student learning and providing information for them on this work. Finally, you will be perceived as working with and being supported by the chair of one of the best departments in the college. This should alleviate any fears that you are focusing on departments which have a reputation for poor teaching and makes it less likely that you will be considered a threat or an inconvenience.

THE NEEDS ASSESSMENT INTERVIEW

I have chosen to concentrate on the interview and focus group methods because they are more practical for faculty development centers. Survey approaches may be used although they require significant time, energy, and sophistication in psychometric procedures. However, for those who would like to become acquainted with that method several good resources for survey approaches include Alreck & Settle (1995), Babbie (1990), Leatherman (1990), Phillips & Holton (1995), Robinson & Robinson (1996), Warshauer (1988), and Wexley & Latham (1991). These books discuss the use of questionnaires and organizational data as sources of information, in addition to individual interviews and group discussions, but their focus is primarily on industrial organizations.

You are now ready to begin your interview with the selected chair. Start by introducing yourself and the reason for your visit. Although the chair may be familiar with your purpose, it is helpful to summarize this information now. In essence, you are there to help the chair with two areas of responsibility—faculty development and teaching and learning. What will you do with the data? It is essential to indicate that the results will be anonymous, but not confidential; that is, you will combine data to report trends across the college, such as:

- Needs identified by faculty
- Number and topics of workshops conducted
- Number of interviews conducted
- Frequency of coaching with individual faculty

In other words, though you will be identifying categories of your work when you include any material in your own annual report writing, you will not provide any information that could identify an individual faculty member or a specific department.

You are probably well-advised to limit yourself to four or five general areas such as those suggested below, beginning with questions that are not threatening and are likely to evoke a positive

response. This acts as an ice breaker, but also gives the chair an opportunity to talk about some achievements or programs initiated and
about which he or she feels good.

1) How is teaching in your department different from teaching in
    other departments?

    •   What is being done to help new faculty with their teaching?

    •   How is student learning measured in your department?

    •   What are faculty members in this department doing to increase
        student learning that you feel particularly good about?

    •   What would you like to see faculty do more of to increase stu-
        dent learning even further?

    •   What areas of teaching and learning are of concern to you?

    •   What expectations do you have for your department in the
        area of teaching and learning?

2) When do you talk about teaching in the department?

    •   What typically triggers such discussions?

    •   Based on your knowledge of faculty syllabi, what kinds of
        knowledge, skills, values, and attitudes do faculty expect a
        student to have acquired by the end of a course?

    •   How do faculty organize and teach their courses to ensure
        that students have gained this knowledge and these skills?

3) How is teaching effectiveness evaluated in your department?

    •   How are student evaluations used to improve the teaching-
        learning process? For faculty development purposes?

    •   In addition to student evaluations, what other sources are
        used to provide feedback to faculty about their teaching?

    •   How are colleague observations used in the department?

    •   To what extent have faculty participated in developing a
        process for handling feedback on teaching observations?

4) How ready are your faculty to talk about or work on any of these
    areas?

- Where do you think would be the best place to begin?

- How can I help you in any of these areas?

- Are there any questions that I should have asked but didn't?

When conducting interviews, try to keep the following issues in mind as well. In order to make the interview most productive, use open-ended questions. All of the questions in the list above are open-ended and encourage interviewees to discuss the topic from their own perspectives. Avoid biased language, such as, "Don't you think that . . . ?" which suggests what answers you would like to hear. Finally, to increase your understanding, use probing questions and comments such as the following:

- Tell me more about that.

- Can you give me an example?

- Could you be more specific?

- Could you say that another way? I'm not sure I understand.

- How often does this occur?

- When and where does this occur?

- When and where does this fail to occur?

- What factors contribute to making this happen?

Finally, thank the chair for the interview. Agree on the next step, which might be to have the chair schedule a meeting on teaching and learning for about an hour either at a regular department meeting or a special meeting. If the department is a large one, meet with six to 12 faculty at a time. Since time in department meetings is precious, the chair will have to have been convinced by your prework with the dean and your interview that spending time in this way would be valuable and would be perceived as such by the rest of the faculty members. You can add that you would very much like to do this because faculty will be more committed to the idea of further work on teaching and learning if they participate in some preliminary discussion.

Actually, this first meeting will raise the consciousness of some faculty and let others see the array of topics that could improve everyone's work on student learning. There are other advantages, such as opening up the topic of teaching and learning for discussion, as this may not have been talked about in the department before. Faculty members who may be apprehensive about possible exposure of their lack of knowledge or who feel that there is nothing for them to learn about teaching will also see that talking about teaching and learning need not be intimidating, that there are many effective teaching methods, and that some of the same problems which they thought they were struggling with alone are shared by others. Rather than focus on improving teaching, you can discuss how the needs of students have changed in recent years and why this new breed of student requires a different teaching approach. If all of the department members participate in a discussion about such topics, it is more likely that commitment to faculty development will be generated.

Conducting a Needs Analysis with Faculty

You are now ready to conduct a group interview with the department faculty. Ask the department chair to introduce you and mention the purpose of your being there. You may want to add other relevant information, such as the fact that this is a pilot study with a department that has a reputation for quality teaching. The plan is to make yourself available as a resource person and to conduct a couple of workshops on student learning in academic departments. Since you would like to understand faculty views about teaching and learning more clearly, you should prepare several questions to guide the discussion. You will want to have a flip chart available on which you will record ideas that surface. Asking faculty to feel free to be open in their comments is not nearly as effective as your general attitude of acceptance of their comments, a liberal use of active listening or paraphrasing to make sure that you understand the points that are being made, and an honest respect for those opinions with which you may disagree.

In order to lead the discussion with faculty, you might use questions such as these:

- Think of a particular course that you have taught. What are the knowledge, skills, attitudes, and values that you would like to have your students demonstrate by the end of the course?

  — How will you construct the course, and what teaching approaches will you use to facilitate this learning?

- — Which teaching methods are most likely to achieve each of your course objectives?

- Describe one of your golden moments (or experiences) in the classroom when things went really well.

  - — What did you do that made this happen?

  - — How might a student describe the same classroom session?

- Describe a typical class session.

  - — How might a student describe the same class?

  - — What made the difference between a golden moment and a typical class?

- How would you construct the first class in the semester to create a learning environment in which students will be motivated and enthusiastic about what they will learn (see also Lucas, 1990)?

I suggest about two dozen other questions that you might ask, each of which is followed by several references that deal with those issues (Lucas, 1994, pp. 115-118).

You can help individuals build on the thoughts of others, capitalize on the excitement of effective teachers to energize the group, use humor or pause to savor humor when it surfaces within the group, and help create synergy. This gives poor and mediocre teachers an opportunity to listen to the perspective of others and may stretch them to increase their own instructional awareness. Your task is to use active listening with those who resist the idea of discussing teaching and show respect for their point of view. Try to avoid a combative position. Summarize what they tell you, and solicit other thoughts. If you begin with your best departments, you will sharpen your own skills in facilitating a group and be able to anticipate even the worst case scenarios by the time you have to deal with the poorest, most resistant teachers. When very negative views are presented, such as, "Teaching is a mystery. No one knows what good teaching is," summarize what you have heard. Pause. Other faculty will probably disagree. If they don't, you could ask, "How can we measure student learning? What are some things we do know about good teaching?"

At the end of this meeting, summarize what has happened. Then ask faculty what workshop topics they would find of particular interest. If there are several such topics, ask them to prioritize.

Designing Workshop Learning Objectives

As a result of conducting a needs assessment, you now have several topics about which faculty members would like to learn more and which have generated some enthusiasm. The next step is to involve at least one or two members of the department in developing learning objectives for these topics. The value of involving faculty at this point is to begin to shift some of the responsibility for the discussion of teaching and learning to the department itself and to enhance the validity of the training you will do by involving some of their own people in the work.

The learning objectives should communicate what your faculty development center and the faculty members intend to do and what the expected outcome or benefit to the participants will be. Objectives should follow the SMART mnemonic, that is, specific, measurable, acceptable to participants, realistic, and timely. "To improve teaching performance in the classroom" is a poor objective for the following reasons:

- It is not specific.

- It is not measurable because there is no baseline against which change can be evaluated.

- There is no guarantee that this will happen.

- It focuses on teaching, which creates defensiveness on the part of faculty instead of on learning, which focuses on student outcomes.

A more realistic learning objective is, "Participants will have an opportunity to share and discuss the selection of appropriate choices of pedagogical methods for achieving specific course objectives." Or, "By the end of this session you should:

- Identify several objectives for an individual class in one of your courses.

- Understand how the choice of appropriate teaching methods is related to the successful achievement of course objectives.

- Understand the measures that can be used to evaluate student learning and satisfaction as a result of different teaching methods.

- Have an opportunity to participate in at least one experiential learning module and evaluate its effectiveness as an approach to teaching skills and attitudes."

You are now ready to decide on the methodology you will use and what part the faculty members who are working with you will take in the workshop. Although all of this takes effort, you will soon have a repertoire of workshop modules on which you can draw as you engage another department in faculty development. You can also ask one or two faculty from a department with which you have worked to accompany you to another department, particularly to a difficult or strongly resistive one. Having other faculty members recount their positive experiences in working with you makes your entry into troublesome departments much easier. Also, you will have created ongoing teaching projects with which faculty are involved in many departments. Then you will only have to visit the departments periodically to obtain progress reports and find out how you can continue to be used as a resource person.

MEASURING OUTCOMES

The outcome of your work with departments can be measured in a variety of ways. At the end of a workshop, a brief questionnaire can be distributed, asking what faculty have learned that they can use to increase student learning outcomes. The questionnaire can also include a couple of questions about what they liked best and least about the workshop and what other topics they would like to address. This information can be shared with the respondents, the chair, and the dean and can be included in your annual report.

Through periodic contacts with the chair of each department with which you have worked, you can ask about the extent to which faculty are discussing teaching and learning in the department and whether there has been any change in student evaluations (if these pass through the hands of the department chair). You can conduct a couple of interviews with faculty members in departments in which you have worked to discover what changes they have observed. You can survey members of these departments to inquire about the extent to which they have used any of the material discussed in the workshops to increase student learning and how these approaches have worked. Most of the work in these areas involves developing brief questionnaires that can be used again and again in different departments. The main idea is to discover and publicize how the work of your center has accomplished strategic college and departmental goals. After such successful beginnings, deans in the other colleges will want you to work with them as well.

SUMMARY

Faculty members need to become reflective practitioners and engage in ongoing professional development in their facilitation of student learning. Although all faculty benefit from increased instructional awareness, when poor and mediocre teachers do not improve, they perform an extreme disservice to generation after generation of college students. These are the faculty members whom two-thirds of chairs feel unsuccessful in helping. These are also the teachers who do not voluntarily present themselves to faculty development programs.

Poor and mediocre teachers typically overestimate the effectiveness of their teaching. It is difficult for faculty who have been teaching for a number of years to admit that they may not be doing a good job of it. Understanding this makes it easier to work with such teachers, listen to them, and respect their resistance. An intervention with faculty is presented that does not single out poor teachers, but enlarges their perspective by exposing them to ideas generated by colleagues in the department and to research on learning.

A method for conducting a needs analysis, working collaboratively with faculty, developing meaningful and measurable objectives for workshops, and evaluating and sharing the results of your interventions with key people is described. Such an intervention can make a significant impact on the teaching and learning outcomes in an institution by embedding your work in the culture of the department.

REFERENCES

Alreck, P., & Settle, R. (1995). *The survey research handbook*. Burr Ridge, IL: Irwin.

Babbie, S. (1990, April). *Survey research methods*. Belmont, CA: Wadsworth.

Barber, L.W. (1990). Self-assessment. In J. Millman & L. Darling-Hammons (Eds.), *The new handbook of teacher evaluation* (pp. 216-228). Newbury Park, CA: Sage.

Boice, R. (1992). *The new faculty member*. San Francisco, CA: Jossey-Bass.

Carroll, J. B., & Gmelch, W. H. (1992). *A factor-analytic investigation of the role types and profiles of higher education department chairs*. San Francisco, CA: The national conference of the American Educational Research Association. (ERIC Document Reproduction Service No. ED 345 629)

Centra, J. A. (1993). *Reflective faculty evaluation: Enhancing teaching and determining faculty effectiveness*. San Francisco, CA: Jossey-Bass.

Cross, K. P. (1977). Not can, but will college teaching be improved? In J. A. Centra, (Ed.), *Renewing and evaluating teaching* (pp. 1-15). New Directions for Higher Education, No. 17. San Francisco, CA: Jossey-Bass.

Feldman, K. A. (1989). Instructional effectiveness of college teachers as judged by teachers themselves, current and former students, colleagues, administrators and external (neutral) observers. *Research in Higher Education, 30,* 137-189.

Leatherman, D. (1990). *The training trilogy: Assessing needs.* Amherst, MA: Human Resource Development Press.

Lucas, A. F. (1994). *Strengthening departmental leadership: A team-building guide for chairs in colleges and universities.* San Francisco, CA: Jossey-Bass.

Lucas, A. F. (1990). Using psychological models to understand student motivation. In M. D. Svinicki, (Ed.), *The changing face of college teaching* (pp. 103-114). New Directions for Teaching and Learning, No. 42. San Francisco, CA: Jossey-Bass.

Phillips, J. J., & Holton, III, E. F. (Eds.). (1995). *In action: Conducting needs assessment.* Alexandria, VA: American Society for Training and Development.

Robinson, D. G., & Robinson, J. C. (1996). *Performance counseling: Moving beyond training.* San Francisco, CA: Berrett-Koehler.

Warshauer, S. (1988). *Inside training and development: Creating effective programs.* San Francisco, CA: Pfeiffer.

Weimer, M. (1990). *Improving college teaching: Strategies for developing instructional effectiveness.* San Francisco, CA: Jossey-Bass.

Wexley, K. N., & Latham, G. P. (1991). *Developing and training human resources in organizations* (2nd ed.). New York, NY: Harper Collins.

Ann F. Lucas is Professor Emerita at Fairleigh Dickinson University, where she served as the Director of the Office of Professional and Organizational Development. She conducts leadership training workshops for department chairpersons, and she has served as a member of the POD Core Committee.

Email: annlucas@aol.com

17

Problem-Based Learning

Richard G. Tiberius

Over three decades ago, in an otherwise modest steel town in southern Ontario, an event occurred that was the educational equivalent of the Big Bang. All contemporary trends in education—learner-centered, cooperative, small-group, problem-based, contextually dependent learning, as well as patient-centered and community-centered education—originated from this seething cauldron of creativity. I am referring, of course, to the educational program, inaugurated in 1969 at the McMaster University Medical School that has come to be known as problem-based learning, or simply PBL.

I do not expect you to believe this distorted picture of educational genesis, but if you ponder it for a moment, it could help you understand the situation you might face if you were asked to help your medical school implement its new curriculum. Imagine yourself seated in an auditorium amid a large number of clinicians and researchers from the medical school. As you look around, you realize how few of them have been to your teaching and learning workshops. Indeed, not many have had any formal training in the methods of teaching. Yet they are present, and you find yourself wishing arts and science teachers would turn out in such numbers. Clearly there is a sense of urgency in the room regarding this new wave in education which, it is widely believed, will drown everyone who fails to stay on top of it.

You discover the sense of urgency is well founded as you chat with your seat mates. The curriculum committee has passed a resolution in favor of conversion to PBL. Arguments raised at the committee are still stinging the ears of those sitting beside you: "We are the only medical school in the district that still has a traditional program!" "Did you know that Harvard has gone PBL?" Skeptics who might have opposed the resolution really did not know much about PBL, and those who lack information have learned, in the culture of the medical faculty, to keep their heads down.

The lecturers are introduced amid the squeaking of writing arms and the rustle of notebooks. The speakers turn out to be two visiting medical educators from an advanced (one that has already "gone PBL") medical school. The definition appears benign enough: "Problem-based learning is learning that begins with problem solving. The problem comes first. The theory and facts are learned afterward, as they are needed to solve the problem." (Barrows & Tamblyn, 1980). This sequence has made sense to a lot of educators from Dewey to Kolb. Nothing spooky here, you think.

The problem begins with their first overhead, a lurid confirmation of the Big Bang theory. At the very top, in 36-point characters, are the letters "PBL." Radiating from below the acronym, as if it were the sun, are lines connecting the various educational derivatives— student-centered, cooperative, active learning, and so on. The implication is that PBL provides all of these features in the same way that a drug has multiple effects. Still later you find that the drug has multiple forms. You are told to strive for the purist form of PBL, to accept no substitutes. There will be a tutor whose role is to facilitate the discussion. A student will read aloud the first problem sheet. The group will then attempt to address the problem. A scribe will be appointed to write down the facts and the underlying mechanisms that are identified by the group. In a third column, the scribe will write the so-called "learning issues." Learning issues are gaps in knowledge or understanding that have been uncovered in the course of their discussion, gaps that must be filled to solve the problem. At the end of the first session, the learning issues will be parceled out to members of the group who will go off to the library to study them in preparation for the second session. During the second session, after participants have reported their findings to one another, the problem solving discussion will proceed and new learning issues will be identified. These will be assigned to various members and reported at the final session.

It begins to look like PBL is a carefully spelled out formula which, if followed precisely, will deliver the promised effects. You begin to feel the nausea that educators feel when confronted with rigid formulas for learning. You begin to recognize that these derivatives of PBL are actually basic principles of teaching and learning that can be traced back in history anywhere from 50 years to several thousand.

The dean of the Medical School, in his concluding remarks, has announced that the director of the Educational Development Unit on the main campus has agreed to take on the task of training PBL tutors and that you are going to coordinate the program. The dean asks you to stand as hundreds of eager faces look in your direction. You are flushing, almost tearful. Your response is taken as academic modesty.

The hectic months that follow leave you little time for reflection. You are busy setting up a team of developers to train a vast number of faculty in the required procedures. Gradually you begin to regret your role as it becomes apparent that a slogan is a poor substitute for an understanding of educational principles and that mastery of a procedure is a woefully insufficient guide to a new approach to teaching. You wish that someone who had sat in your seat before would have written a chapter in a handbook warning you of the pitfalls.

I dearly hope that this chapter can help. I began with this worst case scenario because I believe that faculty developers who are asked to help transform their traditional medical school—or any school or unit for that matter—into a PBL school need to prepare for such a scenario or for an approximation of it. Medical schools that are desperate to conform to the new wave have a tendency to treat PBL as a slogan and the accompanying curriculum as a mass movement.

The word slogan derives from an ancient war cry used among the Scottish Clans, the *Sluagh-Ghairm*. Slogans have some important advantages in curriculum change, as Ilene Harris (1987) has pointed out. Probably their most important function is legitimating actions. PBL as a slogan can provide a morale boost for the traditional medical school suffering the narcissistic injury of a poor accreditation. The headlines "Traditional Medical School Goes PBL" is much more likely to have an impact on accreditation bodies than "Traditional Medical School Follows Well-Accepted Educational Principles."

Second, slogans have the emotional and social appeal necessary to mobilize a busy faculty who may not take education as their first priority. A war cry gets everybody's attention. Third, slogans focus attention. Aspects of the curriculum that had been ignored before, such as the amount of lecturing or the lack of integration among subjects, are suddenly pushed to the forefront. Administrators start counting the number of lecture hours. Journal articles that have been ripped out of their bindings at the library are given new meaning as faculty begin to reexamine the competitiveness in the old curriculum. Finally, slogans provide an indispensable shorthand. The phrase "PBL" packs a whole lot of meaning.

My main purpose, however, is not to extol the virtues of slogan language but to draw attention to some of the problems that may arise from its use. Again, I draw from Ilene Harris' (1987) excellent analysis of slogan language in medical curricula: Slogans are ambiguous to specific recommendations. While faculty may be committed to doing it, they are not sure what it is. Slogans exclude complementary emphases. Moreover, slogans tend to mask complex issues such as the educational principles underlying the new curriculum. These problems of slogan language and of curriculum reform as a mass movement create some serious pitfalls that the developer must take care to avoid. Before these pitfalls are addressed, a brief description of the principles themselves is necessary.

PBL, used in a circumscribed sense, refers to just one of a number of educational tenets that underlie the philosophy of medical education developed at McMaster University. As a slogan, PBL means much more. It implies that by following a set of simple procedures, teachers can reap the benefits of the major curricular changes of the 20th century. It masks the complexity underlying the actual changes in the new medical curricula. Pallie and Carr (1987), writing about the McMaster philosophy, lament:

> ...it is common to encounter major misconceptions and interpretations about what goes on and why. In fact, more than one visitor has chosen to present his own views after a brief visit and sometimes, like the tourist, uses the freedom to improvise on and interpret what he presumes to be going on...Even within the diffuse body of McMaster faculty, individualistic variations exist in the perceptions of what goes on, and should go on. (p. 60)

TENETS AND SOUND PRINCIPLES

Notice that Pallie and Carr do not use the phrase problem-based learning in the broader sense. They write about an educational philosophy built upon a number of tenets. As developers, we recognize these tenets as sound principles of education that have their origins in writings and research that predate McMaster University. The developer who is helping medical faculty adjust to this new curriculum must help them appreciate these educational principles.

Learning is problem-based, not discipline-based. This principle rejects the time-honored idea that biomedical information had to be learned in blocks corresponding to the academic disciplines. For the purpose of transferring to clinical practice, information is more effectively learned in the context of clinical problems rather than disciplines. The corollary follows that the basic sciences are not considered obligatory antecedents to clinical studies.

Learning in small groups fosters interaction and active engagement of the learner. This principle calls for a reduction in the number of lecture hours in favor of small-group discussion. The assumption underlying the principle is that small-group learning sessions foster interaction and active engagement of the learner. In contrast, students attending lectures are usually more passive, unless a lecturer is particularly skilled at stimulating learner engagement.

Learning is student-directed rather than teacher-directed. The students define their own learning objectives within the tutorial sessions, assisted by the tutor. Tutors are usually faculty with a background in clinical medicine but are not necessarily experts in the subject matter that they are teaching. They have been trained to facilitate an inquiry and problem solving process and to help students define their own learning objectives. The tutors serve primarily as guides and occasionally as sources of information. In the latter capacity, they are careful to respond to students' questions rather than tell students what they ought to be learning. Students learning to define their own learning objectives is considered part of a life-long skill of self-directed learning that they must acquire to maintain competence in a field the half-life of which is five years.

Learning is cooperative rather than competitive. Students learn to share information with their tutorial groups. They learn how others can differ from their own point of view, even after reading the same sources, and to adjudicate between conflicting views.

Learning is contextually grounded rather than context free. Because learning takes place in a problem context that is more similar to the situations in which it will be used, the information is more likely to transfer to actual practice. In the language of the theorists of "cognitive apprenticeship" (Brown, Collins, & Duguid, 1989), the learning is "situated" in authentic contexts.

Learning is patient-centered rather than disease-centered. A patient-centered curriculum encourages the students to look beyond the problem or disease process to the family and psychological situation of the patient.

Learning is community-centered rather than individual patient-centered. This emphasis on the community context is a natural extension of the original McMaster philosophy and one that has grown up more recently. Its development is associated primarily with the Universities of New Mexico (US), Newcastle (Australia), and Limburg (The Netherlands) (Schmidt, Lipkin, de Vries, & Greep, 1989).

PITFALLS

There are also definitely some pitfalls in PBL, and these are as follows.

Exclusion of Complementary Emphases

PBL, used as a slogan, excludes complementary emphases, which is a problem with slogans. That is, they tend to sweep aside anything that is not part of the new program. Prior to our shift to a problem-based curriculum, my own faculty of medicine enjoyed a number of superb lecturers, very highly rated by the students. Several of them were multiple winners of the coveted silver shovel award, which is bestowed on excellent teachers by the students themselves. There is no question that some of our students did learn from listening to lectures, particularly to these lecturers. Yet by and large, these lecturers were swept away by the new curriculum. Losing these effective lecturers was unfortunate and ironic, because lecturing does not have to be excluded from a PBL curriculum. At Bowman-Gray Medical School, I had the privilege of witnessing a lecture that was thoroughly integrated into the medical curriculum. The teacher, who had not prepared a formal lesson, faced an audience of students who had just participated in a series of problem-based learning sessions. He asked them if they had issues or questions that they would like him to explore. After writing these questions on the blackboard and rearranging them slightly to create a list of topics, he presented a series of minilectures on each of the topics with plenty of time in between for interaction. He was functioning as a resource person in the context of a learning event that was clearly student-driven.

Exclusion and Polarization of Some Faculty

A problem with mass movements is that they tend to exclude faculty who are already adhering to the educational principles but not using the approved language. Used as a slogan, PBL tends to exclude faculty who are already practicing sound educational principles and to polarize faculty into converted and saved factions. A good example is found in the story of an anatomy course director who had organized the first year course. Over many years, he had developed a course that was an exemplary manifestation of contemporary educational principles. Students worked in small, cooperative learning groups; they taught one another through interaction; they defined their own learning needs; their learning was set in the context of presenting problems; and they even pursued diagnoses. Yet, when the movement toward PBL gained its full momentum, he was considered obstructive by the curriculum police because he refused to abandon his program in favor of the approved PBL. Fortunately for the school and its students, he stood his ground.

Another problem with mass movements is that they tend to polarize faculty into warring factions—the converted and the unsaved. Curriculum battles can be worthwhile if they are about something substantive, but battles over slogans rarely are. A few years ago, I was invited by the University of The West Indies to present an address, in Trinidad, to an assembly of their three medical schools. At first a profound sense of guilt forced me to refuse the invitation. Trinidad in winter sounds amazing to someone living in Toronto, but I was sure they had the wrong person. My own university had moved to a problem-based curriculum only recently. Moreover, they told me that they were interested in evaluation, not my strong point. Surely they would want to hear from someone from McMaster. I gave them the names of several persons from there who design evaluations. Six months later I got another call from Trinidad urging me to come. This time my role was made a little clearer. Apparently the person who was issuing the invitation had heard me lecture on the subject of the educational principles underlying recent trends in medical education, including PBL. She thought that an opening address on this topic would cool down the fiery debate among the medical schools. The usual competitiveness among the islands and their medical schools was exaggerated by the fact that one had converted to PBL while the other two retained their traditional curricula. The reason for their interest in evaluation was that the traditional schools were demanding evidence for the superiority of the new program before they would consider it. They had hoped that my talk would demonstrate how all three schools could, each in its own way, move toward sound principles of education. I packed my snorkel, and the talk went very well. What they needed was to put the PBL procedure into the larger perspective of the context of contemporary trends in education.

Important Features of the Curriculum

When PBL is taken as a set of magical procedures that ensure the success of the tutorial sessions, then the critical role played by other important features of the curriculum to that success is not appreciated. One such feature is the exam. Put yourself in the position of a medical student for a moment. Your first priority is to survive the exams, both those of the medical school and subsequently of the licensing body. Only a cynic would think this would be your only priority, but if you don't survive these exams, there is no medical career. There will be time later to make yourself an exemplary physician. For now, you need to know what they expect you to know. In traditional curricula, lectures provide the best source of information about the exam. A good set of lecture notes is therefore invaluable, and notes are meticulously copied, edited, and passed from year to year. After all, it is the lecturers who make up the exams, and wouldn't they be more likely to write questions on the same material that they consider important enough to include in their lectures? In the new curriculum, when all the lectures have gone, how do the students "psych out" what might be on the exam?

Since students in PBL tutorials generate their own learning objectives, they cannot be sure that the exam will be based on their learning objectives. It takes only one multiple choice exam based on the teacher's learning objectives to render the tutorial sessions irrelevant in the eyes of the students. After such an exam, students will be much more interested in finding out what the real learning objectives of the tutorial sessions are, the ones that the tutor has tucked away in her or his briefcase, than in generating their own. They will begin to see the PBL sessions as busy work exercises. They will put pressure on the teacher to hand out the real learning objectives prior to the end of the sessions.

The remedy is to use an assessment system that is congruent with the educational principles underlying tutorial, problem-based learning. The so-called Triple Jump and the Progress Test are two such assessment instruments.

Triple Jump. The Triple Jump is the most relevant form of exam possible for a tutorial process because it consists of the process itself, under test conditions. In the first step, the student reads a problem, discusses her or his interpretations with a tutor (the examiner, in this case), and defines a set of learning goals. In the second step, the student goes off to read or use whatever sources he or she thinks might be helpful in fulfilling the learning goals. In a final step, the student returns to the tutor with his or her interpretations and analysis of the problem based on the new information that he or she has gathered. The process provides the tutor with an excellent opportunity to access the student's ability to engage in self-directed learning—defining learning objectives, identifying relevant resources, and problem solving. In addition, the tutor can provide constructive feedback to the student so that the examination becomes a learning process as well.

Progress Test. The Progress Test is designed to meet the requirements of a number of educational principles including self-directed learning, learning through practice, emphasizing abilities beyond knowledge, and the integration of disciplines (Van der Vleuten & Verwijnen, 1990). A Progress Test can best be conceived of as a kind of repeated final examination. It contains many questions (about 250 to 300, in true/false format), together forming a knowledge sample from the entire medical cognitive domain, and it represents the end objectives of the curriculum. This final examination is given four times per year to all students in the medical school—each three months with a test made up of new items, parallel in content to the previous one (Van der Vleuten & Verwijnen, 1990, p. 31).

Because items on the test are drawn from all of the material in the entire undergraduate program, it is uncoupled from the "block" of material prior to it. Students therefore do not cram for it; it does not have the steering effect of a "block" test. Of course, first-year students will not be able to give many answers, but they will learn from the questions about the learning objectives of the medical school. Each year students will do better until, upon graduation, they will be able to answer most of the questions. By raising student awareness of the educational objectives of the program, the test frees students to enjoy their tutorial experience, to learn what they think they need to know rather than what they guess will be on the next exam.

A second feature that is critical to the success of self-directed, problem-based tutorial teaching is the availability of resources. At McMaster, students are able to make appointments with subject matter experts to arrange briefing sessions individually or for their tutorial group. Many medical schools which have a problem-based curriculum make heavy use of what they call resource sessions. Cynics have referred to these sessions as traditional lectures in disguise, but they are not. The teacher defines the topics for the traditional lecture. The students themselves define the topics in the resource sessions. As developers we must ensure that teachers are given the time to provide such resources and are trained in teaching in a student-directed curriculum. Library resources are critical, too, and library staff also need to understand the nature of self-directed learning.

Training for Tutoring

Training in the procedures of tutoring a PBL session is not sufficient. As I wrote above, PBL as a slogan implies that by following a set of simple procedures, teachers can enjoy the benefits of the major curricular changes of the 20th century. The mistaken assumption is that these principles are somehow built into the method. There is a tendency for faculty to believe that they only needed to learn how to perform the functions of the tutor to ensure that their teaching conforms to the major educational principles discussed above. But any set of guidelines can be corrupted by well meaning teachers and students if they do not know the underlying principles. I am reminded of the blackboard game that English teachers play with their classes to demonstrate the difficulty of precise expression. The class is given the task to communicate to the teacher, by verbal means only, how to draw a simple geometric figure like a triangle. The teacher's role is to take advantage of every possible loophole to misinterpret the information. For example, upon hearing the instructions "draw a line" the teacher draws a wavy line, amid shouts of "No, not like that."

Let me give some examples from PBL tutorials. One tutor regularly handed out the learning objectives (the official, teacher version of the objectives) before the end of the sequence so that students could study for the exam (a violation of the principle of self-direction). He saw no harm in this since, as he said, the students still "went through" PBL. What he meant is "going through" the paces, the formal procedure. Another example is from a school in which the place of the tutorial session is defined so precisely within the curriculum that the students knew the problem must be gastrointestinal in nature because of its location within the gastrointestinal block (a violation of the interdisciplinary principle). A final example is of students who make excellent summaries of the information that they gathered, which they then copy and hand out to others, thus obviating the need for discussion and violating the principle of cooperative problem solving.

Inability to follow the spirit of the procedures is only one side of the problem. The other is a rigid adherence to a narrow interpretation of the procedures. Without an understanding of the principles, teachers and students will not have the flexibility to create useful variations on the orthodox method that they learned in their training sessions. Let me give an example from my own experience. Because one of our teaching hospitals is far from the downtown campus, the director of education for that hospital asked permission to redesign their PBL sessions so that students would have to go to that setting only twice a week for three-hour sessions instead of three times a week for two-hour sessions. The reply from the administration was a flat refusal on the grounds that if such a change were made, the result "would no longer be PBL." While it is true that one of the desirable features of the three-day form would be lost, namely the ability of students to correct misunderstandings in the research they did after the first day, the process still has many features that foster desirable goals. The absence of that feature alone does not render the procedure useless to learners.

Extended Training

Tutors need more than a single training session. It does not take very long to learn the mechanics of the PBL tutorial. A typical training period consists of two or three half-day sessions. But there is more to tutoring than knowing the mechanics of the PBL session. Indeed, PBL tutoring can be viewed as employing three separate skills simultaneously (E. Flak, 1993, personal communication):

- The first skill deals with the mechanics of the session such as who reads the problem sheets, who writes on the flip chart, and what the scribe should write.

- The second skill deals with the medical problem itself and the biological issues that arise out of it. Although, according to the theory, the tutor does not have to be an expert, it turns out that tutoring becomes easier as tutors learn more about the cases.

- The final skill involves handling the group dynamics, including knowing when to summarize, when to intervene, how to facilitate evaluation, as well as how to deal with problems such as the dominant speakers, nonspeakers, and group conflict.

A discovery that we made about these three components is that they appear to be mastered in sequence by the tutors. That is, we discovered a natural flow of tutor development from mastering the mechanics of PBL, to understanding the medical background of the problem, to concentrating on group dynamics. During the initial training sessions, teachers were so preoccupied with mastery of PBL mechanics that they paid little attention to group dynamics. In contrast, when we interviewed tutors after their first few years of tutoring, almost all of their requests for further training were for skills in group dynamics. Interestingly, many of these experienced tutors also indicated an interest in gaining a better understanding of the underlying principles. Training should, therefore, take place in stages. The pretutoring phase should consist of training in the mechanics. Then, after some experience with tutoring, teachers should engage in some training in group dynamics and in the principles underlying the new curriculum.

CONCLUSION

If I have made myself clear in this brief chapter, you will appreciate that these sessions on the principles underlying the new curriculum will, in the long run, be the most important element in your training program. Your tutors may not continue tutoring, and your PBL sessions may themselves be discontinued, but the principles that tutors learn will continue to assist them wherever and whatever they teach.

REFERENCES

Barrows, H. S., & Tamblyn, R. M. (1980). *Problem-based learning: An approach to medical education.* New York, NY: Springer.

Brown, J. S., Collins, A., & Duguid, P. (1989). Situated cognition and the culture of learning. *Educational Researcher, 18* (1), 31-42.

Harris, I. (1987). Communicating educational reform through persuasive discourse: A double-edged sword. *Professions Education Research Notes, 9* (2), 2-7.

Pallie, W., & Carr, D. H. (1987). The McMaster medical education philosophy in theory, practice, and historical perspective. *Medical Teacher, 9* (1), 59-71.

Schmidt, H. G., Lipkin, M. Jr., de Vries, M. W., & Greep, J. M. (Eds.). (1989). *New directions for medical education: Problem-based learning and community-oriented medical education.* New York, NY: Springer-Verlaag.

Van der Vleuten, C., & Verwijnen, M. (1990). A system for student assessment. In C. Van der Vleuten & W. Wijnen. (Eds.), *Problem-based learning: Perspectives from the Maastricht experience.* Amsterdam, NL: Thesis.

A Very Brief Annotated Bibliography of PBL

• For the mechanics of tutoring:

Barrows, H. S. (1994). *Practice-based learning: Problem-based learning applied to medical education.* Springfield, IL: Southern Illinois University.

• For helping students get the best out of PBL:

Woods, D. R. (1994). *Problem-based learning: How to gain the most from PBL.* Hamilton, Ontario: W. L. Griffin.

• For a discussion of the problems of implementing PBL:

Kaufman, A. (1985). *Implementing problem-based medical education: Lessons from successful innovations.* New York, NY: Springer-Verlaag.

Richard G. Tiberius is Professor in the Department of Psychiatry and at the Centre for Research in Education in the Faculty of Medicine at the University of Toronto, Canada. His main roles include collaboration with health science faculty on educational research projects, supervision of resident research, and various faculty development activities. He teaches graduate courses in research methods and educational development at the Ontario Institute for Studies in Education, University of Toronto. He has served as a member of the POD Core Committee.

Email: r.tiberius@utoronto.ca

Part V

Addressing Diversity

18

Conceptualizing, Designing, and Implementing Multicultural Faculty Development Activities

Christine A. Stanley

As many colleges and universities increase in size and social and demographic diversity, instructors no longer see the traditional representation of white middle- and upper-class students who have so dominated the classroom population. Rather, we are seeing more students of color, more women, more nontraditional students (older, gay, lesbian, bisexual), more students with disabilities, and other students whose unique characteristics may be visible or invisible. This increase in diversity challenges faculty to take a critical look at how they teach, moving them from traditional modes to ways of designing teaching and learning activities to meet the needs of diverse learners (Marchesani & Adams, 1992). The ideal multicultural classroom embodies a teaching and learning environment in which interdependence is valued, differences are affirmed, communities are strengthened, knowledge is presented from multiple perspectives, and equity and social justice is maintained (Anderson, 1995; Wlodkowski & Ginsberg, 1995). To help meet these instructional challenges, many institutions receive assistance from faculty development units of learning and teaching centers, the primary goal being to support the institution's teaching and learning mission.

In order to respond to the multicultural development needs of faculty, it is imperative that faculty developers be knowledgeable about diversity and multicultural education in academia. To work with faculty in this arena requires careful thought as to how we conceptualize, design, and implement multicultural faculty development initiatives in the faculty, instructional, and organizational development process to enhance the quality of teaching and learning in higher education. The literature in this area is replete with faculty development models that call for our understanding of how we conceptualize multicultural teaching (Adams, Bell, & Griffin, 1997; Anderson, 1995; Jackson & Holvino, 1988; Marchesani & Adams, 1992; Wlodkowski & Ginsberg, 1995). These models share several threads that provide faculty developers with a practical framework from which to assist faculty in the following:

1) The design of an inclusive curriculum

2) The development and exploration of their own multicultural awareness

3) The development of a variety of instructional approaches

4) The development and understanding of students' multicultural awareness

Based on these models and from my own experience working with faculty in this area, this chapter offers a practical guide for new and experienced faculty developers on how to approach multicultural faculty development initiatives.

GETTING STARTED: FACTORS TO CONSIDER

If institutions and faculty developers are going to begin a purposeful multicultural faculty development effort or seek to enhance an existing program, several factors need to be considered.

Institutional Commitment

A multicultural faculty development program cannot be effective in accomplishing its goals without institutional commitment. Without this factor firmly established at the heart of the program, activities will be seen by faculty as not making a difference. Institutional commitment, resources, and verbal support must come from high-level administrators. Program activities should complement existing efforts that foster student diversity such as:

- Offices of minority affairs

- Student life, disability services

- International student services

- Gay, lesbian, or bisexual student services

- Women student services

A multicultural faculty development program should also provide for faculty ownership of program activities to undergird the institutional commitment. Program goals should be established with the guidance of a faculty advisory committee, the membership of which should reflect not only diversity within its members and across disciplines, but also expertise in the area of multicultural teaching.

Program Rationale

Articulating the rationale for a multicultural faculty development program is critical for support, implementation, and evaluation of its activities. It is not unusual for many faculty development units to take charge of coordinating multicultural faculty development activities after the need has been identified. For example, at The Ohio State University the justification for a multicultural faculty development program was born out of data gathered in the late 1980s that revealed low retention rates for black students. These data led to the development of the Teaching for Black Student Retention (TBSR) program that was later expanded to the Multicultural Teaching Program (MTP) and the current Commitment to Success Program. At the centerpiece of these initiatives is the rationale that the classroom is one of the many critical variables contributing to the success of a student's academic experience. A multicultural faculty development program should articulate the meaning of diversity and multicultural teaching. The goal of multicultural faculty development programs in preparing faculty to teach in a diverse classroom is to provide an understanding of how diversity impacts teaching and learning so that behavioral changes can be made to improve the classroom environment for all students (Schmitz, Paul, & Greenberg, 1992).

Theoretical and Pedagogical Rationale

Once institutional commitment and a program rationale are articulated, it is imperative to develop a theoretical and pedagogical framework upon which multicultural faculty development activities will be grounded (Adams et al., 1997; Schmitz et al., 1992; Smikle, 1994). If the goal of the program is to provide faculty with an understanding of how diversity impacts the teaching and learning process, then the framework should reflect this. The theoretical frameworks that have proven most useful for multicultural faculty development activities are those espoused by pluralists. They would argue that interdependence is supported and valued in a diverse classroom and that students are able to explore their differences and to appreciate cultural experiences. Cultural pluralism emphasizes common features between and among groups. The pedagogical frameworks that I have used are those drawn from social justice education practice. Social justice education utilizes principles of cognitive development theory, learning styles, intergroup relations, human relations, experiential education, interactive learning and teaching, and feminist pedagogy (Adams et al., 1997). Social justice education argues for instructors to pay attention to these principles as we examine the classroom environment, particularly the teaching and learning process, where knowledge is explored and instructional approaches are planned to include all participants.

Domains of Teaching

I have found that it is essential to have a conceptual framework to help faculty understand the major domains of multicultural teaching. The dynamics of the multicultural teaching and learning model developed by Jackson and Holvino (1988) and later adapted by Marchesani and Adams (1992) suggest a framework for faculty to encounter the complex task of understanding four dimensions of the teaching and learning process operative within a diverse classroom. These four dimensions—faculty, teaching method, course content, and students—are summarized in Figure 18.1.

The Faculty Developer

Clearly, faculty developers themselves are a significant factor in the implementation or enhancement of the multicultural development effort, and there are several aspects to consider.

Knowledge of self. Working with faculty in the area of multicultural teaching requires that the faculty developer have a high level of self-awareness and sensitivity (Coleman, 1990; Smikle, 1994; Warren, 1994). If we are going to require faculty to look at their own understanding and development of multicultural awareness, it is only natural to take an equally critical look at our own biases and assumptions. We have to know who we are, where we are, what we are about, and why we are doing this work. For example, knowing who we are requires that we take a look at our identity, socialization, and what we are bringing to our charge. As Kardia (1998) appropriately states,

As a faculty developer working on multicultural issues, I need to be able to reflect on a variety of issues including what I know from experience versus what I need to learn from the experiences of others; my own cultural biases and blind spots that may interfere with my interactions with faculty; and how I might be perceived by faculty whose experiences are significantly different from my own. (p. 26)

Knowing where we are takes into account the faculty development unit and the institution with its commitment and vision relating to diversity issues. Knowing what we are about requires that we develop program goals congruent with the unit's mission, and knowing why we are doing this work demands that we empower individuals to share the dialogue around various multicultural issues, such as teaching and learning, philosophy, social justice, and institutional transformation. It is also important to understand that one's identity,

Figure 18.1 *Four Dimensions of Multicultural Teaching*

Faculty
- Know oneself
- Develop monocultural/multicultural socialization
- Examine assumptions and stereotyped beliefs
- Mentor students

Teaching Method (implicit messages)
- Examine the culture of the classroom
- Broaden repertoire of teaching methods to address multiple learning styles
- Establish classroom norms that emphasize respect, fairness, and equity

Course Content (explicit messages)
- Use a curriculum of inclusion
- Represent diverse perspectives
- Draw examples and illustrations from diverse life experiences

Students
- Know your students
- Develop monocultural/multicultural socialization
- Examine assumptions and stereotyped beliefs

Adapted from Jackson & Holvino (1988) and Marchesani & Adams (1992).

whether it be along racial, cultural, or other social diversity lines, will have an impact on how we conceptualize and deliver training in this area. For example, experts generally advise that delivering workshops and seminars as a biracial team rather than as a member of the dominant or target group makes a considerable difference in how a predominantly white audience receives the information.

Knowledge of scholarship. The faculty developer should read a variety of texts that address the social and cultural aspects of teaching for the diverse classroom. Some examples are listed in the reference section of this chapter. The faculty developer must have a working definition of multicultural teaching but, more importantly, must also know how diversity is defined in academia (Anderson, 1995; Asante, 1991; Banks, 1995; Nieto, 1992). Diversity, in some instances, is defined in terms of and associated with multiculturalism, culture, democracy, learning, curriculum change, the learning environment, demographics, instruction, assimilation, and pluralism. One should take a critical look at these definitions, the breadth of their definition, and the implications behind them. One must also be able to conceptualize how these ideas fit within the institution's culture and mission and the faculty development unit.

Audience awareness. It is important that faculty developers give careful thought to the audience in designing and coordinating activities such as workshops, orientations, and consultations. Careful research of one's audience as to reasons, readiness, and long-term plans for any of these activities enables us to better meet the needs of participants and also to help engage interest and increase motivation for change. Knowing our audience also must take into account representation along race, culture, gender, disability, and sexual identity lines. Obviously, some of these characteristics will not be visible, but knowing the makeup of the audience is critical to the success of any workshop. The materials, media, and exercises selected for multicultural faculty development activities should reflect faculty awareness, needs, and ease of implementation (Smikle, 1994).

Professional allies. Faculty developers can learn from individuals who are effective allies—those who have experience in the area of multicultural teaching and education and who are not afraid of "walking the talk." They have worked to develop a better understanding of social and cultural issues, have taken risks, are able to examine their own biases and assumptions, share experiences and resources, and are positive change agents. Effective allies can be faculty, professional colleagues, or staff. According to Ferren and Gellar (1993), for example, many faculty who are already doing work in this area can serve as resource persons, providing information about multicultural issues in their disciplines. Faculty developers can also learn from other faculty developers doing work in this area. I have found that talking with and making site visits to faculty development centers currently coordinating multicultural faculty development programs is essential for professional development and the sharing of ideas and resources for program enhancement.

Contributing to campus policies. Faculty developers must be included in the dialogue on issues that concern multicultural teaching and learning issues in the classroom. This involvement is essential in order to influence institutional transformation so that students, staff, faculty, and administrators identify and understand the current issues surrounding the social and cultural aspects of the institutional environment and take action for change. By serving on key committees that address multicultural education, we begin to develop campus partnerships to affect attitudes and behaviors inside as well as outside the classroom.

DESIGNING MULTICULTURAL FACULTY DEVELOPMENT ACTIVITIES

In designing effective multicultural faculty development programs, it is essential that the content is relevant for the appropriate academic unit, is practical in its use for teaching and learning, raises awareness about multicultural issues in general, identifies institution-wide resources for supporting multicultural teaching, and creates avenues for follow-up.

Workshops

Many higher education faculty grapple with the idea of incorporating issues related to diversity into their courses and/or curriculum. Lack of awareness and insensitivity varies from discipline to discipline (Cooper & Chattergy, 1993) and leads many to espouse the concept that their discipline is culturally neutral. In preparing these workshops faculty developers will first articulate a set of attainable goals. While goals of a workshop are articulated to reflect participants' needs and size of the group, some general guidelines might be:

- To provide a definition and conceptual framework for multi-cultural teaching

- To heighten participants' self-awareness about teaching for diversity and social justice

- To have participants examine how issues of social and cultural diversity manifest themselves in the classroom

- To identify a range of strategies for teaching for the success of all students in the classroom

- To make instructors aware of institutional resources for teaching in a diverse classroom

It is then necessary to develop a framework for the format and content. To do so, I have participants reflect on the four dimensions of multicultural teaching from perspectives of the "what," the "so what," and the "now what" (Borton, 1970). In working with faculty at The Ohio State University, I found it helpful to use these three perspectives in our workshops. The "what" addresses an explanation, definition, or need for the problem that is being addressed. The "so what" addresses why the instructor should care about the problem, and the "now what" addresses how the problem affects instructors and how they might take action to solve it. A general format for a multicultural faculty development workshop might follow the outline shown below.

Introduction and Goals

Topics: Facilitator and participants introduce themselves and explain what they hope to gain from the workshop.

Purpose: Establishes tone and enables facilitators to get a sense of how to meet participants' needs.

Principles of Teaching for the Diverse Classroom (the "What")

Topics:
- Changing demographics of the classroom
- Changing college faculty
- A conceptual framework for defining the problem such as Marchesani and Adams' (1992) four dimensions of multicultural teaching

- Groundrules for participation
- Research that connects relevance of the issue to the discipline such as retention and demographic data

Purpose: Provides a conceptual framework for multicultural teaching and raises assumptions about what constitutes a diverse classroom.

The Changing Classroom Climate for Teaching and Learning (the "So What")

Topics: Common classroom concerns as reported from the research on diverse student groups (may use video vignettes, self-assessment exercises, case studies on teaching and learning behaviors in the classroom to facilitate discussion). Sample case scenarios and self-assessment exercises can be found in Appendices 18.1 and 18.2.

Purpose: Establishes the rationale that the teaching and learning process is complementary, provides examples of how these two relationships operate in the classroom and of behaviors that enhance and impede learning, and focuses on things that will help participants to care and realize ways in which they can make a difference or worsen the problem.

The Need for Changes in Teaching and Learning (the "Now What")

Topics:
- Examples of teaching and learning strategies that facilitate change
- Self-assessment exercises
- Personal contracts
- Multicultural course and curriculum change
- Classroom observations with feedback
- Classroom assessment techniques

Purpose: Provides concrete teaching and learning strategies once areas in need of change have been identified.

Teaching Support Services

Topics:
- Additional resources and opportunities for follow-up such as periodic recommitment seminars

- Further readings on the topic
- Support service units on campus

Purpose: Provides follow-up information to participants who wish to explore and learn further about the topics discussed and leaves them feeling that they are not in this endeavor alone.

Evaluation

Topic: An instrument allowing participants to give facilitators feedback on the organization, content, facilitation, benefits of the workshop, and ideas for follow-up. This instrument can be structured so that feedback is given using ratings on a Likert Scale, open-ended responses, or a combination of both.

Purpose: Gathers formative feedback in order to better structure and facilitate further workshops in this area.

The format above is designed for a two-hour time period. Obviously, individual faculty developers need to make adjustments for length, content, and type of audience. For example, faculty in a sociology department might appreciate the use of qualitative data in presenting the "what" as opposed to faculty in a mathematics department, who might appreciate the use of quantitative data. In a workshop designed for the mathematics department, the author, as part of establishing the "what," worked with a staff member to gather and present recruitment and retention data of underrepresented student populations in that department. These data were integral to setting the tone of the workshop and making the participants more receptive to owning the problem. I have found copresenting with a faculty liaison from the department requesting the workshop helps the faculty developer establish credibility with participants.

Whatever the method chosen for the presentation, the content should be tailored to the discipline or be generic in its content so that it is applicable to most. For example, in using case studies, it is often helpful to work with the faculty liaison in developing scenarios that have really occurred in the classroom or department. Considering the scenario from the perspective both of the student and instructor, faculty find case studies productive and meaningful as they think through ways to develop appropriate actions for change.

Individual Consultation

Individual consultation can involve review of course and curriculum design, as well as syllabi, and is very challenging. For many faculty, integrating multicultural course content is often relegated to a book or article addressing an aspect of diversity. Even more challenging is working with a faculty member who feels that the course does not lend itself well to incorporating issues of diversity. Consultations should start by helping instructors to realize how culture permeates all that we do, and they might begin by examining themselves.

Based on a survey conducted by Weinstein and O'Bear (1992) with a group of 25 faculty, Adams, Bell, and Griffin (1997) suggest that knowing ourselves as instructors should take into account issues such as the following:

- Being aware of one's own social identity

- Confronting our own biases

- Responding to biased comments in the classroom

- Acknowledging our doubts and ambivalence about multicultural issues

- Realizing that students may feel uncomfortable talking about multicultural issues

- Dealing with emotional intensity and fear of losing control

- Negotiating authority

- Disclosing our knowledge and experiences about diversity

- Creating institutional risks and behaviors

Course and Curriculum Design

There are several approaches to integrating multicultural perspectives into the curriculum. The approach discussed here is adapted from Banks (1995) and consists of four levels—the contributions approach, the additive approach, the transformation approach, and the action approach. These levels of modification are explained in Figure 18.2.

The ease of implementation decreases from the lowest to the highest level. Many researchers agree that levels 3 and 4—transformation and action—are what instructors should strive for in course and curricular reform (Banks, 1995; Ginsberg & Wlodkowski, 1997; Green,

1989; Jackson & Holvino, 1988; Ognibene, 1989; Schoem, Frankel, Zuniga, & Lewis, 1993). These two levels also demand a deliberate institutional approach. It is important to remember that the contributions and additive approaches, though easier to implement, have their disadvantages, one of which is that they are easily eliminated if instructors are pressed for time in covering content. Another is that students often view contributions or additives as outside the realm of course content if they are not integrated to promote several perspectives on the content.

Working with multicultural course content and curriculum change requires that instructors take a close look at these approaches

Figure 18.2 *Approaches to Multicultural Curriculum Reform*

Level 1: The Contributions Approach
Heroes, heroines, holidays, food, and discrete cultural elements are celebrated occasionally. For example, the contributions of Black Americans to history are celebrated only in February, Black History Month. Or, an introductory physics course might mention contributions made by the late African American physicist and astronaut Ron McNair.

Level 2: The Additive Approach
Content, concepts, lessons, and units are added to the curriculum without changing the structure. For example, an instructor adds Alice Walker's book, *The Color Purple*, or Shakespeare's *Othello* to a literature course without changing its structure.

Level 3: The Transformation Approach
The structure of the curriculum is changed to enable students to view concepts, issues, events, and themes from the perspectives of diverse ethnic and cultural groups. For instance, a lecture on World War II might describe the contributions and meaning of the war to African Americans and the role played by the Tuskegee Airmen. A 20th century literature course might include scholarship on the writings of James Baldwin, Maxine Hong Kingston, Maya Angelou, Rudolpho A. Anaya, and Leslie Marmon Silko. A general biology or zoology course might address AIDS and discuss the impact and effect of the disease on various communities such as gay, lesbian, and bisexual individuals, women, African Americans, and other populations.

Level 4: The Action Approach
Students make decisions on important personal, social, and civic problems and take action to help solve them. To illustrate, a class studies the effects of institutional discrimination practices in higher education and develops an action plan to improve these practices at their institution.

Adapted from Banks (1995).

and then reflect on how they might incorporate them. Kitano (1997) argues that reforming each level requires considerable planning, experimentation, and revision and that each activity should be a continuous process over time.

Syllabi. It is essential to articulate multicultural goals for the course. Kitano (1997) offers a working model for course and syllabus change and defines a multicultural course as one that appropriately incorporates multicultural content, perspectives, and strategies. In developing such goals, faculty should ask themselves the following questions:

- Is the goal of this course to assist students in acquiring knowledge that reflects the accurate contributions of all individuals?

- Is the goal of this course to present content from multiple perspectives?

- Is the goal of this course to help students value the richness of diversity?

- Is the goal of this course to prepare students to function in a global society?

- Is the goal of this course to support different learning styles?

The overall course and multicultural goals articulated on the syllabus should be consistent with how the course is organized, implemented, and assessed and how the teaching methods are chosen. In addition to the usual information, an effective syllabus that is created from a multicultural perspective should pay attention to the checked items presented in Figure 18.3.

CONCLUSION

Conceptualizing, designing, and implementing multicultural faculty development activities is challenging work. These activities require strong institutional commitment, solid grounding in a variety of theoretical and pedagogical rationales, in-depth exploration around who we are as individuals doing this work, excellent facilitation skills, and continuous professional development. Multicultural faculty development work is also highly rewarding. It encourages us to expand our repertoire of social and cultural experiences as we work with faculty and institutions in higher education to meet the teaching and learning

Figure 18.3 *Syllabus*

Course Information
Includes course title, course number, credit hours, location of the classroom, days and hours of class/lab/studio, etc.

Instructor Information
Includes name, title, office location, office phone number, office hours, teaching associates (TAs).

Textbooks, Readings, and Materials
Includes title, author, date, publisher, and why it or they were chosen. Text(s) should be chosen for representation and treatment of course content and goals. Authors should be chosen for their treatment of multiple perspectives. Readings and materials should be chosen for their representation of diverse perspectives.

✓ **Course Description and Goals**

Includes course and multicultural goals and why these goals are important for teaching and learning. Might include a rationale for instructional methods. Instructional methods should capitalize on students' experiences, learning, and cognitive styles. Course objectives for multicultural teaching and learning should address cognitive, affective, and behavioral domains (Kitano, 1997).

Course Calendar and Schedule
Includes a daily or weekly schedule of class activities such as readings, assignments and due dates, lecture topics, quizzes, and exams. Assessment strategies should provide students with a variety of ways for mastering course content.

✓ **Course Policies**

Includes attendance, lateness, class participation, missed assignments and exams, lab safety, academic misconduct, and grading. Communicates a tone of high expectations for all students and a knowledge of the research on differential interaction patterns of underrepresented groups.

✓ **Available Support Services and Resources**

Includes a statement for students who may require support services from offices such as disability services, academic learning center, tutoring center, library, and computer center. Resources should accommodate the social and cultural characteristics and experiences of the students.

Adapted from Altman and Cashin (1992).

---

needs of an increasingly diverse college student population. Finally, conceptualizing, designing, and implementing multicultural faculty development activities is ultimately of value to everyone. When we as faculty developers embrace any such call to action, we will not only have enriched the pool of educational resources at our institutions, but the academy as well.

REFERENCES

Adams, M., Bell, L., & Griffin, P. (1997). *Teaching for diversity and social justice.* New York, NY: Routledge.

Altman, H. B, & Cashin, W. E. (1992). *Writing a syllabus.* (Idea Paper No. 27). Manhattan, KS: Kansas State University, Center for Faculty Evaluation and Development.

Anderson, J. A. (1995). *Merging effective models of diversity with teaching and learning in the curriculum.* Raleigh, NC: North Carolina State University.

Asante, M. (1991). Multiculturalism: An exchange. *The American Scholar, 60,* 267-76.

Banks, J. A. (1995). Multicultural education: Historical development, dimensions, and practice. In J. A. Banks & C. A. M. Banks (Eds.), *Handbook of research on multicultural education* (pp. 3-24). New York, NY: Macmillan.

Borton, T. (1970). *Reach, touch, and teach.* New York, NY: McGraw Hill.

Coleman, T. (1990). Managing diversity at work: The new American dilemma. *Public Management, 70,* 2-5.

Cooper, J. E., & Chattergy, V. (1993). Developing faculty multicultural awareness. An examination of life roles and their cultural components. In D. Wright & J. Povlacs Lunde (Eds.), *To Improve the Academy: Vol. 12. Resources for Faculty, Instructional, and Organizational Development* (pp. 81-95). Stillwater, OK: New Forums Press.

Ferren, A. S., & Geller, W. W. (1993). The faculty developer's role in promoting an inclusive community: Addressing sexual orientation. In D. L. Wright & J. Povlacs Lunde (Eds.), *To Improve the Academy: Vol. 12. Resources for Faculty, Instructional, and Organizational Development* (pp. 97-108). Stillwater, OK: New Forums Press.

Ginsberg, M. B., & Wlodkowski, R. J. (1997). *Developing culturally responsive teaching among faculty: Methods, content, and skills.* A session presented at the 10th Annual Conference on Race and Ethnicity in American Higher Education, Orlando, FL.

Green, M. F. (Ed.). (1989). *Minorities on campus: A handbook for enhancing diversity.* Washington, DC: American Council on Education.

Jackson, B. W., & Holvino, E. (1988). Developing multicultural organizations. *Journal of Religion and the Applied Behavioral Sciences, 9* (2), 14-19.

Kardia, D. (1998). Becoming a multicultural faculty developer: Reflections from the field. In M. Kaplan & D. Lieberman (Eds.), *To Improve the Academy: Vol. 17. Resources for Faculty, Instructional, and Organizational Development.* Stillwater, OK: New Forums Press.

Kitano, M. K. (1997). What a course will look like after multicultural change. In A. Morey & K. Kitano (Eds.), *Multicultural course transformation in higher education: A broader truth.* (pp. 18-34). Needham Heights, MA: Allyn and Bacon.

Marchesani, L. S., & Adams, M. (1992). Dynamics of diversity in the teaching-learning process: A faculty development model for analysis and action. In M. Adams (Ed.), *Promoting diversity in college classrooms: Innovative responses for the curriculum, faculty, and institutions* (pp. 9-19). New Directions for Teaching and Learning, No. 52. San Francisco, CA: Jossey-Bass.

Nieto, S. (1992). *Affirming diversity: The sociopolitical context of multicultural education.* New York, NY: Longman.

Ognibene, E. R. (1989). Integrating the curriculum: From impossible to possible. *College Teaching, 37* (3), 105-110.

Schmitz, B., Paul, S. P., & Greenberg, J. D. (1992). Creating multicultural classrooms: An experience-derived faculty development program. In L. Border & N. Chism (Eds.), *Teaching for Diversity, 49,* (pp. 75-87). San Francisco, CA: Jossey-Bass.

Schoem, D., Frankel, L., Zuniga, X., & Lewis, E. A. (1993). The meaning of multicultural teaching: An introduction. In D. Schoem, L. Frankel, X. Zuniga, & E. A. Lewis (Eds.), *Multicultural teaching in the university* (pp. 1-12). Westport, CT: Praeger.

Smikle, J. L. (1994). Practical guide to developing and implementing cultural awareness training for faculty and staff development. *Journal of Staff, Program & Organization Development, 12* (2), 69-80.

Warren, J. (1994). A training for cultural diversity. *Literacy Harvest, 3,* 38-45.

Weinstein, G., & O'Bear, K. (1988). Design elements for intergroup awareness. *Journal for Specialists in Group Work, 13,* 96-103.

Weinstein, G., & O' Bear, K. (1992). Bias issues in the classroom: Encounters with the teaching self. In M. Adams (Ed.), *Promoting diversity in college classrooms: Innovative responses for the curriculum, faculty, and institutions* (pp. 39-50). New Directions for Teaching and Learning, No. 52. San Francisco, CA: Jossey-Bass.

Wlodkowski, R.J., & Ginsberg, M.B. (1995). *Diversity and motivation.* San Francisco, CA: Jossey-Bass.

Christine A. Stanley is Assistant Professor in the Department of Educational Administration and Associate Director of the Center for Teaching Excellence at Texas A&M University, College Station, Texas. Prior to this appointment, she was Associate Director of Faculty and TA Development at The Ohio State University. She has been engaged in faculty development activities since 1987. She is the former Chair of the POD Diversity Commission, has served on the POD Core Committee, and she also served as the President of POD in 2000-2001.

Email: cstanley@coe.tamu.edu

APPENDIX 18.1

SAMPLE CASE SCENARIOS TO FACILITATE DISCUSSION ON TEACHING FOR THE DIVERSE CLASSROOM

Directions

Read the following case scenarios that portray some common issues arising in the college classroom. View the situation from the perspectives of the students, then from the instructors' perspectives. What might each be thinking? What suggestions for action do you have for each situation or for avoiding the situation in the first place?

Scenario 1: A department faculty wonders how to be more inclusive in its curriculum.

David Wong is chairperson of his department. The Hispanic student association has sent him a letter urging the department to include the accomplishments of Hispanic scholars and significant issues pertaining to Hispanics in its curriculum. At a department meeting, Wong brings the letter to the attention of faculty and graduate teaching associates. The instructors feel that the students' suggestions are unreasonable since instructors say that they don't generally speak of the source of the scholarship, that their course is "culturally neutral," and that they don't see how they can accommodate these concerns.

Scenario 2: What is the instructor's responsibility?

Clarice Golden is having a classroom discussion on the changing profile of the American family. A student in the class raises the point of gay and lesbian couples having children. Immediately after saying this, another student, Patrick Williams, says half-humorously, "Oh, God, that's sick!" The class laughs. Golden quiets the class, quickly passing over the suggestion as potentially too disruptive, and continues facilitating the discussion on "safer" grounds. After class, Ann, a student in the class, comes to her office and identifies herself as lesbian. She is angry and offended, accuses Golden of homophobia, and asks that she reprimand Williams.

Scenario 3: To intervene or not to intervene?

Jim Burton, an African American senior student, has done poorly on the first two exams in Barbara Ross's course. He doesn't participate in class and has not come to see her outside of class. Even if he does exceptionally well on his final two exams, he will not get a good grade. Ross fears that Burton will not do well and will most likely fail, given his performance to date. She generally leaves it up to students to come see her when they are in trouble, but in this case she thinks that Burton might be shy and makes a point of asking him to see her. In talking with him, she determines that he is not very realistic about his performance and the prospects of reversing his grade. She suggests that he might consider dropping this course and taking a lower-level one so that he will not damage his grade point average. She feels that she has gone out of her way to help Burton and is puzzled when he resents being singled out and thinks that her suggestion is insulting.

Scenario 4: An instructor expresses his concern to you that a student has accused a colleague of patronizing the disabled.

John Green approaches his colleague, Gordon Wexner, and says that Leslie Bicknell, a student in Wexner's class, stopped by the office to express concern over an issue in his class. She explained that she is uncomfortable with his insensitivity toward the disabled. She said that throughout the semester Wexner has consistently pointed out how wonderful it is that Bill Hudson has overcome his disability. He also tends to speak loudly to Bill, which is offensive, since Bill's disability is visual. Wexner gets angry, saying that he is only trying to make Hudson feel welcomed in class and teachers these days are just "damned if they do and damned if they don't." Leslie Bicknell left feeling that Wexner just doesn't get it.

The scenarios have been adapted with permission from The Ohio State University's Teaching for Black Student Retention and Multicultural Teaching Programs.

APPENDIX 8.2

A Sample Self-Assessment Exercise on Teaching Underrepresented Student Populations

Instructions: Circle the response that best describes your behavior. This inventory will not be "scored." It merely serves as a starting point for discussion.

In teaching, advising, or interacting with students, do you find yourself ...

	Usually	Sometimes	Rarely	Never
1) Wondering if a student of color plagiarized when he or she turns in a well-written paper	a	b	c	d
2) Thinking that gay, lesbian, and bisexual students are identifiable by certain mannerisms or physical characteristics	a	b	c	d
3) Requesting verification from students who tell you that they have a learning disability	a	b	c	d
4) Treating all students the same	a	b	c	d
5) Having lower expectations for students of color	a	b	c	d
6) Trying to relate course work and research to a student's life situation	a	b	c	d
7) Transforming course content by using examples and material that are inclusive so as to represent diverse perspectives	a	b	c	d
8) Calling on male students more than female students	a	b	c	d
9) Consciously or unconsciously choosing males to be team or lab leaders	a	b	c	d
10) Wondering why all students of color sit together in class	a	b	c	d
11) Being sensitive to the needs of adult learners	a	b	c	d
12) Finding yourself surprised when a student of color performs well in your class	a	b	c	d
13) Expecting more from Asian American students than from other minority students	a	b	c	d

	Usually	Sometimes	Rarely	Never
14) Wishing that older students wouldn't talk about their life experiences so much	a	b	c	d
15) Feeling uncomfortable talking about sensitive issues in class	a	b	c	d
16) Trying to find out what special needs and abilities your students have	a	b	c	d
17) Nominating students of color for awards and fellowships	a	b	c	d
18) Interrupting or calling on women and students of color	a	b	c	d
19) Getting irritated when a student of color shows up at your office without an appointment	a	b	c	d
20) Expecting women to have math anxiety	a	b	c	d
21) Being insensitive to the fact that students labeled "Hispanic" frequently prefer a more specific designation (i.e., Puerto Rican, Mexican) based on their family origins	a	b	c	d
22) Making an extra effort to include reticent students in class discussions	a	b	c	d
23) Relying on past test scores as sole predictors on how a student will perform	a	b	c	d
24) Varying your teaching strategies to meet students' learning styles	a	b	c	d
25) Challenging your assumptions about the performance and expectations of your students	a	b	c	d

This self-assessment has been adapted with permission from The Ohio State University's Teaching for Black Student Retention Program.

19

Methods for Addressing Diversity in the Classroom

Lee Warren

Since the 1970s, the student population at many colleges and universities has changed dramatically. Once mostly white, middle class, sometimes only male, one can now find people of every color, class, and gender in higher education. Walking around campus, there is variety of every sort, everywhere.

At the same time, institutional structures, faculty, and staff have not always kept pace with the changes in student populations. Many faculty members are bewildered by the astonishing array in their classrooms and choose to proceed as if nothing has changed. These faculty teach the same material in the same ways and criticize students for being unable to keep up. Others are confused but are trying to adapt to the new populations. Still others have been working with the change all along, have welcomed the diversity, and have been making wonderfully innovative changes in their content and pedagogy.

The task for faculty developers is to find ways to address diversity issues in the classroom so that faculty who need help can learn without retreating into defensive postures. While it is true that more often than not we preach to the converted in workshops on diversity, it is difficult to get the diehards into the room. It is also true that more and more confused faculty members come to such workshops, and the converted often gain important new insights and teaching techniques.

This chapter addresses three methods that I have used to open discussions about diversity. These approaches are designed to minimize the defensiveness that can so easily arise. These approaches are as follows:

- Written and videotaped cases, used to discuss race and gender issues

- Case-in-point experiential teaching/learning, which can be used to address any diversity issue
- A workshop designed to address class issues

WRITTEN AND VIDEOTAPED CASES

When addressing issues of race and gender with faculty, I most often turn to cases. There are many available, and the method is both provocative and relatively safe. I use cases (as opposed to giving lectures or presenting Ten Easy Tips on the subject) because this method involves participants in finding their own insights and solutions to the problems raised. They can then make these insights and solutions appropriate to their own context, teaching, and personality styles, not to mention their own stages of readiness or development. Therefore, I do not come into these workshops with the answers, a strategy particularly inappropriate to these topics, but rather with the questions. The case discussion becomes the property of the participants, and we discuss the issues at their level and from their experience. The defensiveness that is easily called forth when an outsider comes in to give the answers, or simply when the topic is race or gender, is thus obviated.

My goals in using cases are twofold: 1) to increase participants' awareness and understanding of classroom dynamics, and 2) to increase the number of strategies they have available for use in their own classrooms. In using cases, one always starts with the story as given.

We first discuss at length what exactly is going on in the classroom portrayed: who the players are, what the teaching strategy is, what the teacher-student and student-student dynamics are, and whether or how race or gender is affecting either the content or the process of the discussion. I want people to see and understand more about how race and gender affect classroom interactions, to be able to name dynamics as they occur. Inevitably, discussion will include stories from participants' own classrooms, as well as the material in the case.

After some time spent on analysis, we move to action questions such as, "If you were the teacher in this classroom and this event occurred, what would you do now?" We brainstorm strategies, question and critique them, and work toward a range of possibilities for this particular case. People talk from their own experience and explore new possibilities.

Case discussions are always astonishingly varied. People see things in the cases and come up with suggestions that are endlessly surprising, to each other and to the facilitator. No one person sees all the possibilities in a well-put-together case. One of the advantages of these discussions is to see how limited one's own perceptions and assumptions are and thus to become more open to others' views. Consequently, one of the results is to walk away with an enhanced range of interpretive views and action strategies.

One videotaped case, for example, features an Asian woman who is silent during an active classroom discussion. The teacher ponders whether to call on her but decides not to because "all Asian women are like that. That's just the way they're brought up." When participants in a recent discussion of the case were asked why she is quiet, they quickly came to a number of conclusions: she is bored, physically out of the circle, sick, had a fight with her boyfriend or her mother is dying, has not done the homework, does not speak English well, is offended by the comments of the other students, or has been culturally conditioned not to speak in groups. Many participants were certain, at first, that their interpretation was correct and were astonished to see how many other views of the case there were. This, in fact, is part of the lesson: We cannot make assumptions about students; we need to ask. The range of opinions was equally varied when participants thought about whether she should be asked to speak and, if so, how the teacher might go about doing so.

Videotaped cases work well for several reasons. One is the powerful immediacy of film: participants see and hear the story unfold and are quickly drawn into the tensions and passions of the story. They are also useful when participants have not had a chance to read a case in advance. There are, of course, some written cases short enough to use on such occasions, but usually a video is easier. With this in mind, our center has produced two videotaped collections of cases: *Race in the Classroom* and *Women in the Classroom*. Each tape contains five short classroom vignettes which are used to trigger discussion. Many videotapes on the subject of race or gender, we found, were too simplistic and proposed too easy answers. Our tapes, while short, are deliberately complex, as are good written cases. A number of other good videotapes, from other universities, are also available such as *Inequity in the Classroom* (1991) from Concordia University and

Teaching in the Diverse Classroom (1991) from the University of Washington.

Many written cases on diversity topics are available, too. Harvard has developed several which I enjoy using because of their richness and complexity. They are collected in *Teaching and the Case Method* (Barnes, Christensen, & Hansen, 1994). William Welty and Rita Silverman (1993) at Pace University in New York have also developed an entire collection of teaching cases and, with the American Association of Higher Education, run yearly conferences to discuss using cases.

CASE-IN-POINT EXPERIENTIAL LEARNING

Another form of the case method that can be used for addressing issues of diversity is the case-in-point experiential method. In this instance, one uses the class itself—its members and its interactions—as the case. The facilitator constantly watches for dynamics that illustrate some aspect of race, gender, or class (or whatever other topic might be the subject of the meeting) and also thinks of ways to use these dynamics as productive cases for discussion. The cases can focus on dynamics among the participants or between participants and the facilitator. Everyone's behavior is subject to analysis and can be used for learning.

Of the three methods addressed in this chapter, this approach is the most risky but has the greatest learning potential. The learning comes from an intensive assessment of what just occurred. Over time, participants also become able to spot cases and to initiate the case-in-point discussion. Their ability to spot the cases, name and interpret them, and work them productively is one sign of their learning.

For example, in a session on diversity in the classroom, one might begin by simply asking participants what they notice in the room. During the session, inevitably a number of behaviors will illustrate the topic: Men may talk more frequently or at greater length than women, whites may dominate the discussion, whites may back off and become silent once their domination is noted, people of color may enter the discussion with an attack, middle class people may be bewildered at the kinds of things said about class by lower class people.

Any of these behaviors may be productively discussed and used as both starting point and demonstration of the points being made. An enormous amount of learning could occur, for example, if, after trying to have such a discussion, people analyzed what happens when whites and people of color try to talk about race together. Using the group's own behavior as the text or case means that the learning can be immediate and intensely personal. People see how they have behaved, thought, or felt in the situation and can use that as a way to explore both their own position and the complexities of such interactions.

People learn from this kind of discussion at many levels. Learning is intense, personal, emotional, and intellectual. It is also profoundly individual in that people learn very different things in these sessions depending upon what they need to learn and are capable of learning at the moment. Individuals are able to process such discussions at widely varying levels and with widely varying insights.

Leading these discussions, however, is difficult. Facilitators must be on the alert for developing cases, must find ways to introduce them that will enable learning to occur, must be willing and able to be the target of the discussion themselves, and must be able to contain the strength and range of emotions that are likely to arise. They must also be able to keep the conversation focused on what is happening in the room, on the here and now, and on the specific. Groups often like to avoid the hard work of such discussions by talking about what has happened elsewhere and by becoming abstract and general. Outside references and stories can sometimes be quite useful to further illustrate what is occurring in the room, but they are an easy distraction and are usually presented so generally that the group cannot make good use of them for specific insights.

Leading such discussions sometimes feels like riding a wildly careening bronco. But the ride is worth it. Learning can be so deep and so transformational that people's lives are changed by the experience.

CLASS IN THE CLASSROOM WORKSHOP

Several years ago my colleague, Peter Martynowych, and I developed a workshop on the issue of class in the classroom, which is the diversity issue least addressed. It is an often invisible form of difference, and many academics pretend it does not exist. When submitting this workshop as a proposal to an academic conference, for example, one reviewer rejected it, wondering whether the social class diversity among conference participants was enough to make the process worthwhile. To my mind, this comment was the most persuasive argument I could think of for offering the workshop at that conference.

I should say at the same time that faculty at some schools talk about and teach to issues of class all the time. Generally, these faculty members teach at schools that target working class adults, and many community and state colleges fall into this category. Interestingly, my impression is that institutions that attract working class people of the usual student age are less likely to address class directly through their course content and pedagogy than are those attracting working adults.

This workshop is more personal than case discussions and less risky than the case-in-point method. I like to use it in part because I do not know of any cases about class, but even more because it is a good way to raise consciousness about a factor in our lives that is pervasive, powerful, and rarely articulated.

Workshop Goals and Structure

Part one. In the first part, our purpose is to increase participants' self-awareness of class. We start by asking them to divide themselves by class into three groups: lower class, middle class, and upper middle/upper class. This task is in itself the cause of considerable debate, and such questions as the following arise:

- What is class?

- Where are the divisions?

- What do these names mean (e.g., lower class, working class, blue collar, working poor, poverty class)?

- How does one know what class one belongs to?

- Should we think about our families of origin or our current status?

- What if our families changed class as we grew up?

- I lived on a farm and we always had enough money; what class do I belong to?

- My parents were highly educated but never made a lot of money; which class do I belong to?

- We were actually quite wealthy, but continued to live in our old blue collar neighborhood. What is my class?

We then further divide people into groups of three or four and ask them to talk about the advantages and disadvantages of their class background to their college education. We chose this question because it makes the point that there are positives and negatives to every class position. The upper classes obviously have notable advantages, but there are also disadvantages attached to those classes, and the lower classes have significant advantages as well.

At this point the room erupts into sound. It is very difficult to persuade participants, after some time, to come back to the whole group. Many people say that this is the first time they have ever talked about these things and that it opens a floodgate for them.

Part two. In the second part, we bring participants back to the whole group and ask them to report the advantages and disadvantages each class brought to their learning experiences. Our purpose is to increase people's imaginative understanding of class experiences other than their own.

We produce their lists on poster paper and hang them on the walls for all to keep in mind as the workshop continues. When the workshop time period is long enough, we encourage groups to ask questions of each other, to clarify meanings, and to clear up misunderstandings. Discussion at this point is sometimes quite heated, as people express old hurts or current political stances.

Part three. In the third part we turn to the practical. Our goals here are to turn from our awareness to our pedagogy and to give people something concrete to leave with. We again ask participants to form groups of three or four, but this time of mixed class. Their task is to discuss changes they would make to address the class differences among their students, based on the findings of the previous exercise. Specifically, they should think about pedagogy, course content, curriculum, and the institutional setting. Depending on the length of the workshop, we either have each group address all of these dimensions or, in a briefer period, pick one and come up with two suggestions for things they would do differently. Again, we reconvene the group and share insights, thus providing participants with a number of potential strategies.

Findings

What we discover in these workshops is worth discussing, even if only briefly, because so little is written about the topic of class as a diversity issue. I have found only a few articles and two books about the experience of working class academics (Barney Dews, & Leste Law, 1995; Ryan & Sackrey, 1984). Others are surely around, but they are difficult to find, and while there are occasional articles about the class experiences of students, as far as I know they have not yet been anthologized.

Our findings are poignant, eye-opening, and provocative. Lower class people talk about the difficulties of making their way in dominantly middle class academic institutions. They talk about feeling as if they have no right to be there, do not know the rules or the system and often do not know whom or how to ask, and do not have the right language. They are afraid of being found out and become silent about their background. They have a poor educational background and so are behind academically, lack access to assumed opportunities, feel a lot of pressure to avoid failing, and at the same time have less time for academic work because of the need to earn money. They also talk about the difficulties of going home, where they no longer fit in socially, and about the difficulties of fitting in socially with students of other classes, who have more money and more social sophistication.

Yet they also talk with pride of the experiences and strengths of their class background. They are focused, goal-oriented, and motivated; they have a good work ethic, strength of character, and a strong sense of possibility; they know the value of an education, are able to communicate with others, and show both courage and a willingness to take risks. They understand diversity, appreciate what they have, and are proud of being able to both work and study. They are tuned to collaboration and group-building.

Middle class people say they feel protected and thus both naive and confident. They assume higher education will be available to them and value it, work hard, and count on their parents' steadiness and skills behind them. They are confident and believe they will succeed no matter what. Moreover, they are disciplined, hard-working, resilient, and at home in the world of ideas. They also feel a responsibility to contribute.

At the same time, some feel their sense of security is tenuous and that the need to earn money is both an advantage and a disadvantage. They feel academically behind in some areas, and some sense that they do not know how to network or play the game on the big stage.

Upper class people are quite clear, and often embarrassed, about their advantages: They feel they have a voice, know how to work the system, have good academic and social preparation for the academy, assume their higher education, and have a safety net, which enables them to take risks. They have a sense of infinite possibility and freedom to be themselves; parental support; no fear of authority; infinite possibility; choices of career and colleges; and exposure to the world of travel, education, and art. They value success, community responsibility, hard work, and excellence.

Not surprisingly, it is more difficult for them to name disadvantages. They talk about a limited perspective that leaves them insensitive to others' issues and perspectives and a difficulty in communicating and socializing with other classes. They take their privileges for granted. They did not choose their education, but rather they were doing what was expected of them. They experience race and gender as continuing barriers (they were the only group that mentioned race and gender). And, like the lower classes, they feel they have to be careful about their class background: Fearing that they will be "found out," they hide their social identity.

Practical Suggestions

In the third part of the workshop, participants have come up with a large number of suggestions for making the academy more open to everyone, and this continues to be a rich field for discussion at each workshop.

For the curriculum, they have suggested including issues about class diversity in the core curriculum and in majors, opening the canon to people of lower classes, creating learning agreements, and building in experiential and service-learning.

In terms of pedagogy, they have suggested that instructors do the following:

- Talk with students before class begins in order to be able to start where they are

- Discuss class backgrounds in class, explicitly look for class-based perspectives on the material

- Help students see and understand others' perspectives and recognize factions in the classroom

- Encourage personal reactions to the material and build on them

Since students come from many classes, faculty should:

- Make group norms explicit and explain the system at the beginning of the term
- Use multiple learning strategies
- Stress active learning
- Develop study groups and other forms of collaborative learning
- Check automatic interpretations based on one's own class background and note value-laden language
- Be sensitive to the difficulties and pain of individual students
- Model acceptance of various classes as a way to foster growth among their students

In institutional terms, participants have suggested some college-wide discussions about what it means to be educated as well as about the purpose of the institution and the values it embodies and promotes. They talk about developing better student support systems, safety nets, and specific strategies for welcoming students of lower classes. They point out that institutions need to find ways to motivate and reward change if they want faculty to change. And the whole institution needs to adjust its attitudes to create increased collegiality and community.

Explanations

Not surprisingly, lower class students have a harder time in institutions of higher learning—academically, socially, personally, and systemically. Their difficulties are often neither recognized nor addressed; the academy is largely oriented toward the middle and upper middle classes in values and expectations. At the same time, however, these students have the strengths of motivation, hard work, and an appreciation of education, also often unrecognized.

Class seems to be most noticed by those at each extreme and remains to a large extent invisible to the middle. This is consistent with the usual patterns in which privilege and difference are often unseen by those in the dominant position: Men often do not see the privileges they have that women do not; whites often do not see the privileges they have compared to people of color. This holds true with regard to class: Those most aware of class are lower class people. Many in the middle class simply assume the system and the modes of discourse within it as a given, and they do not see how class-based they are, nor how privileged they are within the system. This blindness is shared by students, faculty, and staff at most colleges and universities and is part of what makes it so difficult for lower class students to find their way.

While upper class people certainly have the edge on privilege, they, or at least those who attend these workshops, are often embarrassed and defensive about their social position. Their embarrassment is typical of the advantaged, whether it be race, class, or gender, when in dialogue with others less advantaged. It is important to recognize that class distinctions are difficult for everyone in this country. Our national belief is that we are a classless society and that class should not matter, but class is evident everywhere and matters immensely. The disjunction between our held belief and reality makes this a difficult area to understand and accept. We need to be sensitive to the embarrassment in this context of the most privileged, as well as to the more easily recognized difficulties of the least privileged.

Class is rarely discussed, particularly in groups of mixed class. Hence, the participants' reactions to the activities in this workshop. Lower class people, those who have been most aware of class all along, are thrilled to have the chance to address the issue out loud—to talk about their experience, to find confirmation from others, to explore differences as well as similarities in their experience. The middle- and upper-middle class people have more difficulty addressing the issues. The middle class people have to struggle more to see how their class background has affected their education. Upper class people have to struggle with their embarrassment about their privileges in order to articulate their advantages.

Talking about these issues together has been and continues to be an interesting and often exhilarating experience. The tensions and triumphs that arise are not surprising as people struggle to relate to each other on an explicitly class-based basis. This is difficult work, but critical to the creation of an academic environment open to all its members.

While class is largely invisible, especially by comparison to race and gender, it is not entirely so, and the signals lead to what is part of the problem. Students' class backgrounds are often identified by their accent, their choice of words, their clothing, the examples they use in discussion, their levels of preparation, their levels of confidence, and even their silence or ease in participation. Most instructors react to these signals unconsciously, but strongly, favoring one group or the other. One of the purposes of this workshop is to make these signals and our reactions to them more conscious, thus giving us greater choice in how we work with groups of students.

CONCLUSION

There are, of course, other methods for addressing issues of faculty development in relation to the diversity issues critically important in higher education today. The three explained above—cases, case-in-point experiences, and the class workshop—have a number of qualities in common which I would look for when designing a workshop or any other kind of activity on this topic.

- They are based on an active learning model.
- They involve experiential learning.
- They all use stories as a basis for learning.
- They permit people to learn at their own pace, to learn what they need to learn or are capable of learning at that time.
- Their pedagogy is inductive: People move from the particular experience to the general.
- They are bottom-up in design, rather than top-down (grassroots design).
- The facilitator comes to the session with questions, issues, and facilitation skills, but not with the answers.
- The learning is multifaceted: personal, experiential, emotional, intellectual, ethical, and practical.

For all of these reasons, workshops of this sort are particularly useful for the discussion of diversity. They are designed for topics of great complexity; one hopes to help people not only see more clearly, but also learn new strategies for behavior. These are pedagogies designed to create change, both personal and systemic.

REFERENCES

Barnes, L. B., Christensen, C. R., & Hansen, A. (1994). *Teaching and the case method.* Boston, MA: Harvard Business School Press.

Barney Dews, C.L., & Leste Law, C. (Eds.). (1995). *This fine place so far from home: Voices of academics from the working class.* Philadelphia, PA: Temple University Press.

Derek Bok Center (Producer). (1992). *Race in the classroom: A multiplicity of experience* [videotape]. Cambridge, MA: The Derek Bok Center, Harvard University. Distributed by Anker Publishing.

Derek Bok Center (Producer). (1996). *Women in the classroom: Cases for reflection* [videotape]. Cambridge, MA: The Derek Bok Center, Harvard University. Distributed by Anker Publishing.

Office on the Status of Women (Producer). (1991). *Inequity in the Classroom* [videotape]. West Montreal, Quebec, Canada: Office on the Status of Women, Concordia University.

Quigley, B. (Producer), & Nyquist, J. (Executive Producer). (1991). *Teaching in the Diverse Classroom* [videotape]. Seattle, WA: Center for Instructional Development and Research. Distributed by Anker Publishing.

Ryan, J., & Sackrey, C. (Eds.). (1984). *Paradise: Academics from the working class.* Boston, MA: South End Press.

Welty, W., & Silverman, R. (1993). *Using cases to improve college teaching: A guide to more reflective practice.* Washington, DC: American Association for Higher Education.

Lee Warren is Associate Director of the Derek Bok Center for Teaching and Learning at Harvard University. In addition to faculty and TA development, her interests focus on race and gender issues in the classroom, case teaching, and leadership training. She has been involved with faculty development and POD for ten years.

Email: lawarren@fas.harvard.edu

20

What We Value, We Talk About: Including Lesbian, Gay, Bisexual, and Transgender People

Christine Imbra and Helen Rallis

As colleges and universities confront the challenge of making institutions inclusive, it is crucial that we recognize the full breadth and value of diversity on our campuses. Our knowledge and awareness of many different groups have been greatly increased by the growing body of literature on racial and cultural diversity. However, all too often lesbian, gay, bisexual, and transgender (LGBT) people are left out of this diversity equation and thus left out of faculty development efforts aimed at creating inclusive campus environments.

The purpose of this chapter is to provide faculty developers with an understanding of how they can help faculty include LGBT people—their issues and cultures—in curriculum and institutional life. We do this by first placing LGBT issues in the context of the larger framework of diversity issues because we believe that successful inclusion of any group should be part of a campus-wide commitment to diversity, rather than through a piecemeal, group-by-group approach. The goal is to have faculty and administrators learn to integrate the ideas and information on LGBT issues as part of a their overall efforts of valuing diversity. Doing so requires reexamining our teaching philosophies, methods, and content to understand how these can unwittingly perpetuate dominant culture privilege at the expense of those who are not part of the dominant culture.

In order for faculty to be willing to learn how to be specifically and deliberately inclusive of different groups in their classes, they need to believe that doing so is important. We begin, therefore, by showing the importance of the role faculty play in shaping students' attitudes about diversity. Against this background we then provide information and ideas for faculty developers to use in guiding faculty and administrators to include LGBT issues on their campuses.

BACKGROUND

Across the country there are increasing efforts by faculty developers to teach faculty the importance of recognizing the diversity among students. Teaching in ways that incorporate differences among students is not about making exceptions or fragmenting the curriculum to pander to special interests. Rather, it is about recognizing people as individuals who learn in multiple ways and bring with them an extensive culture and background that influences the way they learn and the way they perceive the world.

If our goal as teachers is to teach all students, then it is critical that we teach in ways that enable all students to succeed. A common fear and misconception about teaching with multicultural perspectives is that standards will be lowered. We can still pursue academic excellence as the ultimate goal, but recognizing and encouraging multiple ways to achieve this goal enables more students to accomplish at their highest level. To illustrate, there has been an increasing recognition of the value of cooperative learning strategies—what once might have been called cheating is now recognized as cooperative team learning.

Being inclusive is not only about how we teach, it is also about what we teach. Our choice of course content and the examples we use to illustrate concepts reflect the values we hold and the groups we recognize as being important. Some faculty react defensively to this argument. They may deny that their teaching and/or curriculum is biased in favor of the dominant culture. This may be because they fail to recognize the extent to which traditional teaching methods and content draw from the dominant culture. For example, faculty have claimed that they are not racist even when they acknowledge that their curriculum reflects primarily white examples. They defend this by saying that it is about time, not prejudice—that they don't have time to include examples from different races or cultures. They say the race, gender, or culture of people is not important, but rather the contribution of that person. Nieto (1992) notes another common misconception: the belief that teaching in multicultural ways is only needed if one is teaching students of color.

What these perceptions fail to recognize is the socially constructed power of dominant culture privilege. Teaching in inclusive ways provides a model for all students, not just for those who share similar characteristics with the group or individual addressed. It shows by example the value of difference and also creates an awareness among all aspects of dominant culture privilege. These differences do not seem important if you are a member of the dominant culture and if you have not experienced the pain of systematic isolation, invisibility, or overt discrimination that comes with being a member of a minority or marginalized group. When you belong to such a group, however, having this difference recognized and valued can become extremely important.

Teachers—whether in public schools, colleges, or universities—play a vital role in building students' self esteem. We influence students' knowledge, understanding, and the value they place on people who are different from them. In a story describing her experiences as a white teacher in a multiracial, multicultural school, Vivian Paley (1979) provides us with important insights into the power teachers have. She describes how her reactions to children greatly influenced how children felt about themselves.

> As I watched and reacted to black children, I came to see a common need in every child. Anything a child feels is different about himself which cannot be referred to spontaneously, casually, naturally and uncritically by the teacher can become a cause for anxiety and an obstacle to learning. (Paley, 1979, preface)

Recounting a lesson she learned from Mrs. Hawkins, the parent of one of her students, Paley illustrates the fallacy in the ethnocentric assumption that we should treat students equally, as if they are all the same:

> Mrs. Hawkins told me that in her children's previous school the teacher had said, "There is no color difference in my classroom. All my children look alike to me."
>
> "What rot" said Mrs. Hawkins. "My children are black. They don't look like your children. They know that they are black, and we want it recognized. It's a positive difference, an interesting difference, and a comfortable natural difference. At least it could be so, if you teachers learned to value differences more. What you value, you talk about." (Paley, 1979, p.12)

In the above extracts, Paley's examples are about working with African American children, but her point is true for any person, regardless of age, who is in some way different to the dominant culture. Thus, we could revise her example and substitute any group here:

...this student is not like other students. S/he knows s/he is gay/deaf/biracial/older-than-average age and wants it to be recognized. It is a positive difference, an interesting difference, and a comfortable, natural difference. At least it could be so if colleges and universities learned to value differences more. What they value, they talk about and integrate into all aspects of formal and non-formal campus life...

The image we all have of ourselves is influenced to varying degrees by the way others treat us. This influence is felt most strongly in our formative years, but continues into adulthood. Thus, working with students at the college level plays a role in the image they are constructing of themselves. Our verbal and nonverbal feedback in all interactions sends messages about how we view them. As Mrs. Hawkins notes, whether or not we intend this to happen, what we talk about—in class, in informal conversations, or in any setting where we interact with people—sends a powerful message about what we value. And equally powerfully, our failure to mention certain issues or people speaks volumes about what and who we consider unimportant.

Although Paley and Hawkins were talking about young children, this need to belong, to be recognized, to have your background and experiences not only accepted but seen as important to who you are is a common human need. Different people have different levels of need for recognition, and each person places different emphasis on what aspects of their personal background are important to them. Thus, as teachers we should not presume that because someone is from a particular group, they necessarily see this as an important part of who they are. Conversely, however, we should not presume to discount this necessarily as unimportant.

This uncertainty about how to respond to and value differences is intimidating to faculty, especially if they lack the background knowledge about the many differences students bring to their classes. It often feels like a Catch 22—where no matter what you do, you will offend someone. A natural response is to avoid any mention of difference, and this is the least offensive option. But the effect of this is to further perpetuate and entrench the status quo and the persistence of dominant cultural norms and privilege.

BREAKING THE SILENCE

The following describes the role of faculty developers and provides suggestions for ways in which they can help faculty and administrators understand and incorporate LGBT issues into curriculum and institutional life:

- Raise awareness among faculty and administrators of the need to include LGBT issues within campus-wide diversity training efforts

- Coordinate workshops on LGBT issues, preferably as part of ongoing education, to create an inclusive campus environment

- Collect resources and reference materials, as part of the campus instructional development library, on LGBT issues in the classroom and work environment

- Provide follow-up discussion groups and one-on-one consultation with faculty, helping them integrate what they have learned into their classrooms

- Integrate LGBT and other diversity issues on an ongoing basis in all faculty development efforts, modeling for others the concept of education that is multicultural and inclusive.

The appendices provide resources and handouts for possible workshop activities and can be used by faculty, administrators, counselors, staff, and students. The items can be used as reference materials or as part of a workshop. Most of the ideas presented are best introduced in half-day workshops or in a number of sessions in a workshop series that addresses the broader issues of creating inclusive college campus environments. Not all activities described in the following section need to be included, nor do they have to be presented in the order in which they appear. It is best to pick and choose material based on the level of experience of the workshop participants and expertise of the presenters. On our campus these workshops have been coordinated by our Instructional Development Service, but facilitated by LGBT faculty, staff, and outside resource people.

SUGGESTIONS FOR WORKSHOP CONTENT

Workshops, or any kind of session, need to be tailored to the specific audience and context. We offer the following as suggestions for content topics that have worked well in our setting.

Understanding Vocabulary, Language, and Concepts Used by and about the LGBT Community
(*Breaking the Silence, 1993*)

This handout of definitions is a valuable reference sheet and can be used at the start of a workshop to introduce participants to commonly used terminology (Appendix 20.1).

Symbols of Pride for the LGBT Community
(*Breaking the Silence, 1993*)

This handout provides workshop participants with an understanding of the history behind some of the symbols commonly found in the LGBT community (Appendix 20.2).

What Do You Know About Gay/Lesbian Lifestyles?
(*O'Bear, 1989*)

This survey is a valuable tool for raising the awareness of workshop participants about some of the myths surrounding the LGBT community. It stimulates people to explore their own preconceived notions about LGBT people and helps them become more aware of differences between reality and stereotypes or myths (Appendix 20.3).

Supportive Data for Responses to the Survey
(*O'Bear, 1989*)

Once participants have completed the survey on what they know about gay/lesbian lifestyles, the workshop facilitator can then follow up by explaining the myths surrounding LGBT issues (Appendix 20.4).

The Heterosexual Questionnaire

This questionnaire may be used at the start of a workshop or following the survey of what people know about gay/lesbian lifestyles. It is also an effective icebreaker. Tell participants that for the purpose of this exercise they should assume they are heterosexual. Hand out the questions and have participants reflect for a few minutes on their responses to each question. Then have people divide into small groups and share their reactions to the questions with others in their group. Finally, as a large group, share reactions, questions, and comments. These can be recorded on a flip chart for reference later in the workshop or in subsequent workshops (Appendix 20.5).

Klein Sexual Orientation Grid
(Klein, Sepekoff, & Wolf, 1985)

Instruct workshop participants to use the scale to rate themselves on each of the different variables that define sexual orientation. Follow this with a discussion of each of the variables and how they help us understand the complexity of human sexuality. Invite participants to share their reactions, especially as they compare each variable in terms of past, present, and ideal ratings (Appendix 20.6).

Examining Homophobic Attitudes and Positive Attitudes Toward LGBT People

We suggest first having participants work in pairs or small groups with three steps for this activity.

1) Each group should discuss situations they have experienced or observed where the issue of sexual orientation arose. Have someone in the group record a summary of the situation in the form of a vignette on an overhead transparency or poster paper. Encourage groups to come up with a variety of situations showing varying attitudes, both positive and negative, towards LGBT people. Put these aside until after the next step of this activity.

2) Explain each level of the Riddle Homophobia Scale (O'Bear, 1989) (Appendix 20.7).

3) Have groups exchange the vignettes that they wrote and analyze the situations using the Riddle Scale. Participants should try to identify the level of the person (or people) in the vignette as reflected in their attitude toward LGBT people.

4) As a large group, put up each transparency or poster and share the analyses of each. Use this discussion as a means of

showing how people operate at different stages at different times. Generate ideas on what can be done in each vignette to move the person/people to a more positive level. An important point to emphasize through this activity is the need to recognize at what level people are functioning if we are to help them develop a more positive attitude.

Panel of LGBT Speakers

Invite LGBT people, preferably students, faculty, administrators, and staff from the campus, to share their stories about being lesbian, gay, bisexual, or transgendered. Follow this with questions from workshop participants. (In the workshops we have conducted, this has been one of the activities most highly valued by participants.)

Case Study Analyses

Using sample case studies provided by participants and facilitators, or stories shared by panel speakers, have participants analyze the case(s) in groups. A useful framework is to identify the primary issues, problems, and perspectives on the problems and then generate possible solutions. Different groups can analyze different cases or all groups can analyze the same case, and then share or compare their findings.

Suggestions for Those Working with LGBT Individuals (PFLAG)

At the end of the workshop or workshop series, it is important to devote time to providing people with concrete, specific ways in which they can use what they have learned. Begin with the handout of suggestions and then have people brainstorm other ideas, in particular those they can take and use in their own work contexts. If there are sufficient numbers of people, it may be helpful to group them according to job descriptions. Conclude with a large group summary and discussion of all ideas (Appendix 20.8).

Connect LGBT Issues and Community to Campus-Wide Conversation on Education about and for Diversity

The workshop facilitator should include a discussion of the importance of incorporating this new understanding of LGBT issues into the larger context of an institution that is striving to be inclusive of all diversity. This may be done by sharing the introductory discussion presented at the start of this chapter. Specific and directly useful examples are usually generated if participants work in pairs or small groups.

All should share an overview of a course they teach or their job responsibilities, giving examples of ways in which they bring in names of people, reference to society, or social institutions—any ways in which people are mentioned in the course of their work. With a partner or other group members they can brainstorm specific ways in which their terminology, content, and perspectives can be made more inclusive.

This activity is particularly valuable if participants bring in hard copies of syllabi, course materials, textbooks, readings, university brochures, campus housing information, policy manuals—any materials that refer to people. It may help if the facilitator models a few examples, inviting the group as a whole to analyze the inclusiveness of something as simple as a brochure advertising clothing and supplies from the university bookstore. Other examples include cartoons, clothing catalogs, and greeting cards. These provide powerful visuals and conversation starters, and help participants make the connection within their own work context.

As Paley (1979) stated in her book about teaching children from different races and cultures, it is critical that people understand the importance of talking about LGBT people spontaneously, casually, naturally, and uncritically. The power of breaking the silence by including the LGBT community in the everyday flow of curriculum, classroom conversation, and campus life in general, can be enormous, not only in helping LGBT people, their friends, and their families to feel a part of the campus, but also in teaching all people to accept and value the full spectrum of diversity.

Provide Ongoing Support

This will enable workshop participants to receive support and guidance as they work to integrate what they have learned into their work environment. During these meetings, the faculty developer should connect back to activities from the workshops, particularly those that guided participants in making their conversations and work context more inclusive. People should be encouraged to share examples they have tried in using more inclusive language and in creating materials that demonstrate inclusivity. Faculty developers can collect examples of these to use in future workshops and to publish in campus instructional development newsletters. These can also be shared with the institutions' public relations people so they can integrate them as they update handbooks, brochures, and other information about campus life.

As stated earlier, this is not an exhaustive list of activities, merely a starting point for faculty developers as you begin your journey in providing full inclusion of the LGBT community into training seminars and workshops. We encourage and challenge you to expand this list by developing and designing other activities for use on your campuses. We have also provided a short list of resources to assist you in further inquiry into LGBT issues.

CONCLUSION

It seemed only fitting that three years ago one of our faculty developers was awarded a coveted University of Minnesota teaching award for outstanding contributions to undergraduate education, even though she does not presently teach undergraduate students. This award recognized not only the outstanding efforts of an individual faculty developer, but by extension the whole field of faculty development.

Although faculty developers may not always be involved in face-to face teaching of students, through work with individual and groups of faculty members, the impact of faculty developers on students can be far greater than that of any other single teacher on our campuses. As teachers of teachers, faculty developers plant the seeds of instructional and organizational development and greatly influence the extent and direction in which these grow. Certainly instructional change can and does occur without the support of faculty developers, but the extent of acceptance of this change and the skill with which it is implemented can be considerably enhanced through your direct and active support.

It takes courage to speak out, to break the oppressive silence surrounding lesbian, gay, bisexual, and transgender people at our institutions. As instructional and organizational leaders, faculty developers can make a big difference in creating educational environments that celebrate all diversity and thus move us toward our ultimate goal of having every student be successful. This chapter is a contribution toward making this possible.

REFERENCES

Breaking the silence. (1993, November 1). Final report of the select committee on lesbian, gay, and bisexual concerns. Minneapolis, MN: University of Minnesota.

Klein, F., Sepekoff, B., & Wolf, T. (1985). Sexual orientation: A multi-variable dynamic process. *Journal of Homosexuality, 11* (1/2), 35-49.

Nieto, S. (1992). *Affirming diversity: The sociopolitical context of multicultural education.* New York, NY: Longman.

O'Bear, K. (1989, March). *Opening doors to understanding and acceptance: Facilitating workshops on lesbian, gay and bisexual issues.* Materials presented at the ACPA meeting, Washington, DC.

Paley, V. G. (1979). *White teacher.* Cambridge, MA: Harvard University Press.

RESOURCES

The following is a short list of national LGBT resources. Many other organizations that address LGBT issues exist and can be accessed through the World Wide Web by using word or organization searches, or by visiting your institutional library's reference section.

And Justice For All
P.O. Box 53079
Washington, DC 20009
202-298-9362

Human Rights Campaign
1101 14th Street NW
Washington, DC 20005
202-628-4160
http://www.hrcusa.org/

Lambda Legal Defense and Education Fund, Inc.
666 Broadway, Suite 1200
New York, NY 10012
212-995-8585

National Gay and Lesbian Task Force
2320 17th Street NW
Washington, DC 20009-2702
202-332-6483
http://www.ngltf.org/

People for the American Way
2000 M. Street NW
Washington, DC 20036
202-467-2388

People United to End Homophobia
P.O. Box 60881
Phoenix, AZ 85082-0881
602-351-3080

PFLAG (Parents and Friends of Lesbians and Gays)
1101 14th Street NW, Suite 1030
Washington, DC 20005
202-638-4200
info@pflag.org (email address)
http://www.pflag.org (web address)

Helen Rallis is an Associate Professor of Education at the University of Minnesota, Duluth. She teaches undergraduate and graduate courses in secondary, elementary, and special education and in educational technology. Her research and teaching interests include teaching methodology, multicultural and social studies education, and educational technology.

Christine Imbra is a doctoral student at the University of Minnesota in the Department of Educational Policy and Administration. Her emphases are leadership and higher education. Ms. Imbra's research interests include leadership, lesbians in the academy, moral development, and systemic oppression.

Email: hralis@d.umn.edu

APPENDIX 20.1
DEFINITIONS

The following handout provides a vocabulary of words and concepts used by and about the LGBT community. It is important to note, however, that not all individuals in the LGBT community embrace all of the language. For example, the word "gay" is frequently used to include all gay male, lesbian, and bisexual people, much like "man" is frequently used to include all humankind. Some lesbians and bisexuals find the word inappropriate for them and rarely use it to describe their community. Another example is the word "queer." When used by persons in the LGBT community, it has a very different meaning and connotation than when used by someone outside the LGBT community who may be using it in a condescending way.

The key issue is that this list has not been generated by consensus among the LGBT community. Our suggestion is that you ask people what they want to be called—for example gay versus lesbian, black versus African American, Native American versus American Indian, and so on—and how they feel about particular terms.

Bisexual: A person who experiences the human need for warmth, affection, and love from persons of either gender. Sometimes this includes sexual contact.

Coming Out: Stating openly that one is lesbian, bisexual, gay, or transgender, in contrast to "staying in the closet" by hiding one's sexuality either from oneself or from others.

Domestic Partnership: Two individuals of the same gender who are in a committed relationship of indefinite duration with an exclusive mutual commitment similar to that of marriage.

Gay: This term is frequently used generically to include all lesbian, homosexual male, and bisexual individuals.

Gay Male: A man who experiences the human need for warmth, affection, and love from persons of the same gender. Sometimes this includes sexual contact.

Gender: An individual's basic self-conviction of being male or female. This conviction is not entirely contingent upon the individual's biological sex. The exact process by which boys and girls come to see themselves as male or female is not known. However, research indicates that gender identity develops some time between birth and three years of age.

Lesbian: A woman who experiences the human need for warmth, affection, and love from persons of the same gender. Sometimes this includes sexual contact.

LGBT: Lesbian, Gay, Bisexual, and Transgender; term includes both sexual orientation and gender identification.

LGBT Lifestyles: Some people refer to LGBT individuals in terms of their "lifestyle"; this includes some LGBT individuals themselves. For the most part, members of the LGBT community prefer to think of their lives as just that; their life, not a lifestyle.

Heterosexism: The system of oppression that reinforces the belief in the inherent superiority of heterosexuality and heterosexual relationships and negates gays', lesbians', bisexuals', and transgenders' lives and relationships.

Heterosexual: A person who experiences the human need for warmth, affection, and love from persons of the opposite gender. Sometimes this includes sexual contact.

Heterosexual Privilege: The basic civil rights that a heterosexual person automatically receives that are denied to gay, lesbian, bisexual, or transgender persons simply because of who they are.

Homophobia: Negative feelings, attitudes, actions, or behaviors against lesbians, gay men, and bisexuals. It is likewise a fear of one's own same-sex sexual or affectional feelings as well as a fear of being perceived as gay, lesbian, or bisexual.

Homosexual: A term coined in 1869 by an early psychiatrist named Kertbery to describe a person who has "an other than normal sexual urge which renders them physically and psychically incapable." Since the word was originally used to describe a pathology, most gay, lesbian, and bisexual people today do not like to use this term to define themselves. Homosexuality per se is no longer considered to be pathological by the American Psychiatric Association, the American Psychological Association, the American Medical Association, and many other professional organizations. The word "homosexual" is often used as a descriptor when discussing concrete behaviors (e.g., to describe same-sex behaviors or fantasies.)

In the Closet: A phrase used to describe an individual who has not divulged her or his sexual orientation to all or some friends, family, coworkers, and/or the public.

Outing: Divulging the sexual orientation of an individual without her or his permission.

Queer: Used by some to refer to themselves, or the community, or a person who is gay, lesbian, bisexual, or transgender. Some people feel it is a more inclusive term for issues of race, class, and gender, while others detest it and view it as a pejorative term.

Sex: An act, or series of acts, that humans engage in as part of the expression of their sexual nature and their desire for love and affection.

Sexual Orientation: The orientation within human beings which leads them to be emotionally and physically attracted to persons of one gender or the other or both. One's sexual orientation may be heterosexual, homosexual, bisexual, or asexual.

Transgender: Persons who feel that their gender identity is different than their biological sex. Some transgender persons wish to change their anatomy to be more congruent with their self-perception. Others do not have such a desire. There is no correlation between sexual orientation and transgender issues. Transgender persons can be heterosexual, gay, lesbian, or bisexual.

Adapted from Breaking the Silence *(1993).*

Appendix 20.2
Symbols of Pride for the LGBT Community

Black Triangle: Once emblazoned on the uniform of prostitutes and lesbians by Nazis in the concentration camps. Now the black triangle is worn to honor the women previously persecuted.

Freedom Rings or Freedom Triangles: Rings or triangles in the colors of the rainbow flag, worn as a necklace or bracelet as a symbol of pride.

Lambda sign: The 11th letter in the Greek alphabet, Lambda is a universal gay icon.

Pink Triangle: The symbolism of the pink triangle dates back to World War II, when Jews were forced by the Nazis to wear a yellow Star of David on their coats. Homosexuals, many of whom were also put to death in the concentration camps, were forced to wear pink triangles. The pink triangle has since been adopted by the LGBT community as a symbol of the fight against oppression and for total acceptance. Today the pink triangle is worn as a symbol of pride, thus redefining a symbol once used for persecution.

Rainbow Flag: In 1978, when San Francisco was grieving the assassinations of Harvey Milk, the city's first openly gay Supervisor, and Mayor George Moscone, the organizing committee for "Speak Out for Justice" called for the development of a permanent symbol which could be used by gay men and lesbians celebrating and saluting their community. San Francisco artist Gilbert Baker, inspired by the five-striped "Flag of Races" (red, black, brown, yellow, and white), designed a Rainbow Flag. A crew of artists hand-made and dyed the first eight-striped Rainbow Flags, which made their debut at the 1978 Gay and Lesbian Freedom Day March in San Francisco. The eight-colored flag was affectionately called "New Glory" and was enthusiastically cheered by thousands of people who lined the streets.

The original eight colors were pink for sexuality, red for light, orange for healing, yellow for the sun, green for natural serenity, turquoise for art, indigo for harmony, and violet for spirit. In 1979 the Paramount Flag Company introduced the six-striped flag through its outlet, the Flag Store. Over the years, the Rainbow Flag has gone through many permutations.

Popular sentiment, however, has kept the current six-color flag in promi-
nence: red, orange, yellow, green, blue, and purple. The brilliant six-stripe
flag represents the diversity of the lesbian/gay community and the hope
for unification encompassing all its diversity.

The Rainbow Flag has been an internationally accepted lesbian and
gay symbol since it was first accepted by the International Association of
Lesbian and Gay Pride Coordinators in 1985. Today one can see "lesbian
and gay rainbows" in cities throughout the United States and abroad, a
unique and beautiful banner displaying rightful pride in its heritage and its
legacy.

Adapted from Breaking the Silence *(1993).*

APPENDIX 20.3
WHAT DO YOU KNOW ABOUT GAY/LESBIAN LIFESTYLES?

For many people, much of what they think they know about gay/lesbian
lifestyles is based on myths and not reality. Sorting out the myths and realities
can lead to greater self-awareness which motivates us to learn more and become
more accepting of those whose sexual orientation may be different from our
own.

Read each statement below and circle "SA" if you strongly agree with the
statement, "A" if you agree with it, "N" if you are neutral, "D" if you disagree
with it, and "SD" if you strongly disagree.

SA = Strongly Agree   **A** = Agree   **N** = Neutral   **D** = Disagree   **SD** = Strongly Disagree

---

SA A N D SD   1) Gay/lesbian people can usually be identified by certain mannerisms or physical characteristics.

SA A N D SD   2) In a lesbian/gay relationship one partner usually
plays the "husband"/"butch" role and the other
plays the "wife"/"femme" role.

SA A N D SD   3) We do not know what causes homosexuality.

SA A N D SD   4) Most gay/lesbian people could be cured by having
really good sex with a member of the other sex.

SA A N D SD   5) The majority of child molesters are gay/lesbian.

SA A N D SD   6) Most lesbians/gays regard themselves as members
of the other sex.

SA A N D SD   7) Homosexuality is not "natural," that is, it does not exist
in nature; therefore, this proves it is dysfunctional.

SA A N D SD   8)   Lesbian/gay people should not be teachers because they will try to convert their students to their lifestyles.

SA A N D SD   9)   Gay/lesbian people have made a conscious decision to be gay/lesbian.

SA A N D SD   10)   There are very few "bisexuals"; most people are either completely homosexual or heterosexual.

SA A N D SD   11)   There are some significant differences between the lifestyles of lesbians and gay men.

SA A N D SD   12)   Homosexuality is a type of mental illness and can be cured by appropriate psychotherapy.

SA A N D SD   13)   One homosexual experience as an adolescent will play a large part in determining whether a person will be homosexually oriented as an adult.

Adapted from O'Bear, K. (1989). Opening doors to understanding and acceptance: Facilitating workshops on lesbian, gay and bisexual issues. *Materials presented at the ACPA meeting in Washington, DC.*

APPENDIX 20.4
WHAT DO YOU KNOW ABOUT GAY/LESBIAN LIFESTYLES? SUPPORTIVE DATA FOR RESPONSES TO INDIVIDUAL ITEMS

1) Gay/lesbian people can usually be identified by certain mannerisms or physical characteristics. Gays and lesbians come in as many different shapes, colors, and sizes as do heterosexuals. Only a very small percentage can be identified by stereotypic mannerisms and characteristics. In fact, many heterosexuals portray a variety of the so-called gay stereotypic characteristics. Some members of different subcultures may tend to mimic or imitate specific behaviors in an effort to fit in. (Note: Discuss how members of popular subcultures tend to look alike and act alike, such as: members of fraternities and sororities, administrators, athletes, punkers and new wavers, etc.)

2) In a lesbian/gay relationship one partner usually plays the "husband"/"butch" role, and the other plays the "wife"/"femme" role. This is an old pattern that was evident in some gay/lesbian relationships when they had only the traditional heterosexual relationship as a model. Today, most lesbians/gays work to develop relationships based on the principles of equality and mutuality where they are loved and appreciated for who they are, not for the roles they are supposed to play. There is no right or wrong way that prescribes how to divide roles between partners. Often lesbians/gays perform preferred tasks and share those that are less desirable (i.e., laundry, cleaning, paying bills, etc.).

3)   We do not know what causes homosexuality. This is by far one of the more controversial issues for gays. It is not yet known what specifically causes either homosexuality or heterosexuality. Some believe it is predetermined genetically or hormonally. Others maintain that all humans are predisposed to all variations of sexual/affectional behavior and learn a preference or orientation. Clearly, further research is needed in this area. Caution: Some people may ask the question of causation in an attempt to "find a cure." It may be more helpful to de-emphasize the importance of exploring the causation issue by citing how homosexuality has existed in cultures around the world for centuries. It has been a constant part of societies throughout history. The question, therefore, may not be what causes it, but how can we come to better understand and accept all of the complexities of sexuality?

4)   Most gay/lesbian people could be cured by having really good sex with a member of the opposite sex. There are no "cures." Many gays have had satisfying heterosexual experiences in their lifetime. Gays who, out of desperation or fear, choose to enter a heterosexual relationship "to get cured" may cause undue misery and pain to themselves and their partners. Most gays would never choose to be sexually active with members of the other sex and would resent and challenge the inference that heterosexuals have a corner on the market of "good sex."

5)   The majority of child molesters are gay. Over 90% of child molestation is committed by heterosexual men against young girls. The overwhelming majority of gays have no interest in pre-adolescent children.

6)   Most lesbians/gays regard themselves as members of the opposite sex. Most, if not all gays, are comfortable with their femaleness or maleness. Being gay must not be confused with being transsexual, where one feels trapped in the body of the wrong sex, and therefore may seek surgery to rectify the matter.

7)   Homosexuality is not "natural," that is, it does not exist in nature; therefore, this proves it is dysfunctional. From a scientific point of view, it is "natural." Any animal, including humans, is capable of responding to homosexual stimuli. Research suggests that homosexuality is almost universal among all animals and is especially frequent among highly developed species. There has been evidence of homosexuality in all human cultures throughout history. In fact, one anthropological study of non-Western cultures found that 64% of their sample considered homosexuality "normal and socially acceptable" for certain members of the society.

8)   Lesbian/gay people should not be teachers because they will try to convert their students to the gay lifestyle. Homosexual conversion/seduction is no more common than is heterosexual seduction. Most gay teachers live with the fear that they will be fired immediately if they are "found out." Most, if not all, gays have no desire to "convert" students. Unfortunately, their efforts to provide support for younger gays may be misconstrued and misrepresented. If, in fact, the data are correct that suggest that sexual orientation is established between ages three and six, then contact with teachers would have no effect on students.

9)   Gay/lesbian people have made a conscious decision to be gay. (Refer to question #3 for the issue of causation.) While researchers continue to disagree on the specific "causes" of homosexuality, they mostly agree that there is some sort of predisposition or genetic relationship involved. The decision may not be whether one is going to be gay or not, but rather whether one is going to acknowledge the existence of personal homosexual feelings and behaviors. Coming out is a very complex and difficult process. It may take a long time for many gays to choose to accept their sexual orientation as valid and normal. Those who struggle with their gay identity may suffer enormous anxiety, pain, and anger as they work to rectify the inherent incongruence between societal messages and their own feelings and preferences.

10)   There are very few "bisexuals"; most people are either completely homosexual or heterosexual. Data suggest that few people are either predominantly heterosexual or homosexual. Most people fall somewhere on the continuum between these two ends of the scale and thus have the capacity to experience both affectional and sexual feelings for members of both sexes.

11)   There are some significant differences between the lifestyles of gay men and lesbians. Ideally, there should be no inherent or prescribed differences in intimate relationships of any kind; however, current societal pressures on all men and women often result in distinct differences. All men, not just gay or straight, are typically expected to be macho and allowed to engage in more short-term relationships than women. Consequently, it may be more difficult for gay men to develop and maintain long-term and stable monogamous relationships. In addition, many women are socialized to believe that long-term monogamy is right. Those who maintain that people are people regardless of gender may in fact feel more free to choose from among a variety of lifestyles. Until this happens, all gay men and lesbians suffer from the predominance of heterosexual sex roles in a society where few gays have chosen to provide alternative role models for the public eye.

12)   Homosexuality is a type of mental illness and can be cured by appropriate psychotherapy. In 1973, the American Psychiatric Association removed homosexuality from its list of mental disorders. In 1975, the American Psychological Association went further to state that, "Homosexuality, per se, implies no impairment in judgment, stability, reliability, or general social or vocational capacities." Most, if not all, psychiatrists have had little real success in their attempts to "cure" gays though psychotherapy.

13)   One homosexual experience as an adolescent will play a large part in determining whether a person will be homosexually oriented as an adult. Many young boys and girls (far more than 10% of our population) have homosexual experiences in their childhood as part of the natural exploration of one's sexuality. If this statement were true, then the percentage of gays in the population would be far greater than 10%.

Adapted from O'Bear, K. (1989).

APPENDIX 20.5
THE HETEROSEXUAL QUESTIONNAIRE

1) What do you think caused your heterosexuality?

2) When and how did you first decide you were a heterosexual?

3) Is it possible your heterosexuality is just a phase?

4) Is it possible your heterosexuality stems from a fear of others of the same sex?

5) If you've never had an intimate relationship with a person of the same sex, how do you know you wouldn't prefer a same-sex relationship?

6) If heterosexuality is normal, why are a disproportionate number of mentally impaired persons heterosexuals?

7) To whom have you disclosed your heterosexual tendencies? How did they react?

8) Your heterosexuality does not offend me as long as you don't try to force it on me. Why do heterosexuals feel compelled to convert others into their lifestyle?

9) If you choose to nurture children, would you want them to be heterosexual knowing the problems they may face?

10) The great majority of child molesters are heterosexuals. Do you really consider it safe to expose children to heterosexual teachers?

11) Why do you insist on being so obvious and making a public spectacle of your heterosexuality? Can't you just be what you are and keep it quiet?

12) Heterosexuals are noted for assigning themselves and each other to narrowly restricted stereotyped sex roles. Why do you cling to such unhealthy roles?

13) How can you enjoy a fully satisfying sexual experience or deep emotional rapport with a person of the opposite sex when the obvious physical, biological, and temperamental differences between you are so vast? How can a man understand what pleases a woman or vice-versa?

14) Why do heterosexuals place so much emphasis on sex?

15) With all the societal support marriage receives, the divorce rate is spiraling. Why are there so few stable relationships between heterosexuals?

16) Do heterosexuals hate and distrust others of their own sex? Is that what makes them heterosexual?

17) Why are heterosexuals so promiscuous?

18)   Why do you make a point of attributing heterosexuality to famous people. Does it justify your own heterosexuality?

Several variations of this questionnaire have circulated for years. The original author is unknown, but our thanks go to those who initially developed the concept for a questionnaire of this type.

APPENDIX 20.6
KLEIN SEXUAL ORIENTATION GRID

Directions: Use the following scale to rate each of the variables in each of the three time periods.

1 = Other sex only

2 = Other sex mostly

3 = Other sex somewhat more

4 = Both sexes equally

5 = Same sex somewhat more

6 = Same sex mostly

7 = Same sex only

Variables	Past	Present	Ideal
a) Sexual Attraction			
b) Sexual Behavior			
c) Sexual Fantasies			
d) Emotional Preference			
e) Social Preference			
f) Self-Identification			
g) Hetero/Gay Lifestyle			

Definitions of Variables:
a)   Sexual Attraction: Which sex/es are you attracted to?
b)   Sexual Behavior: With whom do you have sex?
c)   Sexual Fantasies: Whether they occur in fantasies, daydreams, or dreams, which sex/es are in your fantasies?
d)   Emotional Preference: With whom are you emotionally close? For whom you feel love?
e)   Social Preference: With whom do you spend your socializing time?
f)   Self-Identification: How do you label/identify yourself?

g) Hetero/Gay Lifestyle: In what "world"/culture and with whom do you spend your time? Mostly in the gay/lesbian culture? Or in the heterosexual culture?

Klein, F., Sepekoff, B., & Wolf, T. (1985).

APPENDIX 20.7

RIDDLE HOMOPHOBIA SCALE

In a clinical sense, homophobia is defined as an intense, irrational fear of same sex relationships that becomes overwhelming to the person. In common usage, homophobia is the fear of intimate relationships with persons of the same sex. Below are listed four negative homophobic levels, and four positive levels of attitudes towards lesbian and gay relationships/people. They were developed by Dr. Dorothy Riddle, a psychologist from Tucson, Arizona.

Homophobic Levels of Attitude

Repulsion	Homosexuality is seen as a "crime against nature." Gays/lesbians are sick, crazy, immoral, sinful, wicked, etc. Anything is justified to change them: prison, hospitalization, negative behavior therapy, electroshock therapy, etc.
Pity	Heterosexual chauvinism. Heterosexuality is more mature and certainly to be preferred. Any possibility of becoming straight should be reinforced, and those who seem to be born "that way" should be pitied, "the poor dears."
Tolerance	Homosexuality is just a phase of adolescent development that many people go through and most people grow out of. Thus, lesbians/gays are less mature than straights and should be treated with the protectiveness and indulgence one uses with a child. Lesbians/gays should not be given positions of authority because they are still working through their adolescent behavior.
Acceptance	Still implies there is something to accept. Characterized by such statements as "you're not lesbian to me; you're a person!" or "What you do in bed is your own business," or "That's fine with me as long as you don't flaunt it!"

Positive Levels of Attitudes

Support	The basic ACLU position. Work to safeguard the rights of lesbians and gays. People at this level may be uncomfortable themselves, but they are aware of the homophobic climate and the irrational unfairness.
Admiration	Acknowledges that being lesbian/gay in our society takes strength. People at this level are willing to truly examine their homophobic attitudes, values, and behaviors.

| Appreciation | Value the diversity of people and see lesbians/gays as a valid part of that diversity. These people are willing to combat homophobia in themselves and others. |
| Nurturance | Assumes that gay/lesbian people are indispensable in our society. They view lesbians/gays with genuine affection and delight, and are willing to be allies and advocates. |

O'Bear, K. (1989)

APPENDIX 20.8

SUGGESTIONS FOR THOSE WORKING WITH LESBIAN, GAY MALE, BISEXUAL, AND TRANSGENDER INDIVIDUALS

Do not be surprised when someone "comes out" to you. They have probably tested you with a series of trial balloons over a period of time. Based on your previous responses they have decided that you can be trusted.

Respect confidentiality. If a LGBT individual shares with you her or his sexual orientation, it is a sacred trust that must be respected.

Be informed. Most of us are the products of a homophobic society paralyzed by misinformation and fear. We all have a responsibility to inform ourselves about diverse communities.

Examine your own biases. Do not attempt to understand the life of another if you need more information or assistance. Do not add to the burden of an individual struggling with these issues.

Maintain a balanced perspective. Remember that LGBT individuals are more similar to you than they are different.

Understand the meaning of sexual orientation. Each person's sexual orientation is what is natural for that person. It is not a matter of sexual preference, which implies that a person has a choice.

Be supportive. Keep the door open for further conversations.

Do not try to guess who is LGBT. Undoubtedly you will be wrong more often than not. We live in a world of stereotypes that do individuals an injustice. Do not be guilty of perpetuating myths and stereotypes.

Challenge bigoted remarks and jokes. If you do not, you perpetuate injustice through silence.

Adapted from literature distributed by PFLAG (Parents and Friends of Lesbians and Gays).

Part VI

A Guide to Faculty Development Committees: Goals, Structures, and Practices

21

The Basics of Faculty Development Committees

Joyce Povlacs Lunde and Madelyn Meier Healy

It is not surprising that the continued call to improve learning in higher education today is also a compelling call to improve teaching. If we wish to promote better learning in our institutions, then the faculty members who are responsible for instruction should be given the resources and support needed to improve their teaching and to grow professionally. Because in most colleges and universities, committees are the chosen vehicles to address issues, solve problems, and make recommendations, it is also not surprising that the charge of establishing a faculty development program is often given to a campus committee.

The POD Network in Higher Education is a source of information for assistance in establishing faculty development programs on campuses. Frequently, the POD executive directors, its Core Committee, or its members are asked how one goes about doing faculty development on a campus. Often these questions focus on the establishment and functions of a faculty development committee (FDC). Perhaps a committee is already formed and given a general charge, but how to make faculty development happen is often not clear. This guide to faculty development committees is designed to help answer questions about the nature, goals, structures, activities, and functioning of faculty development committees.

DEFINITION OF FACULTY DEVELOPMENT

One of the first things individuals organizing a faculty development committee (FDC) will do is review the purpose for its being called into existence. At the same time, it may also benefit from reviewing what the term faculty development designates in higher education today. Definitions are important for those beginning faculty development programs in order to clarify needs and identify resources.

Faculty development includes the traditional support of faculty members through sabbaticals and research support; a focus on faculty members as teachers and their in-class teaching skills; a perception of faculty members as scholars and professionals with attention to career planning, grant-writing, publishing, and administrative skills; and consideration of faculty members as whole persons who benefit from attention to wellness, interpersonal skills, and stress management.

Instructional development includes curriculum planning, course design, and principles and applications of student learning theory.

Organizational development covers the structure and functioning of the institution, team building, and personnel issues.

Gradually, over several decades, faculty development has emerged as the umbrella term for most faculty-centered approaches, at least in general usage. It stands for a collection of those activities designed to encourage faculty members to improve and to grow by making planned changes in their expertise, skills, attitudes, career paths, or personal lives for the betterment of the invididual, the students, and the institution.

THE STRUCTURES FOR FACULTY DEVELOPMENT

A faculty development center often exists along with the faculty development committee. In general, POD members are apt to be coordinators of faculty development at their institutions. These coordinators are frequently members of the faculty who had come from a variety of disciplines to assume the leadership of a faculty development program.

When an office or a center for faculty development exists, there is likely to be a relationship between it and the faculty development committee. Often the committee serves in an advisory capacity to the center, and the center's coordinator chairs the committee or serves as a member. The two entities sometimes work together on events and share expenses. In other cases, programs of a center and of a committee are really one and the same.

In addition to a designated center or office, other institutional areas which offer services in faculty development include the office of the vice president of academic affairs, the faculty senate, the president, and deans. Other academic or personnel committees also provide some faculty development services.

GOALS OF FACULTY DEVELOPMENT COMMITTEES

The goals of a faculty development committee (FDC) are usually formulated based on whatever initially prompts attention to improving the environment for teaching and learning. Establishing an FDC is a solution to a perceived need to promote a positive climate for learning or inquiry. On the whole, the goals of FDCs can be classified in the expected categories of instructional improvement and professional development. Each institution, however, will have a unique combination of approaches and activities. An FDC may be designed to address needs which are perceived to be particularly important at the time to faculty, administration, a granting agency, or some combination of these groups. Those goals may be revised or added to as the FDC begins. In some cases, the FDC may assume more responsibilities such as conducting an orientation for teaching assistants and new faculty, coordinating all faculty development activities on campus, or awarding research and travel grants.

ACTIVITIES OF FACULTY DEVELOPMENT COMMITTEES

FDC-sponsored activities can be divided into two major areas: the allocation of funds and the provision of faculty development activities. Allocation of funds supports discipline and classroom-based research, professional travel, and curriculum development. Activities such as workshops, conferences, luncheon discussions, and retreats are designed to support classroom instruction and overall professional development. Major topics addressed in workshops and conferences vary. Typical topics might be:

- Teaching strategies
- Applying for and winning a grant/leave
- Writing across disciplines
- Computers in instruction
- Fostering critical thinking
- Lecturing skills

- Teaching in a multicultural classroom
- Cooperative learning groups
- Grading practices
- General education curricula
- Planning courses
- Life/career planning
- Affirmative action
- Syllabus construction
- Compiling a teaching dossier
- Verbal skills
- Use of audiovisual tools
- Adult learners
- Writing research papers
- Advising students
- Fostering community
- The difficult classroom
- The intellectual environment

SECRETS TO SUCCESSFUL FACULTY DEVELOPMENT COMMITTEES

Administrative support and faculty ownership are essential elements and are a necessary prerequisite to offering successful programs in faculty development. In addition, committees with successful programs are careful in the kinds of resources they bring to faculty, their image in promoting events, and in their own functioning as a decision-making body. Successful faculty development committees pay attention to all of these areas as discussed in more detail below.

The Role of the Administrator

Administrative support is critical to the success of a program. This support comes, as one might expect, in the form of funding. It also means verbal, clear pronouncements in support of programming and faculty participation, and it means some sort of visible participation on the part of the administrator.

Faculty Ownership

Another key to faculty development is support from the faculty or ownership. Successful FDC leaders know the culture, politics, and governance structure so that its programming meets needs in the context of the institution. Members of the FDC respect and have confidence in faculty colleagues; their input is solicited, and key faculty leaders attend sponsored functions. Also, as mentioned, the FDC needs to play a balancing act between administrators and faculty. Faculty initiative is important, and programs perceived as dictated from the top down will not work.

The Nature of the Committee

Ideally, the FDC should not be a traditional committee which has a limited agenda and reacts to issues brought before it. Advice regarding the formation of the FDC and preserving its flexibility includes beginning informally. At the outset, involve interested faculty, and remain outside the governance system. Wider acceptance can come later.

Members should be respected, influential, idea persons, independent thinkers, and should also be representative of the constituency the FDC is to serve. From the beginning, it is important to see that members are committed, buy into the program, understand it, care about it, and are energetic and willing workers.

Successful Programming

FDCs typically meet a variety of needs by providing an assortment of activities. Programs are determined by assessing needs and interests, conducting interviews and visitations, using written questionnaires, and drawing on committee members' ideas as representative of the larger community.

Once needs and topics have been established, workshop leaders need to be chosen—with great care. External persons can be used to stimulate fresh insights and approaches and to bring special expertise which might be lacking on campus. Internal persons can be used to promote local expertise and, usually, to save money. Workshop leaders should be prepared for the audience they will face, and they should be expected to model effective teaching methods themselves.

Other characteristics of successful programs are:

- Present topics which have a demonstrated impact on classroom teaching

- Relate workshops to a theme

- Deliberately build community among participants

- Serve refreshments

- Offer regular publications which are on time and carefully edited

Patience is both a virtue and a necessity when implementing faculty development committees. Faculty development can and probably should grow slowly; successful programs take time. At least initially, do not evaluate the programs by attendance alone.

THE FUNCTIONING OF FACULTY DEVELOPMENT COMMITTEES

Perhaps an area of activity often overlooked in the academic world of committees is the nature of committee functioning. The FDC should function as an autonomous group with a distinctive role or mission; it should engage in meaningful tasks and not serve as a rubber stamp or merely pass along bureaucratic policies.

Members need to be proactive and have persons involved who do the work to carry out the program. A coordinator or facilitator often oversees implementation and follow-through, but there should be at least one committee member who is willing to serve as the arms and legs of the committee. Committee work should be structured with goals in mind; members should receive agendas before meetings; and, whenever feasible, subcommittees should be formed to investigate and report on specific topics of concern. Evaluation of progress and process should be frequent.

The FDC should have its own funding and budget, separate from general funds. While external funding might launch a program or be useful for special needs, the FDC should not depend on outside sources for funds to continue its activities. If the committee manages funds or allocates grants, it is important to establish and publish clear guidelines for expenditures and allocation.

It is advisable to offer training for FDC members. Sources for such training include holding special retreats, providing current literature in faculty development for each member, supporting the development of ideas as pilot projects, and funding attendance at external workshops and conferences such as the annual POD conference.

Compensation and/or recognition should be accorded to committee members. Since they often work for long hours, they need compensation either through release time or special celebrations, recognition, or travel opportunities.

22

Questions and Answers about Faculty Development Committees

Joyce Povlacs Lunde and Madelyn Meier Healy

In this chapter we answer some specific questions which we have been asked from time to time by those interested in initiating a faculty development committee (FDC) on their campus. The answers offered need to be considered in the context of the individual campus culture.

1) What can an academic dean or administrator do to get faculty development started?

The administrator who asks this question is often aware of the caveats against unilateral administrative mandates in faculty development. An important, positive role academic administrators play is to share their visions for their institution and explain how faculty development might contribute to that vision.

Practical steps an administrator might take to initiate a faculty development program include:

- Convening a faculty task force of campus leaders

- Setting aside funds for faculty to manage for such items as a needs assessment, consultant visits, and immediate programming

- Sending task force members to faculty development conferences

- Encouraging other administrators and governing boards to be supportive

Other roles an administrator can play are highly dependent on campus culture, but behavior can range from attending almost all the meetings and sponsored events to a strictly hands-off policy. The important thing is that administrative support is both tangible and visible.

2) How does faculty development relate to faculty evaluation?

In general, most systems of evaluation for personnel decisions are kept separate from the faculty development program as far as data relating to individuals are concerned. However, improvement activity must support professional advancement on campus if it is not to be viewed as marginal. The course to steer is a narrow one. On the one hand, faculty development committees should not be directly involved in administering a reward system for the institution. On the other hand, they can, for example, conduct research and provide information on identifying qualities of effective teaching; test out standardized evaluation instruments; investigate innovative ideas in documenting teaching activity, such as portfolio evaluation; bring to campus external experts in the field of evaluating faculty performance; and arrange for workshops for faculty, administrators, and others to define scholarship and teaching in the context of the campus culture. Academic administrators and members of promotion and tenure or personnel committees should take leadership roles in seeing that professional development, including improvement in teaching, is encouraged, recognized, and rewarded.

3) What do we do if a key, supportive administrator leaves?

Sometimes an FDC is on a roll, but then comes the blow. The administrative champion leaves. What should the committee do? Preventive measures are important. In the first place, the champions of faculty development should number more than one administrator. Department chairs or heads, division leaders, and senior faculty should be brought on board as soon as possible. The kind of initial training recommended for members of faculty development committees is also good for administrators. If a key administrator does leave, then members of the committee need to be involved in writing the position description, serving on the search committee, and interviewing candidates. What priorities for faculty development do candidates hold? What is their past record? Are their definitions of faculty development consistent with those of the committee and the campus culture? Once the new administrator is hired, the FDC should conduct a personalized training program in faculty development for that individual. The committee should be prepared to demonstrate faculty support for the program, and, if possible, document its achievements.

4) What can we do to make faculty development a desirable committee assignment?

Faculty development committees need to be nurtured. Retreats, off-campus conferences, and regular meetings build community and a shared purpose. Committee meetings themselves should be testing grounds for ideas even as they follow good practice in group processes. Equal attention should be paid to getting tasks done and to remaining sensitive to the needs and feelings of the members. Successes should be celebrated. Once the FDC is functioning as a community, the word will soon be out that it is a prestige assignment

5) How can we improve attendance at faculty development events?

It is natural to worry about attendance at workshops and conferences, and those experienced in faculty development programming know that attendance at sponsored programs can vary drastically from event to event, sometimes without apparent cause. There is no one solution to a problem of low attendance; and most faculty scorn being required to attend, but some actions might be taken. Before the event, those planning the activity should be in touch with the target group. Does the event meet a clear need? Do workshop flyers and announcements make the event sounding exciting? Are there schedule conflicts? Are the faculty at large involved in the event, as, for example, hosting guests, evaluating activities, or serving as panelists? Is the publicity out in time? Is preregistration requested?

If an event fails to attract the expected audience, then analysis is in order. Are faculty burned out on workshops? Was the last one a flop? A quick telephone survey of no-shows or non-attendees might give needed feedback and also recruit an audience for the next time around. Finally, numbers are not the only measure. A program drawing ten persons excited about conducting classroom research projects constitutes a success.

6) How much can a committee do?

The enthusiasm exhibited in the FDC retreat in May can sadly dissipate by September. The FDC needs to set priorities and plan implementation based on how many willing workers it actually has.

Successful programming often depends on looking after details. For example, someone has to see that memos and newsletters are written, edited, published, and mailed; that workshop planning gets to the nitty-gritty of room reservations and refreshments; and that guest speakers and workshop leaders are met at airports and hosted graciously. Tasks such as these need to be shared among committee members, even if there is a coordinator, and not simply assigned to support staff to carry out. Activities which keep FDC programs and resources visible, such as a newsletter or memo, combined with perhaps some informal luncheons and one or two major workshops might be all that can be handled. It might be both comforting and beneficial to recognize that other kinds of committees (for example, curriculum) can and often do faculty development kinds of things.

7) If faculty colleagues are skeptical or resistant to change, what can a faculty development committee do?

Most faculty development programs start with faculty members seeking new and challenging ideas to improve teaching or address issues of professional development. It is difficult to be patient in the face of skeptical attack, but those promoting new ideas and innovations in faculty development often confront bedrock myths and perceptions of academic life. For example, many among us still believe that good teachers are born, that the popular teacher is academically suspect, and that teaching well is not rewarded and never will be. Those starting programs often hear the complaint that the faculty members who really need it do not come. Effective teachers, it might be pointed out, need faculty development and are knowledgeable consumers of its programs. Over time, with attractive programming meeting the needs of various groups, the base of participation can be expanded to include even those who need the program.

8) What is the relationship between a faculty development committee and a faculty union?

The relationship between a faculty union and an FDC should and can be a compatible and mutually supportive one. Both groups are concerned about the interests and well being of their members. One strategy likely to encourage this compatibility is to have the faculty development committee chair or coordinator meet with the union leaders at least yearly to discuss what concerns and professional development needs are expressed to them by the faculty at large. The FDC should be clear about what subjects relate to bargaining issues and avoid these as topics in programs for workshops or other events. Other strategies depend upon the campus culture, but often faculty development is viewed as an asset by faculty union leadership.

9) If we have a committee, do we also need a coordinator or a center for faculty development?

To answer this question, the problem to address is the need for the FDC's program to be carried out effectively and efficiently. As noted previously, faculty development coordinators/centers and committees are frequently found in association. Coordinators lead in the initiation and development of ideas and program design; facilitate communication among faculty, administrators, and staff; and oversee program implementation, follow-up, evaluation, and feedback. Faculty development coordinators or directors of faculty development centers often carry the history, goals, and dreams around in their heads and thus are passionate champions and dedicated change agents. As long as the FDC has champions who have both the responsibility and the authority to carry out the work of faculty development, then the program has a chance to have major impact on the individuals and the institution. With or without a campus coordinator or center, the many and varied tasks and functions must be divided among FDC members who are held accountable for their accomplishment. On smaller campuses, committee coordinators often come from the faculty, serve limited terms (such as three years), and train their successors before they return to their former roles.

10) What is the bottom line of all faculty development activity?

Establishing a faculty development committee to improve the climate for teaching and learning means that the work of the committee should undergo continuous evaluation. Assessing student gains has been a major preoccupation of higher education in recent years. To link student gains with faculty development programs is an ambitious research hypothesis. If the big question cannot be immediately tackled, then perhaps some of the smaller ones might:

- How do faculty members evaluate events sponsored by the committee?

- What kind of unsolicited testimonials do you have?

- Do surveys or observations reveal changes in faculty class-room practices?

- What documentary evidence can you collect that faculty are growing professionally?

The bottom line is found in positive attitudes, more active inquiry, and better learning. The FDC needs to devise a plan to capture, evaluate, and report these gains to its constituencies.

23

A Faculty Development Committee Checklist

Joyce Povlacs Lunde and Madelyn Meier Healy

Readers of this book and their institutions are likely to be at various stages of faculty development. The material of this chapter can be used whether the faculty development committee is just getting started or has been in existence for a period of time already.

The following statements about the characteristics of faculty development programs and committees, given below in the form of a checklist, are offered to stimulate thought and discussion. The checklist might be used to analyze the current status of planning in a committee already in existence or diagnose the needs of one still in a discussion stage. None of these statements is intended to be absolute. After all, faculty development is developmental. For example, if committee members lack knowledge of current trends and practices in faculty development, then training can be arranged. If the planners want the committee to function at a high level, then exercises devoted to teaching skills in group processes might be incorporated into a committee retreat early in its life. If there is no evaluation plan, one might be developed. FDC planners or members might use a scale of 1-5 to evaluate the ease of accomplishing each of the statements in the checklist.

A FACULTY DEVELOPMENT CHECKLIST

Membership of the FDC

____Members are enthusiastic advocates for faculty development.

____Members are broadly representative of major divisions or disciplines of the institution.

____Most of the members are elected or identified by faculty groups.

____Faculty diverse in ethnic background, race, culture, and academic ranks are encouraged to seek committee membership.

____The number of members is sufficient to plan and carry out activities, but not so large that decision-making is cumbersome (range: 6-14).

____Respected faculty members and leaders are involved as initial committee members.

____Training in faculty development is offered for members.

____Members have joined the POD network to be in touch with national resources and contacts.

Collegewide Involvement

____Faculty have the major role in planning and administering the FDC.

____Key academic administrators have given and continue to give visible and tangible support to the FDC.

____The FDC role is clearly defined and communicated on campus.

Needs Assessments

____Faculty, student, and institutional needs assessments are conducted.

____Needs assessments have multiple data-collecting strategies, including surveys, open-ended questions, personal interviews, and focus groups.

____Results of needs assessments give direction to planning activities.

Financial Support

____Budget is allocated yearly as part of internal funding of the college.

_____Budget includes resources for external presenters and consultants, supplies, printing, travel and training for FDC members, educational materials, secretarial support.

_____Release time is allocated for FDC members when their time spent in planning and carrying out workshops is substantial.

_____External funding, when available, supplements internal funding and does not replace it.

_____Budget is proposed and implemented by the FDC.

FDC Functioning

_____Someone has been identified to coordinate and facilitate FDC planning and provide continuity over time.

_____A member of the committee or a coordinator has the responsibility of managing the budget.

_____An agenda is used for planning meetings.

_____A yearly plan has been developed.

_____Techniques and strategies of team building are employed within the committee.

_____A method of communication with the faculty and administration, such as newsletters, liaison appointees, end-of-year reports, and feedback sessions, is functioning.

Programs

_____A variety of topics is planned to meet a variety of faculty needs and interests.

_____An evaluation or feedback instrument is part of each activity.

_____A plan for evaluating the overall program and direction of faculty development is put into operation.

_____Faculty development activity is kept separate from the tenure/promotion process.

24

Resources For Faculty Development Committees

Joyce Povlacs Lunde and Madelyn Meier Healy

The nature of faculty development committee (FDC) work calls for special resources and expertise for committee members. Faculty development is a field of its own, and more and more studies coming out of a variety of disciplines are expanding our knowledge of it and of the practice of teaching and learning in higher education. In this section we direct attention to an array of resources available in faculty development. It is impossible to cite all the literature, conferences, and workshops readily available, but we offer a few examples of what some of the resources are and where to find them. The contributors to this book, whose names and email addresses are given at the end of their respective chapters, might also be consulted in locating material or lending their expertise to address specific needs.

CONFERENCES AND ORGANIZATIONS

Committee members benefit from attending conferences focused on faculty development. The POD annual conference, usually held in October, offers a preconference workshop for beginning a faculty development program. The National Council for Staff, Program, and Organizational Development (NCSPOD) provides staff development resources especially for the two year colleges. The National Institute for Staff and Organizational Development (NISOD), which is affiliated with the American Association of Community and Junior Colleges, also has an annual conference, usually held in the fall. With sponsorship of the POD Network, an Institute for New Faculty Developers is held every two years during the summer. The annual conference of the American Association of Higher Education (AAHE) held in March or April each year is a good source for information on trends in higher education and for identifying any of a number of interest groups and associated meetings, all relevant to faculty development. The American Educational Research Association (AERA), which holds its annual conference each spring, has a special interest group on faculty development and evaluation.

Still other conferences provide teaching faculty an opportunity to present teaching and curriculum innovations across the disciplines. For example, the International Society for Exploring Teaching Alternatives (ISETA), which also has a fall conference, is a place where those interested in guided design, mediated instruction, and other innovative approaches to learning might come together and share their projects. Another annual conference, the National Conference on Successful College Teaching, is held in late winter usually in Orlando, Florida, and is for those sharing innovations in teaching; it is sponsored by the Center for Higher Education at North Texas University (Denton) and the Institute of Higher Education and the Division of Continuing Education at the University of Florida (Gainesville). The Lilly Conferences, held in several regions of the country, focus on teaching and learning. The Great Lakes Colleges Association (GLCA) focuses on faculty in liberal arts colleges. The Canadian Society for Teaching and Learning in Higher Education hosts an annual conference. Web sites for these and other organizations and conferences will provide further current information.

Many states and regions have conferences for classroom faculty and for faculty development practitioners. Examples include the annual summer Faculty College sponsored by the University of Wisconsin State System, which served as a model for one initiated by the public institutions in Nebraska.

Almost all of the conferences mentioned above invite proposals for presentations and feature the sharing and exchange of ideas among the participants. Other kinds of national workshops are offered by specialized organizations. For example, the Center for Faculty Evaluation and Development in Manhattan, Kansas, offers workshops and seminars for administrators directed toward issues of faculty development and evaluation. Two other organizations which specialize in human relations training include NTL (formerly, National Training Laboratories) located in Alexandria, Virginia, and University Associates, with home offices in San Diego, California. The programs of NTL and University Associates may be of particular interest to those seeking training in personal and organizational development.

PUBLICATIONS

Print and other media resources for faculty development in higher education constitute a growing field. Publications of Anker Publishing, Greenwood Press, New Forums Press, Jossey-Bass, and Stylus will be of interest. *The Journal of Staff, Program, and Organizational Development* is a useful resource as well. Also of interest to faculty members who wish to implement improvement projects in their classes and encourage others is the work *Classroom Assessment Techniques: A Handbook for College Teachers* (Angelo & Cross, 1993).

POD's publications are useful in helping FDC members develop knowledge of the field and to share that knowledge with others. *To Improve the Academy*, an annual publication of POD published by Anker Publishing, contains a variety of articles in instructional, organizational, and personal development for faculty. Also available for distribution from POD is a subscription to the *Essays on Teaching Excellence*, a series of essays on college teaching which might be circulated as part of a campus newsletter or used in workshops, seminars, and individual consultation. These short and succinct pieces could also be valuable for educating new members of FDCs. The subscription is also available in html format.

Many members of FDCs and coordinators of programs on individual campuses who publish newsletters for their own faculty are glad to add names to their mailing list and to give permission to duplicate and distribute articles upon request.

Of special interest to FDC members should be those publications which address issues of group functioning and team building. If complaints about committee meetings are at all justified, improving the way committees do business and work groups get tasks done should be a high priority for faculty development committees. A few publications about committee functioning in general, which contain stimulating exercises often in a lighter vein, are those by Bradford (1976), Dunsing (1977), Francis and Young (1979), and North (1980). The Bergquist and Phillips three volumes of *A Handbook for Faculty Development* (1975, 1977, 1981), early works in faculty development, are still worthwhile and contain much material useful to committees to assist them in improving their functioning.

QUESTIONNAIRES AND INVENTORIES

Sometimes already prepared and published questionnaires and inventories are useful in team building as well as assessing faculty needs. For example, the questionnaires based on "Seven Principles for Good Practice in Undergraduate Education" (Chickering & Gamson, 1987) include an Institutional Inventory and a Faculty Inventory (Chickering, Gamson, & Barsi 1989). The Kolb *Learning Styles Inventory* (1976) might be used to stimulate discussion about how students learn.

SPECIAL INTEREST GROUPS

In addition to the resources cited above, recent years have seen a tremendous growth in special interest groups which have faculty development components, including the following:

- Conferences and publications on critical thinking
- Creative thinking
- General education
- International education
- Writing across the disciplines
- The beginning student
- The senior student
- Retention
- Ethics
- Diversity
- Honors
- Undergraduate research
- Assessment of learning
- Evaluation of faculty
- The reward structure
- Classroom research
- Training for teaching assistants

The *Chronicle of Higher Education* is a good place to start to find the specific organizations and conferences associated with these and similar topics.

HUMAN RESOURCES

Last, but not least, are the many individuals, particularly members of POD, who can serve as workshop leaders, program evaluators, or consultants. While POD as an organization neither facilitates consultation nor endorses individual consultants, it is a network of people who willingly share resources and expertise with each other. In general, most POD members, who are listed in the POD annual directory, are happy to answer questions via email or over the telephone or, if there is a match of need and expertise, they may visit a campus as a consultant

Subscribing to the *Chronicle of Higher Education* and becoming members of the American Association for Higher Education (AAHE) as well as of POD are basic ways of tapping into the rich array of publications, networks, conferences, and workshops available to practitioners of faculty development in higher education today. Even a very quick examination of the resources available proves that no member of a faculty development committee needs to remain uninformed or untrained for long.

REFERENCES

Angelo, T., & Cross, K. P. (1993). *Classroom assessment techniques: A handbook for college teachers.* San Francisco, CA: Jossey-Bass.

Bergquist, W. H., & Phillips, S. R. (1975, 1977, 1981). *A handbook for faculty development* (Vols. 1-3). Washington, DC: Council for the Advancement of Small Colleges [now Council of Independent Colleges].

Bradford, L. P. (1976). *Making meetings work: A guide for leaders and group members.* La Jolla, CA: University Associates.

Chickering, A., & Gamson, Z. (1987). Seven principles for good practice in undergraduate education. *The Wingspread Journal, 9* (2): special section.

Chickering, A., Gamson, Z., & Barsi, L. (1989). *Inventories of good practice in undergraduate education.* Racine, WI: The Johnson Foundation (Wingspread).

Dunsing, R. J. (1977). *You and I have simply got to stop meeting this way.* New York, NY: AMACOM [A division of American Management Associations].

Francis, D., & Young, D. (1979). *Improving workgroups: A practical manual for team building*. La Jolla, CA: University Associates.

Kolb, D. (1976). *Learning Styles Inventory*. Boston, MA: McBer and Company.

North, J. (1980). Guidelines and strategies for conducting meetings. *POD Quarterly. 2*, 79-91.

Joyce Povlacs Lunde is Professor Emerita at the University of Nebraska, Lincoln. She served as an instructional consultant in the university's Teaching and Learning center and also in the Office of Professional and Organizational Development within the Institute of Agriculture and Natural Resource, and in the Department of Agricultural Education. Joyce has been a POD member since 1976 when she became involved in faculty development through a training program sponsored by the Council for the Advancement of Small Colleges (now the Council of Independent Colleges).

Madelyn Meier Healy is Professor Emerita at Kean University, where she served as director of the Center for Professional Development. Previously at Kean, she had been a counselor educator, a department chair, the associate dean and acting dean of the School of Education, and coordinator of graduate studies. She has been actively involved in POD for a number of years.

Email: jlunde1@unl.edu
          drmhealy@aol.com

BIBLIOGRAPHY

Adams, M., Bell, L., & Griffin, P. (1997). *Teaching for diversity and social justice.* New York, NY: Routledge.

Albright, M., & Graf, D. (Eds.). (1992). *Teaching in the information age: The role of educational technology.* New Directions for Teaching and Learning, No. 51. San Francisco, CA: Jossey-Bass.

Alreck, P., & Settle, R. (1995). *The survey research handbook.* Burr Ridge, IL: Irwin.

Altman, H. B., & Castron, W. E. (1992). *Writing a Syllabus.* (Idea Paper No. 27). Manhattan, KS: Kansas State University Center for Faculty Evaluation and Development.

Ambrose, S. (1995). Fitting programs to institutional cultures: The founding and evolution of the university teaching center. In P. Seldin & Associates (Eds.), *Improving college teaching.* Bolton, MA: Anker.

Anderson, J. A. (1995). *Merging effective models of diversity with teaching and learning in the curriculum.* Raleigh, NC: North Carolina State University.

Angelo, T. A. (Ed.). (1998). *Classroom assessment and research: An update on uses, approaches and research findings.* New Directions for Teaching and Learning, No. 75. San Francisco, CA: Jossey-Bass.

Angelo, T. A., & Cross, K. P. (1993). *Classroom assessment techniques: A handbook for college teachers.* San Francisco, CA: Jossey-Bass.

Asante, M. (1991). Multiculturalism: An exchange. *The American Scholar, 60,* 267-76.

Association of American Colleges and Universities. (1985). *Integrity in the college curriculum: A report to the academic community.* Washington, DC: Association of American Colleges and Universities.

Atkinson, L. et al. (1981). *Introduction to psychology.* New York, NY: Harcourt Brace Jovanovich.

Austin, A., & Baldwin, R.G. (1991). *Faculty collaboration: Enhancing the quality of scholarship and teaching.* (ASHE-ERIC Higher Education Report No. 7)

Babbie, S. (1990, April). *Survey research methods.* Belmont, CA: Wadsworth.

Banks, J. A. (1995). Multicultural education: Historical development, dimensions, and practice. In J. A. Banks & C. A. M. Banks (Eds.), *Handbook of research on multicultural education* (pp. 3-24). New York, NY: Macmillan.

Barber, L.W. (1990). Self-assessment. In J. Millman & L. Darling Hammons (Eds.), *The new handbook of teacher evaluation* (pp. 216-228). Newbury Park, CA: Sage.

Barnes, L. B., Christensen, C. R., & Hansen, A. (1994). *Teaching and the case method.* Boston, MA: Harvard Business School Press.

Barney Dews, C.L., & Leste Law, C. (Eds.). (1995). *This fine place so far from home: Voices of academics from the working class.* Philadelphia, PA: Temple University Press.

Barrows, H. S. (1994). *Practice-based learning: Problem-based learning applied to medical education.* Springfield, IL: Southern Illinois University.

Barrows, H. S., & Tamblyn, R. M. (1980). *Problem-based learning: An approach to medical education.* New York, NY: Springer.

Bates, A. W. (1996). *Technology, open learning & distance education.* Madison, WI: Magna.

Bennett, W. J. (1984). *To reclaim a legacy.* Washington, DC: National Endowment for the Humanities.

Bennett, J. B., & Figuli, D. J. (1990). *Enhancing departmental leadership.* New York, NY: American Council on Education/Macmillan.

Bergquist, W. H., & Phillips, S. R. (1975). *A handbook for faculty development (Vol. 1).* Washington, DC: Council for the Advancement of Small Colleges.

Bergquist, W. H., & Phillips, S. R. (1977). *A handbook for faculty development (Vol. 2).* Washington, DC: Council for the Advancement of Small Colleges.

Bergquist, W. H., & Phillips, S. R. (1987). *A handbook for faculty development (Vol. 3).* Washington, DC: Council for the Advancement of Small Colleges.

Boice, R. (1992). *The new faculty member.* San Francisco, CA: Jossey-Bass.

Bonwell, C., & Eison, J. (1991). *Active learning: Creating excitement in the classroom.* (ASHE-ERIC Higher Education Report No. 1)

Bordonaro, T. (1995-96). Improving the performance of teaching assistants through the development and interpretation of informal early evaluations. *The Journal of Graduate Teaching Assistant Development, 3,* 21-26.

Borton, T. (1970). *Reach, touch, and teach.* New York, NY: McGraw Hill.

Bouton, C., & Garth, R. (Eds.) (1983). Learning in groups. *New Directions for Teaching and Learning, No. 14.* San Francisco, CA: Jossey-Bass.

Boyer, E. (1986). *College: The undergraduate experience in America.* Princeton, NJ: Carnegie Foundation for the Advancement of Teaching.

Bradford, L. P. (1976) *Making meetings work: A guide for leaders and group members* La Jolla, CA: University Associates.

Braskamp, L. A., & Ory, J. C. (1994). *Assessing faculty work: Enhancing individual and institutional performance.* San Francisco, CA: Jossey-Bass.

Breaking the silence. (1993, November 1). *Final report of the select committee on lesbian, gay, and bisexual concerns.* Minneapolis, MN: University of Minnesota.

Brinko, K. T. (1993). The practice of giving feedback to improve teaching: What is effective? *Journal of Higher Education, 64* (5), 54-68.

Brinko, K. T., & Menges, R. J. (Eds.). (1996). *Practically speaking: A sourcebook for instructional consultants in higher education.* Stillwater, OK: New Forums Press.

Brown, D. G. (1999). *Always in touch: A practical guide to ubiquitous computing.* Winston-Salem, NC: Wake Forest University Press. Distributed by Anker Publishing.

Brown, D. G. (Ed.). (2000). *Interactive learning: Vignettes from America's most wired campuses.* Bolton, MA: Anker.

Brown, D. G. (Ed.). (2000). *Teaching with Technology: Seventy-five professors from eight universities tell their stories.* Bolton, MA: Anker.

Brown, J. S., Collins, A., & Duguid, P. (1989). Situated cognition and the culture of learning. *Educational Researcher, 18* (1), 31-42.

Carroll, J. B., & Gmelch, W. H. (1992). *A factor-analytic investigation of the role types and profiles of higher education department chairs.* San Francisco, CA: The national conference of the American Educational Research Association. (ERIC Document Reproduction Service No. ED 345 629)

Centra, J. (1979). *Determining faculty effectiveness.* San Francisco, CA: Jossey-Bass.

Centra, J. A. (1993). *Reflective faculty evaluation: Enhancing teaching and determining faculty effectiveness.* San Francisco, CA: Jossey-Bass.

Chickerinjg, A., & Gamson, Z. (1987). Seven principles for good practice in undergraduate education. *The Wingspread Journal, 9* (2): special section.

Chickering, A., Gamson, Z. & Barsi, L. (1989). *Inventories of good practice in undergraduate education.* Racine, WI: The Johnson Foundation (Wingspread).

Chism, N. V. N. (Ed.). (1987). *Institutional responsibilities and responses in the employment and education of teaching assistants.* Columbus, OH: The Ohio State University, Center for Teaching Excellence.

Chism, N. V. N. (1998). The role of educational developers in institutional change: From the basement office to the front office. In M. Kaplan & D. Lieberman (Eds.), *To improve the academy: Vol. 17. Resources for faculty, instructional, and organizational development* (pp. 141-154). Stillwater, OK: New Forums Press.

Chism, N. V. N. (1999). *Peer review of teaching: A sourcebook.* Bolton, MA: Anker.

Clark, D. J., & Bekey, J. (1979). Use of small groups in instructional evaluation. *Insight to teaching excellence,* VII.I. Arlington, TX: The University of Texas at Arlington.

Clark, D. J., & Bekey, J. (1979). Use of small groups in instructional evaluation. *POD Quarterly, 1,* 87-95.

Clark, D. J., & Redmond, M. (1982). *Small group instructional diagnosis: Final report.* (ERIC Document Reproduction Service No. ED 217954)

Coleman, T. (1990). Managing diversity at work: The new American dilemma. *Public Management, 70,* 2-5.

Cook, C., & Sorcinelli, M. D. (1999, March). Building multiculturalism into teaching development programs. *AAHE Bulletin, 51* (7), 3-6.

Cooper, J. E., & Chattergy, V. (1993). Developing faculty multicultural awareness. An examination of life roles and their cultural components. In D. Wright & J. Povlacs Lunde (Eds.), *To Improve the Academy: Vol. 12. Resources for Faculty, Instructional, and Organizational Development.* (pp. 81-95). Stillwater, OK: New Forums Press.

Cross, K. P. (1977). Not can, but will college teaching be improved? In J. A. Centra (Ed.), *Renewing and evaluating teaching* (pp. 1-15). New Directions for Higher Education, No. 17. San Francisco, CA: Jossey-Bass.

Cross, K. P. (1998). Classroom research: Implementing the scholarship of teaching. In T. A. Angelo (Ed.), *Classroom assessment and research: An update on uses, approaches, and research findings.* New Directions for Teaching & Learning, No. 75, (pp. 5-12). San Francisco, CA: Jossey- Bass.

Cyrs, T. E., Smith, F. A., & Conway, E. D. (1994). *Essential skills for television teaching.* Las Cruces, NM: New Mexico State University.

Dale, E. (1998). *An assessment of a faculty development program at a research university.* Unpublished doctoral dissertation, University of Massachusetts at Amherst.

Dawson, J., & Caulley, D. (1981). The group interview as an evaluation technique in higher education. *Educational Evaluation and Policy Analysis, 11, 4.*

Davis, B. G. (1993). *Tools for teaching.* San Francisco, CA: Jossey-Bass.

Derek Bok Center (Producer). (1992). *Race in the classroom: A multiplicity of experience* [videotape]. Cambridge, MA: The Derek Bok Center, Harvard University. Distributed by Anker Publishing.

Derek Bok Center (Producer). (1996). *Women in the classroom: Cases for reflection* [videotape]. Cambridge, MA: The Derek Bok Center, Harvard University. Distributed by Anker Publishing.

Diamond, N., & Smock, R. (1985, October). *Description and evaluation of the senior clinical interview process.* Paper presented at the tenth annual conference of the Professional and Organizational Development Network in Higher Education, Somerset, PA.

Duning, B. S., Van Kekerix, M. J., & Zaborowski, L. M. (1993). *Reaching learners through telecommunications.* San Francisco, CA: Jossey Bass.

Dunsing, R. J. (1977). *You and I have simply got to stop meeting this way.* New York, NY: AMACOM [A division of American Management Associations].

Eble, K., & McKeachie, W. (1985). *Improving undergraduate education through faculty development.* San Francisco, CA: Jossey-Bass.

Ekler, W. J. (1994). The lecture method. In K. W. Prichard & R. M. Sawyer (Eds.), *Handbook of college teaching: Theory and applications* (pp. 85-89). Westport, CT: Greenwood Press.

Eison, J., & Sorcinelli, M. D. (1999, January). *Improving teaching and learning: Academic leaders and faculty developers as partners.* Presentation at the Seventh AAHE Conference on Faculty Roles and Rewards, San Diego, CA.

Erickson, B. L. (1986). Faculty development at four-year colleges and universities: Lessons learned. *Proceedings of faculty evaluation and development: Lessons learned* (pp. 33-48). Manhattan, KS: Kansas State University, Center for Faculty Evaluation and Development.

Erickson, F. (1986). Qualitative methods in research on teaching. In M. C. Wittrock (Ed.), *Handbook of research on teaching* (3rd ed., pp. 119-161). New York, NY: Macmillan.

Erickson, G. (1986). A survey of faculty development practices. In M. Svinicki, J. Kurfiss, & J. Stone (Eds.), *To improve the academy: Vol. 5. Resources for faculty, instructional, and organizational development* (pp. 182-196). Stillwater, OK: New Forums Press.

Erikson, E. H. (1974) *Dimensions of a new identity.* New York, NY: Norton.

Evertson, C. M., & Green, J. L. (1986). Observation as inquiry and method. In M. C. Wittrock (Ed.), *Handbook of research on teaching* (3rd ed., pp. 162-213). New York, NY: Macmillan.

Falk, D., & Carlson, H. (1995). *Multimedia in higher education.* Medford, NJ: Information Today.

Feldman, K. A. (1989). Instructional effectiveness of college teachers as judged by teachers themselves, current and former students, colleagues, administrators and external (neutral) observers. *Research in Higher Education, 30,* 137-189.

Ferren, A. S., & Geller, W. W. (1993). The faculty developer's role in promoting an inclusive community: Addressing sexual orientation. In D. L. Wright & J. Povlacs Lunde (Eds.), *To Improve the Academy: Vol. 12. Resources for Faculty, Instructional, and Organizational Development* (pp. 97-108). Stillwater, OK: New Forums Press.

Flanders, N. A. (1970). *Analyzing teaching behavior.* Reading, MA: Addison-Wesley.

Fink, L. D. (1992). Orientation programs for new faculty members. In M. D. Sorcinelli (Ed.), *New and junior faculty.* New Directions for Teaching and Learning, No. 50. San Francisco, CA: Jossey-Bass.

Fink, L. D. (1995). Evaluating your own teaching. In P. Seldin (Ed.), *Improving college teaching* (pp. 191-203). Bolton, MA: Anker.

Fisch, L. (1983). Coaching mathematics and other academic sports. In M. David, M. Fisher, S. C. Inglis, S. Scholl (Eds.),*To improve the academy: Vol. 2. Resources for student, faculty and institutional development.* (pp. 3-6). Orinda, CA: John Kennedy University.

Francis, D., & Young, D. (1979). *Improving workgroups: A practical manual for team building.* La Jolla, CA: University Associates.

Fisch, L. (1988). *On academic bonding.* Unpublished manuscript.

Gabriel, D. (1987). Characteristics of successful developmental educators. *Review of Research in Developmental Education, 5* (1), 1-5.

Gaff, J. G. (1975). *Toward faculty renewal.* San Francisco, CA: Jossey-Bass.

Ginsberg, M. B., & Wlodkowski, R. J. (1997). *Developing culturally responsive teaching among faculty: Methods, content, and skills.* A session presented at the 10th Annual Conference on Race and Ethnicity in American Higher Education, Orlando, FL.

Gmelch, W. H., & Miskin, V. D. (1993). *Leadership skills for department chairs.* Bolton, MA: Anker.

Gray, P. J., Diamond, R. M., & Adam, B. E. (1996). *A national study on the relative importance of research and undergraduate teaching at colleges and universities.* Syracuse, NY: Syracuse University, Center for Instructional Development.

Green, M. F. (Ed.). (1988). *Leaders for a new era.* New York, NY: American Council on Education/Macmillan.

Green, M. F. (Ed.). (1989). *Minorities on campus: A handbook for enhancing diversity.* Washington, DC: American Council on Education.

Green, M. F. (1990). Why good teaching needs active leadership. In P. Seldin & Associates (Eds.), *How administrators can improve teaching* (pp. 45-62). San Francisco, CA: Jossey Bass.

Harris, I. (1987). Communicating educational reform through persuasive discourse: A double-edged sword. *Professions Education Research Notes, 9* (2), 2-7.

Harvey, D., & Brown, D. R. (1996). *An experiential approach to organization development* (5th ed.). Upper Saddle River, NJ: Prentice Hall.

Hecht, I. W. D., Higgerson, M. L., Gmelch, W. H., & Tucker, A. (1999). *The department chair as academic leader.* Phoenix, AZ: American Council on Education/Oryx.

Heenan, T. A., & Jerich, K. F. (Eds.). (1995). *Teaching graduate students to teach: Engaging the disciplines.* Urbana-Champaign, IL: University of Illinois at Urbana-Champaign, Office of Instructional Resources and the Office of Conferences and Institutes.

Hilsen, L. (1988). Some possible suggestions for establishing a positive classroom climate. In L. Hilsen (Ed.), *Establishing and maintaining a positive classroom climate* (pp. 9-14). Duluth, MN: Instructional Development Service, University of Minnesota, Duluth.

Hilsen, L. (1988). Visualization exercise: Classroom climate. In L. Hilsen (Ed.), *Establishing and maintaining a positive classroom climate* (p. 8). Duluth, MN: Instructional Development Service, University of Minnesota, Duluth.

Hoge, R. D. (1985). The validity of direct observation measures of pupil classroom behavior. *Review of Educational Research, 55,* 469-483.

Hoover, K. (1980). Questioning strategies. In *College teaching today: A handbook for postsecondary instruction* (pp. 120-149). Boston, MA: Allyn and Bacon. (See also chapters on Discussion Methods, pp. 120-149, and Analyzing Reality: The Case Method, pp. 199-223).

Jackson, B.W., & Holvino, E. (1988). Developing multicultural organizations. *Journal of Religion and the Applied Behavioral Sciences, 9* (2), 14-19.

Johnson, G. R. (1987). Changing the verbal behavior of teachers. *Journal of Staff, Program & Organization Development, 5,* 155-158.

Johnson, D. W., Johnson, R. T., & Smith, K. (1991). *Cooperative learning: Increasing college faculty instructional productivity.* (ASHE-ERIC Higher Education Report No 4)

Kardia, D. (1998). Becoming a multicultural faculty developer: Reflections from the field. In M. Kaplan & D. Lieberman (Eds.), *To Improve the Academy: Vol. 17. Resources for Faculty, Instructional, and Organizational Development.* Stillwater, OK: New Forums Press.

Kaufman, A. (1985). *Implementing problem-based medical education: Lessons from successful innovations.* New York, NY: Springer-Verlaag.

Kitano, M. K. (1997). What a course will look like after multicultural change. In A. Morey & K. Kitano (Eds.), *Multicultural course transformation in higher education: A broader truth.* (pp. 18-34). Needham Heights, MA: Allyn and Bacon.

Klein, F., Sepekoff, B., & Wolf, T. (1985). Sexual orientation: A multi-variable dynamic process. *Journal of Homosexuality, 11* (1/2),35-49.

Kolb, D. (1976). *Learning Styles Inventory.* Boston, MA: McBer and Company.

Kolb, D. A. (1984). *Experiential learning: Experiences as the source of learning and development.* Englewood Cliffs, NJ: Prentice-Hall.

Leaming, D. R. (1998). *Academic leadership: A practical guide to chairing the department.* Bolton, MA: Anker.

Leatherman, D. (1990). *The training trilogy: Assessing needs.* Amherst, MA: Human Resource Development Press.

Lewis, K. (1987). *Taming the pedagogical monster: A handbook for large-class instructors.* Austin, TX: Center for Teaching Effectiveness, University of Texas at Austin.

Lewis, K., & Johnson, G. R. (1986). *Monitoring your classroom communication skills: A programmed workbook for developing coding skills using Johnson's Cognitive Interaction Analysis System (CIAS) and Expanded CIAS.* Unpublished programmed workbook and audiotape for skill training in CIAS. Available from Center for Teaching Effectiveness, Main Building 2200 (G2100), The University of Texas at Austin, Austin, TX 78712-1111.

Lewis, K. G. *Developing questioning skills.* An unpublished handout available from the Center for Teaching Effectiveness, Main Building 2200 (G2100), The University of Texas at Austin, Austin, TX 78712-1111.

Lewis, K. G. *Evaluating discussion.* An unpublished handout available from the Center for Teaching Effectiveness, Main Building 2200 (G2100), The University of Texas at Austin, Austin, TX 78712-1111.

Lewis, K. G. (1986). Using an objective observation system to diagnose teaching problems. *Journal of Staff, Program & Organization Development, 4,* 81-90.

Lewis, K. G. (1991). Gathering data for the improvement of teaching: What do I need and how do I get it? (pp. 65- 82). In M. Theall & J. Franklin (Eds.), *Effective practices for improving teaching.* New Directions for Teaching and Learning, No. 48. San Francisco, CA: Jossey-Bass.

Lewis, K. G. (1993). Section II: Development Programs for TAs. In K.G. Lewis (Ed.), *The TA experience: Preparing for multiple roles* (pp. 95-237). Stillwater, OK: New Forums Press.

Lewis, K. G. (1996). Collecting information via class observation. In K. T. Brinko & R. J. Menges (Eds.), *Practically speaking: A sourcebook for instructional consultants in higher education* (pp. 29-51). Stillwater, OK: New Forums Press.

Lewis, K. G., & Lunde, J. P. (Eds.). (2001). *Face to Face: A sourcebook of individual consultation techniques for faculty/instructional developers. (2nd ed.).* Stillwater, OK: New Forums Press.

Lindquist, J. (Ed.).(1978). *Designing teaching improvement programs.* Berkeley, CA: Pacific Soundings Press.

List, K. (1997). A continuing conversation on teaching: An evaluation of a decade-long Lilly Teaching Fellows Program 1986-96. In D. Dezure & M. Kaplan (Eds.), *To improve the academy: Vol. 16. Resources for faculty, instructional, and organizational development* (pp. 201-24). Stillwater, OK: New Forums Press.

Lucas, A. F. (1986). Effective department chair training on a low-cost budget. *Journal of Staff, Program, and Organization Development, 4* (4), 33-36.

Lucas, A. F. (1990). Using psychological models to understand student motivation. In M. D. Svinicki (Ed.), *The changing face of college teaching* (pp. 103-114). New Directions for Teaching and Learning, No. 42. San Francisco, CA: Jossey-Bass.

Lucas, A. F. (1994). *Strengthening departmental leadership: A team-building guide for chairs in colleges and universities.* San Francisco, CA: Jossey-Bass.

Marchesani, L. S., & Adams, M. (1992). Dynamics of diversity in the teaching-learning process: A faculty development model for analysis and action. In M. Adams (Ed.), *Promoting diversity in college classrooms: Innovative responses for the curriculum, faculty, and institutions* (pp. 9-19). New Directions for Teaching and Learning, No. 52. San Francisco, CA: Jossey-Bass.

McKeachie, W. (1998). *Teaching tips: A guidebook for the beginning college teacher* (10th ed.). Lexington, MA: D.C. Heath.

Meyers, C., & Jones, T. B. (1993). *Promoting active learning strategies for the college classroom.* San Francisco, CA: Jossey-Bass.

Michaelsen, L. K. (1994). Team learning: Making a case for the small-group option. In K. W. Prichard & R. M. Sawyer (Eds.), *Handbook of college teaching: Theory and applications,* (pp. 139-154). Westport, CT: Greenwood.

National Education Association. (1996). *The politics of remedy: State legislative views on higher education.* Washington, DC: National Education Association.

National Institute of Education. (1984). *Involvement in learning: Realizing the potential of American higher education.* Washington, DC: National Institute of Education.

Nelson, W. C., & Siegel, M. E. (1980). *Effective approaches to faculty development.* Washington, DC: Association of American Colleges.

Nemko, M., & Simpson, R. D. (1991). Nine keys to enhancing campus-wide influence of faculty development centers. In K. J. Zahorski (Ed.), *To improve the academy: Vol. 10. Resources for faculty, instructional, and organizational development* (pp. 83-88). Stillwater, OK: New Forums Press.

Nieto, S. (1992). *Affirming diversity: The sociopolitical context of multicultural education.* New York, NY: Longman.

North, J. (1980). Guidelines and strategies for conducting meetings. *POD Quarterly. 2,* 79-91.

Nyquist, J. D. (1986). CIDR: A small service firm within a research university. In M. Svinicki (Ed.), *To improve the academy: Vol. 5. Resources for faculty, instructional, and organizational development* (pp. 66-83). Stillwater, OK: New Forums Press.

Nyquist, J. D., Abbott, R. D., Wulff, D. H., & Sprague, J. (Eds.). (1991). *Preparing the professoriate of tomorrow to teach.* Dubuque, IA: Kendall/Hunt.

O'Bear, K. (1989, March). *Opening doors to understanding and acceptance: Facilitating workshops on lesbian, gay and bisexual issues.* Materials presented at the ACPA meeting, Washington, DC.

Oblinger, D., & Rush, S. C. (Eds.). (1995). *The learning revolution: the challenge of information technology in the academy.* Bolton, MA: Anker.

Office on the Status of Women (Producer). (1991). *Inequity in the Classroom* [videotape]. West Montreal, Quebec, Canada: Office on the Status of Women, Concordia University.

Ognibene, E. R. (1989). Integrating the curriculum: From impossible to possible. *College Teaching, 37* (3), 105-110.

Osterman, D., Christiansen, M., & Coffey, B. (1985). *The feedback lecture* (Idea Paper, No. 13). Manhattan, KS: Kansas State University, Center for Faculty Evaluation and Development.

Paley, V. G. (1979). *White teacher.* Cambridge, MA: Harvard University Press

Pallie, W., & Carr, D. H. (1987). The McMaster medical education philosophy in theory, practice, and historical perspective. *Medical Teacher, 9* (1), 59-71.

Pew Foundation. (1994, April). To dance with change. *Policy Perspectives, 5* (3), A1-A12.

Phillips, J. J., & Holton, III, E. F. (Eds.). (1995). *In action: Conducting needs assessment.* Alexandria, VA: American Society for Training and Development.

Pintrich, P. R. (1994). Student motivation in the college classroom. In K. W. Prichard & R. M. Sawyer (Eds.), *Handbook of college teaching: Theory and applications* (pp. 23-44). Westport, CT: Greenwood.

Pittas, P. (2000). A model program from the perspective of faculty development. *Innovative Higher Education, 25,* 97-110.

Povlacs, J. (1985, March). *More than facts.* University of Minnesota, Duluth Instructional Development, 1-2, 4.

Powney, J., & Watts, M. (1987). *Interviewing in educational research.* London, England: Routledge & Kegan Paul.

Prosser, M., & Trigwell, K. (1993). Development of an approach to teaching questionnaires. *Research and Development in Higher Education, 15,* 468-473.

Quigley, B. (Producer), & Nyquist, J. (Executive Producer). (1991). *Teaching in the Diverse Classroom* [videotape]. Seattle, WA: Center for Instructional Development and Research. Distributed by Anker Publishing.

Robinson, D. G., & Robinson, J.C. (1996). *Performance counseling: Moving beyond training.* San Francisco, CA: Berrett-Koehler.

Rutherford, L. H., & Grana, S. (1994). Fully activating interactive TV: Creating a blended family. *T.H.E. Journal, 22* (3), 86-90.

Rutherford, L. H., & Grana, S. (1995). Retrofitting academe: Adapting faculty attitudes and practices to technology. *T.H.E. Journal, 23* (2), 82-86.

Ryan, J., & Sackrey, C. (Eds.). (1984). *Paradise: Academics from the working class.* Boston, MA: South End Press.

Schmidt, H. G., Lipkin, M. Jr., de Vries, M. W., & Greep, J. M. (Eds.). (1989). *New directions for medical education: Problem-based learning and community-oriented medical education.* New York, NY: Springer-Verlaag.

Schmitz, B., Paul, S. P., & Greenberg, J. D. (1992). Creating multicultural classrooms: An experience-derived faculty development program. In L. Border & N. Chism (Eds.), *Teaching for Diversity, 49,* (pp. 75-87). San Francisco, CA: Jossey-Bass.

Schoem, D., Frankel, L., Zuniga, X., & Lewis, E. A. (1993). The meaning of multicultural teaching: An introduction. In D. Schoem, L. Frankel, X. Zuniga, & E. A. Lewis (Eds.), *Multicultural teaching in the university* (pp.1-12). Westport, CT: Praeger.

Seldin, P. (1984). *Changing practices in faculty evaluation.* San Francisco, CA: Jossey-Bass.

Seldin, P. (1997). *The teaching portfolio: A practical guide to improved performance and promotion/tenure decisions* (2nd ed.). Bolton, MA: Anker.

Seldin, P. (1999). *Changing practices in evaluating teaching.* Bolton, MA: Anker.

Shih, M., & Sorcinelli, M. D. (2000). TEACHnology: Linking teaching and technology in faculty development. In M. Kaplan & D. Lieberman (Eds.), *To improve the academy: Vol. 18. Resources for faculty, instructional, and organizational development* (pp. 151-163). Bolton, MA: Anker.

Silberman, M. (1996). *101 strategies to teach any subject*. Boston, MA: Allyn and Bacon.

Simon, A., & Boyer, E. G. (Eds.). (1970). *Mirrors for behavior: An anthology of classroom observation instruments*. Philadelphia, PA: Research for Better Schools. (ERIC Document Reproduction Service No. ED 031 613)

Smikle, J. L. (1994). Practical guide to developing and implementing cultural awareness training for faculty and staff development. *Journal of Staff, Program & Organization Development, 12* (2), 69-80.

Smith, R. A. (1995). Reflecting critically on our efforts to improve teaching and learning. In E. Neal & L. Echlin (Eds.), *To improve the academy: Vol. 14: Resources for faculty, instructional, and organizational development* (pp. 5-25). Stillwater, OK: New Forums Press.

Sorcinelli, M. D. (1985, April). *Faculty careers: Personal, institutional, and societal dimensions*. Paper presented at the meeting of the American Educational Research Association, Chicago, IL.

Sorcinelli, M. D. (1988). Encouraging excellence: Long-range planning for faculty development. In E. Wadsworth (Ed.), *A handbook for new practitioners* (pp. 27-31). Stillwater, OK: New Forums Press.

Sorcinelli, M. D. (1992). *The career development of pretenure faculty: An institutional study*. Amherst, MA: University of Massachusetts at Amherst.

Sorcinelli, M. D. (1999a). Enhancing department leadership and management. *The Department Chair, 9* (3), 4-6.

Sorcinelli, M. D. (1999b). Post-tenure review through post-tenure development: What linking senior faculty and technology taught us. *Innovative Higher Education, 24*, 61-72.

Sorcinelli, M. D., & Aitken, N. (1995). Improving teaching: Academic leaders and faculty developers as partners. In W. A. Wright & Associates (Ed.), *Teaching improvement practices: Successful strategies for higher education* (pp. 311-323). Bolton, MA: Anker.

Sorenson, D. L. (1994). Valuing the student voice: Student observer/consultant programs. In E. C. Wadsworth (Ed.), *To improve the academy: Vol. 13. Resources for faculty, instructional, and organizational development* (pp. 97-108). Stillwater, OK: New Forums Press.

Svinicki, M. D. *Some applied learning theory*. An unpublished handout available from the Center for Teaching Effectiveness, Main Building 2200 (G2100), The University of Texas at Austin, Austin, TX 78712-1111.

Svinicki, M. D., & Dixon, N. M. (1987). Kolb model modified for classroom activities. *College Teaching, 35*, 141-146.

Taylor-Way, D. (1988). Consultation with video: Memory management through stimulated recall. In K. G. Lewis & J. T. Povlacs (Eds.), *Face to face: A sourcebook of individual consultation techniques for faculty development personnel* (pp. 159-191). Stillwater, OK: New Forums Press.

University of Massachusetts (1998). *Annual report (1997-98).* University of Massachusetts at Amherst, Center For Teaching.

Van der Vleuten, C., & Verwijnen, M. (1990). A system for student assessment. In C. Van der Vleuten & W. Wijnen. (Eds.), *Problem-based learning: Perspectives from the Maastricht experience.* Amsterdam, NL: Thesis.

Verduin, J. R., Jr., & Clark, T. A. (1991). *Distance education: The foundations of effective practice.* San Francisco, CA: Jossey-Bass.

Warren, J. (1994). A training for cultural diversity. *Literacy Harvest, 3,* 38-45.

Warshauer, S. (1988). *Inside training and development: Creating effective programs.* San Francisco, CA: Pfeiffer.

Watkins, K. (1983). Handling difficult questions and situations. *Innovation Abstracts, 5* (24). Available from National Institute for Staff and Organizational Development, SZB 348, Austin, TX 78712-1293.

Weimer, M. (1990). *Improving college teaching: Strategies for developing instructional effectiveness.* San Francisco, CA: Jossey-Bass.

Weinstein, G., & O'Bear, K. (1988). Design elements for intergroup awareness. *Journal for Specialists in Group Work, 13,* 96-103.

Weinstein, G., & O' Bear, K. (1992). Bias issues in the classroom: Encounters with the teaching self. In M. Adams (Ed.), *Promoting diversity in college classrooms: Innovative responses for the curriculum, faculty, and institutions* (pp. 39-50). New Directions for Teaching and Learning, No. 52. San Francisco, CA: Jossey-Bass.

Welty, W., & Silverman, R. (1993). *Using cases to improve college teaching: A guide to more reflective practice.* Washington, DC: American Association for Higher Education.

Wexley, K. N., & Latham, G. P. (1991). *Developing and training human resources in organizations* (2nd ed.). New York, NY: Harper Collins.

Wheeler, D. W., & Schuster, J. H. (1990). Building comprehensive programs to enhance faculty development. In J. H. Schuster, D. W., Wheeler, & Associates (Eds.), *Enhancing faculty careers,* (pp. 275-297) San Francisco, CA: Jossey-Bass.

Wlodkowski, R.J., & Ginsberg, M.B. (1995). *Diversity and motivation.* San Francisco, CA: Jossey-Bass.

Woods, D. R. (1994). *Problem-based learning: How to gain the most from PBL.* Hamilton, Ontario: W. L. Griffin.

Zahorski, K. (1993). Taking the lead: Faculty development as institutional change agent. In D. L. Wright & J. P. Lunde. (Eds.), *To improve the academy: Vol. 12. Resources for faculty, instructional, and organizational development* (pp. 227-245). Stillwater, OK: New Forums Press.

INDEX